# Private Education in Modern China

# Private Education in Modern China

᎒᎒

## PENG DENG

Westport, Connecticut
London

**Library of Congress Cataloging-in-Publication Data**

Deng, Peng.
    Private education in modern China / Peng Deng.
      p.    cm.
    Includes bibliographical references and index.
    ISBN 0–275–95639–3 (alk. paper)
    1. Private schools—China—History—20th century.  2. Education
and state—China—History—20th century.  3. Missions—China—
Educational work—History—20th century.  4. Church schools—China—
History—20th century.  I. Title.
    LC54.C6D46  1997
    371.02′0951—dc21      97–5584

British Library Cataloguing in Publication Data is available.

Library of Congress Catalog Card Number: 97–5584
ISBN: 0–275–95639–3

First published in 1997

Praeger Publishers, 88 Post Road West, Westport, CT 06881
An imprint of Greenwood Publishing Group, Inc.

Printed in the United States of America

The paper used in this book complies with the
Permanent Paper Standard issued by the National
Information Standards Organization (Z39.48–1984).

10 9 8 7 6 5 4 3 2 1

*To the memory of my dear mother,*
*Li Enluo.*

# Contents

*Photo essay follows page 89.*

# List of Tables

# Preface

This book is a tribute to a glorious tradition in China, to hundreds of thousands of people, some I know and some I do not know, who are carrying on the tradition heart and soul. It is also a work of appreciation for all the love and support I have received from my colleagues, students, and their parents at Huaxin International School in Shenyang, China.

In the 1994-95 academic year, I took a leave of absence from High Point University in North Carolina, where I hold a teaching position, to go to the largest metropolis in northeast China. My mission was to set up Huaxin International School, one of the forty-odd private schools in Shenyang. As the founding headmaster of the school, I had to meet and deal with people whom I would never have known otherwise. Although born and reared in China, I had to learn nevertheless to interpret government guidelines and regulations and to win over officials whose support was crucial to the school's survival. As the headmaster of a private school, I had to also spend a considerable amount of time with demanding parents to convince them that their children were in loving hands. Nothing came easy and every day passed with some challenge. In the end, however, that year proved to be the most thrilling experience of my life.

The experience opened up a field that had been obscure to me until then: the fate of private education in modern China. Reading deep into the night after my daily routine as headmaster I pondered repeatedly several questions: Why did private schools totally disappear in China in the 1950s? Why, thirty years after its demise, is private education making a comeback? And, if certain socio-political preconditions are necessary for the rise of private education, what does the current resurgence of private schools tell us? In my experiences with officials and ordinary Chinese, I almost always sensed an uneasiness about private schools. I could not help wondering about the origin of this attitude and noticing the often contradictory policy of the Chinese government vis-à-vis private schools. Such were the questions that have haunted me ever since; the following study represents my effort to answer them.

In imperial China, governmental schools were no more than the thin top of the educational pyramid, designed for educating would-be bureaucrats. For hundreds of years, private education was both the cradle of talents and source of true scholarship. In modern times, the emergence of new private schools occurred at a time when China was moving away from an ancient educational system, which revolved around the civil service examination. Even in the twentieth century, private schools maintained numerical superiority for decades, despite the trend toward state control and centralism in education.

The present Chinese school system has resulted not only from the combined efforts of government officials and public school educators, but also from the laudable work of at least four generations of private school educators. Although the government took all the credit for advances in modern education, from time to time, it subjected private education to unjust and selfish treatment.

This phenomenon has not received proper attention from Chinese or Western scholars, which reinforces the view that China's institutional history has lagged far behind her intellectual history. While the educational revolution of the past century has been studied relatively extensively by both Chinese and foreign scholars, private education has remained by and large an unexplored field. This is largely because of the bias of both the Chinese government, which treated public education as its domain, and the many Chinese educational reformers who promoted public education as part of the nation-building in modern China. This was natural in an era of nationalism, when both internal and external conditions seemed to favor a strong central government. Western imperialism before World War II and Japanese aggression in the 1930s and 1940s gave rise to an intense desire among the Chinese elite for a rich nation with a strong military. For such a glorious goal, the Chinese people seemed willing to sacrifice many things deemed precious elsewhere in the world.

The price of radical nationalism was extremely high. The emergence of an all-powerful state took away the already minimal freedom of the Chinese and damaged an incipient civil society that had arisen largely as a product of Western influence. One of the many casualties of the ongoing Chinese revolution in the 1950s was private education. In retrospect, it is indeed amazing that Chinese educators overwhelmingly acquiesced and even actively cooperated in the state takeover of private schools. The Communist victory was so absolute that, with the exception of Western missionary societies which helplessly resisted the takeover, not a single protest was registered.

Luckily, the political radicalism of the 1950s and 1960s seems to have dissipated by the end of the Cultural Revolution. In the post-Mao era, private education has made a comeback, first hesitantly and timidly, than bursting into full swing in the 1990s. Since education has been a central task of the Chinese state in modern times, the miraculous resurrection of private education has had enormous social and political implications. Indeed, the state of Chinese education remains a dependable barometer of the state of Chinese society and government. The resurgence of private education therefore signifies a radical departure from the socialist model of schooling and indicates some fundamental changes in the relationship between the Chinese state and education. The seeming willingness of the Chinese government to allow a certain degree of autonomy to a significant number of schools at all levels is undoubtedly a giant step of enormous sociopolitical significance.

The primary purpose of this study was to recover the recent past of China's private schools and piece together the epic story of four generations of Chinese educators' heroic and sometimes single-minded pursuit of a dream. This was no easy task because of the difficult access to some sources and because I had to sift the truth from contradictory data and paint the entire picture of private education in modern China from fragmentary information. While each private school has a unique story, only the most successful have their experiences recorded. A critical study of these schools' stories, however, would shed light on China's private schools in general, especially when their histories were combined with such sources as government documents and journalistic writings.

Fully aware of the precariousness of predictions, I nevertheless assume that historical events follow some pattern. It is my belief that, as economic reform and political relaxation in China continue, private education will keep flourishing and, consequently, will receive more attention from scholars. Their studies, in turn, will help both the Chinese government and educators in private schools to maintain a more constructive relationship.

Last but not least, mission schools are discussed in this book because they were non-governmental and because they were treated as private institutions by the Chinese government. These schools were among the first private "modern" schools in China and, in many ways, they spearheaded China's educational reform of the late nineteenth and early twentieth centuries. Both my parents at one time studied at mission schools and my own alma maters—Qiujing Middle School in Chongqing and West China University of Medical Sciences in Chengdu—were mission schools during the Republican period. The experience of missionary education reveals much about the intricate relationship between the Chinese state and private education. It is especially significant today because of a renewed Western interest in Chinese education.

# Acknowledgments

As I add the final touches to this manuscript, I feel all the more indebted to the many people who generously assisted me in its production. The project was made possible by my home institution, High Point University, which permitted me a year of absence in the 1994-1995 academic year to work at Huaxin International School in Shenyang, where I conceived the idea for this study. In summer 1996, the university further provided me with a summer scholarship grant, which enabled me to complete my field work in the People's Republic of China.

From the outset of the project, Patricia Sager and David Bryden at High Point University library, tirelessly secured many books and articles through interlibrary loans with amazing efficiency. My friend, Dr. Sun Yi, at Albion College in Albion, Michigan, spent numerous hours at the University of Michigan Library rounding up articles in Chinese newspapers and periodicals; and Mr. Liu Weiwei, in Chengdu, China traveled hundreds of miles to take photographs for this book.

At our meetings in summer 1996, Professor Zhang Zhiyi and Dr. Wu Ni from the Central Institute for Educational Research in Beijing gave me their newly published works on China's private education, which turned out to be most valuable sources for my work. Professor Wu Zhongkui at Beijing Normal University, Professor Zhang Shuchi at the College of Education, Shenyang University, and Professor Zhang Shiya at Southwest China Normal University in Chongqing offered me invaluable advice at various stages of my research and writing.

I am also thankful to dozens of teachers and administrators whom I interviewed at private schools and private colleges in China. They most graciously shared with me not only dependable sources but also their personal insights into private schools today and in the past.

Above all, my heart-felt gratitude goes to my dear colleagues at Huaxin International School in Shenyang, Liaoning province, for their support and never-failing friendship. Mr. Song Tiancheng, in particular, introduced me to an area and society that I had known very little about. Mr. Wen Feng faithfully collected many newspaper and journal articles for me over a period of two years when he had a full-time job at Huaxin during the day and another at home taking care of his bedridden wife. Professor Liu Mingqiong, who succeeded me as the headmaster of Huaxin International School, enlightened me with her insightful views on many issues.

I know very well that I can never thank everyone enough but hope that, when this book is published and in the hands of persons interested in Chinese education, all the labor of those who helped will not have been in vain.

# Private Education in Modern China

# 1

# Private Education in Pre-Modern China

As the longest continuous civilization on earth, China also has the oldest school system. Schools were apparently established during the formative period of the Chinese state. Sima Qian, a famous historian of the second century B.C., believed that education had reached considerable level by the time of Yu (ca. 2,000 B.C.) while the *Shangshu* (Book of history) of the fifth century B.C. reports that Shun, one of the legendary kings in ancient China, appointed Qi the Minister of Education (*situ*) in charge of the five fields of learning (*wujiao*). By the Zhou period (841-476 B.C.), China had an elaborate system of governmental schools, consisting of the national school (*guoxue*) and local schools (*xiangxue*). While the former was located in the capital, the latter existed at several levels. The local school in a village was called a *shu*, in a township, a *xiang* or *xu*. From the outset the Chinese state showed great interest in education. By the Zhou period, the country's education was supervised by the *dasitu* at the central court and at the local level, it was under the charge of the *zhouzhang* and *dangzheng*.[1]

## BEGINNINGS

Private schools, in contrast to governmental schools, were established, financed, and run by individuals or learned societies. Since its formation in the sixth century B.C., the private school has existed in China for well over two thousand and five hundred years. While the exact date of their inception is open to debate,[2] private schools apparently began their first surge in the late Zhou or Spring-Autumn (Chun-Qiu, 770-476 B.C.) period, when Chinese society was beset by a serious political crisis due to a rise in local power and decline of central authority. The crisis was further intensified by a drastic social change resulting from population growth and the rise of a merchant class. As the feudal system of the early Zhou became dysfunctional, peace was replaced by intra-state political turmoil and inter-state warfare. Since the governmental school system depended on the support of the Zhou court, the collapse of the central power drove learning into the "barbarian lands" (*si yi*).

Ironically, political crisis and social tension also created a period of unprecedented intellectual growth. As political power changed hands from the hereditary nobles to the big landholders and commercial upstarts, responsibility for education shifted from the government to private individuals. The result was a proliferation of private schools and a concomitant golden age of scholar-ship in China's history known as the Period of a Hundred Schools. With perhaps the exception of the Daoists, who harbored a deep distrust of political power and commercial activities and advocated a social escapism, every major school of thought in this period was politically oriented. To expand their political influence, the contending schools worked hard to recruit students. At the same time, feudal lords, knowing the importance of the educated gentlemen (*shi*), spent their fortunes to keep many of these people in their domains. The dispersion of educated people gave Chinese education a broader base and encouraged the rise of private schools.

In the late Zhou period, there were many educators and promoters of education; the most famous was Kong Qiu, or Confucius (551-479 B.C.). A man of great intellect and moral integrity, Confucius is credited with establishing the first private school of some scale in China's recorded history. As a teacher, he had three thousand students and, as a sage, seventy disciples. He successfully ran the largest private school of his time and explored a vast spectrum of issues concerning education. An original thinker, Confucius was the first philosopher in China who clearly defined the role of education and the role of an educator. For him, education was not only the vehicle for practical knowledge but also the sure passage toward moral cultivation. Studies in the Six Classics that he compiled[3] helped nurture moral qualities centered on two potent concepts: *ren*, or benevolence, and *li*, or propriety. Individuals with cultivated morals were then called *junzi*, or gentlemen, who would help the ruler to administer the country wisely, fairly, and effectively. Most notable in Confucius's philosophy was his belief in the democratic nature of education. Although a conservative believing in a social hierarchy, Confucius nevertheless took students regardless of their class backgrounds and, consequently, most of his students came from non-aristocratic families. While he required references and face-to-face interviews with applicants, the tuition he charged for a student from a commoner's family—ten pieces of bacon—was unusually small.

For the cultivation of the *junzi*, Confucius developed the most comprehensive curriculum of his time, which centered on the six arts and a highly innovative and flexible pedagogy. Courses at his school included poetry, history, ethics, and music, and with the assistance of his best students, Confucius compiled a tremendous corpus of classical literature. His class was apparently very lively, involving much dialogue with his students and free discussions. His method was always designed to stimulate his students' interests in the subjects and encourage original thinking. Above all, his teaching had a goal: to put his disciples into action. He spent years traveling through the states in northern China in the hope of finding a wise ruler interested in his social and political agenda. Revered as the first great educator in China's history, Confucius cast a long shadow not only on Chinese education but on Chinese society and the state as a whole. For two thousand and five hundred years, Confucius had numerous critics and in modern times, he was severely criticized for his fundamentally conservative ideology, yet no one else has ever ventured to claim his stature.

The earliest private schools in ancient China occurred in a time of great social and political fluidity. They also prospered during a time of a vigorous search for solutions to the problems facing the Chinese people. The symbiosis of private education and an unprecedented intellectual flowering formed the basis upon which much of the scholarship, and the social and political system in imperial China evolved. Of the many contributions made by Confucius and his contemporaries, the emphasis on the value of learning and the ideal of a government by the talented and well-educated under the "son of heaven" had the most influence on future generations.

Confucius had many rivals and successors. While Mo Zi is considered to be the greatest private educator next to Confucius, others, such as Mencius and Tian Pian, had hundreds of students. In fact, during the ensuing Warring States period (475-221 B.C.), private education was even more prosperous and diverse and private schools even bigger. The funeral of Chunyu Kun, a private educator at this time, for example, was attended by three thousand people. The proliferation of private schools in this period signified the independence of education from the state. Even some governmental schools, such as the palace school at Jixia (*Jixia xuegong*) in the state of Qi, contained elements of private education: teachers at the school were mostly visiting or adjunct scholars, not members of the faculty.

Private education declined drastically for a few decades during the short-lived Qin Dynasty (221-206 B.C.), when the First Emperor shut down all private schools to make way for his legalist policy. The Qin state rose to hegemony by adopting the theory of the legalists who, instead of advocating a virtuous ruler and emphasizing the good potential of mankind, promoted a despotic state and rule by harsh penalties. Although the earlier legalists were eager participants in private education, the legalist advisors to the first emperor of Qin were convinced that the collapse of the previous Zhou dynasty could be attributed to uncontrolled private education. While stripping hundreds of scholars of their right to teach, the Qin state attempted to replace private schools with "social education" through a centralized bureaucracy. However, the effort to eliminate sources of subversive thinking conversely hastened the doom of the regime as it alienated many of the country's educated elite.

In the Han period (206 B.C.-22 A.D.), private education revived, and for decades it almost monopolized the study of the Confucian classics. Private education thrived in this era not only because of the government's financial inadequacy but because of people's yearning for knowledge after a period of devastating chaos. Although most private schools during this time apparently were small, a few enrolled hundreds of students. It also appears that scholars at various lyceums (*jingshe* and *jinglu*) lectured on Legalist and Daoist, as well as Confucian classics. The textual studies of the pre-Qin classics at the private schools in this period laid the foundation for what was later called the Han Learning. A peculiar phenomenon and indicator of the popularity of private education in this period was the practice of the titular student (*zhulu dizi*). A *zhulu dizi* put his name on the roster of a great master even though he seldom or never attended the latter's lectures. A famous scholar could well have thousands of such students. Cai Xuan, a master of the "Five Classics," had a thousand regular students and sixteen thousand titular students.[4] For the master, it was a matter of fame as well as income. For the students, serious independent study plus the name of their teacher meant advance toward officialdom. For people today, such practice appears phony. But in ancient China where communication was difficult and educational provision limited, it largely helped elevate the stature of private masters and disseminate learning.

During the chaotic time between the late Han and the unification of China in the early seventh century, private schools not only persisted between the rise and fall of dynasties and the invasion of nomads from the north but also served as catalysts for the fusion of Confucian ideology and Buddhist philosophy. Once again, the dysfunction of governmental schools was compensated for by the proliferation of private schools, some of which were amazingly productive. For example, Xu Zunming, a Confucian scholar in the Northern Wei period, allegedly taught over ten thousand students during his lifetime. Private schools that borrowed from Buddhist teaching and took to the scenic depths of the mountains were probably prototypes of the private academy (*shuyuan*) of later times.

## CIVIL SERVICE EXAMINATION AND PRIVATE SCHOOLS

A landmark in the history of Chinese education was the full implementation of the civil service examination system during the Tang era (618-896).[5] Militarily energetic, economically prosperous, politically stable, and culturally cosmopolitan, the Tang regime developed the most elaborate school system China had ever seen. The *keju*, or civil service examination system was, in modern parlance, a talent search program based on the Confucian notion of meritocracy. Through formal examinations at different levels, the government was able to discover and select the best and brightest among China's educated population to staff the imperial bureaucracy. Thereafter, the civil service examination remained an administrative cornerstone of the Chinese government and the motor for China's educational system. In subsequent dynasties, the *keju* evolved into a three-tier system at the county, provincial, and capital level. Scholars who passed the exam at the county level were granted the title of *xiucai*, or budding scholar, and thereafter referred to as a qualified candidate (*shengyuan*). Those who succeeded in the provincial exam obtained the title of *juren*, or elevated man. A combination of dedication and luck helped the very few to reach the pinnacle of the capital exam and win the laurel of *jinshi*, meaning advanced scholar. Except for brief periods of dynastic decline, this product of Chinese ingenuity remained almost the exclusive avenue to government positions for China's educated elite for well over one thousand years. In addition to maintaining a high level of administrative talent, the *keju* kept the channels of upward mobility open and prevented the emergence of a permanent hereditary aristocracy.

A dual educational system evolved around the *keju*. For the purpose of maintaining the level of learning and ideological unity, the imperial government in China ran a governmental school system centered in the capital and in seats of provincial and prefectural governments. In the early Tang period, the Chinese government set up a school system in the capital consisting of the Six Schools (*Guozixue, Taixue, Simenxue, Shuxue, Suanxue*, and *Luxue*) and the Two *Guan* (*Hongwenguan* and *Congwenguan*), which supplied most candidates for the degree of *jinshi*. In the Song period (960-1279), governmental schools operated at both the central and provincial levels. The Song system was copied by later dynasties with some modifications. In the Qing period (1644-1911), the state-run school system comprised the Hanlin Academy at the top, provincial schools (*fuxue*), prefectural schools (*zhouxue*), and county schools (*xianxue*).[6] Instructors at these schools gave lectures to scholars aspiring to advanced degrees. In most cases, these schools were in fact learning centers where supervisory personnel promoted and selected promising candidates for government service.

Ironically, the *keju*, which was in theory available to all candidates regardless of their background, made governmental schools relatively unnecessary, for participating in the exam did not require any specific formal education. During the late Tang period, in particular, the test for the degree of *jinshi* (advanced scholar) included poetry and a literary essay, which were not stressed at governmental schools. People with literary potential therefore gravitated to private schools with well-known masters. The result was that private schools contributed more *jinshi* than schools set up by the central government.[7] In the Northern Song (960-1126), the Capital University (*Guozijian*) was attended by no more than one hundred students, whereas participants in the metropolitan examination numbered several thousand. Obviously the majority of the candidates were graduates of local schools, many of which were private. This trend was assisted in part by the great number of books made possible by the use of paper and the printing press.

During the subsequent Ming and Qing periods, the *keju* was opened to virtually all aspirants to officialdom. At this time, a candidate for the degree of "elevated man" (*juren*) and above had to be a *shengyuan*. However, a *shengyuan* did not have to register at a governmental school. At the same time, the *keju* stimulated enormous interest in private schooling among the Chinese people. The problem with the *keju* system was the government's will to impose the orthodox ideology on learning. Consequently the tests were increasingly characterized by ideological rigidity and technical formalism, especially since the Ming period (1368-1644). From time to time, thinking was sacrificed for rote learning, and bookworms were chosen over real talents. "Absurdities of all kinds, including misreading of the Confucian texts, arbitrary and illogical punctuation, and ludicrous allusions, became commonplace."[8] The *keju* therefore became an intellectual straitjacket for China's millions of otherwise creative scholars and indeed a hurdle to the country's progress in modern times. Its abolition in the early twentieth century presaged the demise of a tradition in education.

## SISHU

The vast majority of private schools in traditional China were collectively called *sishu*. They were, by and large, private schools which served local needs for basic literacy and, to a lesser extent, prepared youth for higher learning, even for the civil service examination. The *sishu* dates back at least to the Zhou period and, henceforth, remained the most popular form of schooling in pre-modern China. Although Chinese governments of various times experimented with elementary schools,[9] the *sishu* persisted as the predominant instrument of basic literacy education in imperial and early modern China.

In early modern China, the *sishu* became quite elaborate. Operating in both rural and urban areas, the system was further divided into *zuoguan* or *jiaoguan* (private schools in rich households); *jiashu* (where teachers taught students in their own residence); *sishu* (private schools); *yishu* (charity schools); and *cunshu* (village schools).[10] In general, there were few *zuoguan* or *jiaoguan*, and those that did exist were only for children of the well-to-do, especially official and scholar-gentry families who could afford the money and space. For the gentry in traditional Chinese society, having a *zuoguan* or *jiaoguan* was a way to maintain power and prestige. It not only separated children of gentry families from children of ordinary farmers but, as rich gentry families could always afford better teachers, helped prepare their children for higher level schools and even the civil service examination. At *zuoguan* or *jiaoguan*, girls from rich families might receive a basic education even though women in general were barred from formal education in traditional China. Apparently some girls in rich families became well versed in literature, prose or poetry. But family education, even at its best, only prepared these girls for married life. The village school (*cunshu*) ranked the lowest in the hierarchy of private schools, for it met the needs of families of modest means and its students, with few exceptions, stood little chance of advancing beyond the budding scholar (*xiucai*) level.[11]

Given the largely decentralized state of its educational system, China's academic and ideological uniformity was amazing. All *sishu* offered similar curricula for the purpose of basic literacy (*mengxue*). Courses at a *sishu* usually included reading, handwriting, and composition. Texts, such as *Precepts for Children* (Tongmengxun) by Lu Benzhong, *Rudimentary Learning* (Xiaoxue) by Zhu Xi of the Song era, *Language Text for Children* (Xiao'er yu) by Lu Desheng, and *Children's Decorum* (Tongzi li) by Tu Xiying of the Ming era largely reflected the Neo-Confucian philosophy. They covered moral, historical, as well as literary education.[12]

Most *sishu* were financed by the tuition of students. *Sishu* teachers were most likely to have been unsuccessful candidates in the civil service examination. But these schools made education available to children of families of even moderate means, thereby keeping alive the Confucian ideal of meritocracy and serving as the first rung of the ladder of upward social mobility. The best students at *sishu* had a fair chance to pass the county civil service examination to obtain the title of *xiucai*. Along with the civil service examination, s*ishu* remained the most important instrument for in maintaining social and political stability.

Starting with the Ming period, a new type of private school, the *shexue* (village school) was established under governmental auspices. *Shexue* curricula were geared to the civil service examination, and their best graduates were granted the privileges of a qualified candidate (*tongsheng*) and were eligible for the local civil service examination for the degree of budding scholar (*xiucai*). Funding and administration had to be taken care of by the villagers, invariably under the leadership of the local gentry. In this regard, the *shexue* presaged the *minban* (literally people-run) schools in Communist China. In the late Ming, as the *shexue* entered a period of uncertainty, the charity school (*yixue*) gained momentum. Although promoted by the government as a means to popularize literacy, *yixue* were, in most cases, locally initiated and privately funded. An official notice from Zhou Kai, governor of the Xiangyang prefecture during the reign of the Daoguang emperor, urged the scholar-gentry and merchants to donate money for charity schools in their own localities, since a lack of education had led to a growing crime rate and a decline in morality. The governor rewarded people who donated over three hundred silver taels with an inscribed board; other donors had their names engraved on stone monuments on the side of major thoroughfares.[13] Many charity schools were based on land donations and operated on the income from rental properties. While a board of governors was responsible for management and the hiring of teachers, local governments were often involved in the operation of charity schools. To guarantee the stability of charity schools and protect their property from future disputes and encroachments, their land and finances were often put under official supervision. Curriculum and pedagogy at the *yixue* or *shexue* were, by and large, the same as at other *sishu* even though their students were, in general, from poor families.[14]

At the better *sishu*, students learned to read and write and were exposed to rudimentary texts in Confucian literature; more advanced students delved into Confucian classics in preparation for the civil service examination. Since usually there was no age requirement and no regular time for graduation, students at a *sishu* were at several academic levels. Thus the teacher was expected to tailor the curriculum to suit almost every student. It took great patience and innovation from the teacher to keep students interested while maintaining certain measure of order in the classroom. Thoughtful educators encouraged critical thinking among students even though most *sishu* were only intended to achieve basic literacy.[15] Unfortunately, since education in imperial China evolved around the *keju*, pedagogy was mechanical by modern standards as mastery of Confucian classics at the *sishu* largely depended on rote learning and the practice of the "eight-legged essays" required by the civil service examination. Corporal punishment, especially slapping a child's hand with a ruler, was widespread in accordance with the authoritarian tradition. Facilities at most *sishu* were understandably scarce, and most *sishu* teachers seem to have lived a simple life on a meager income. Moreover, though teachers were supposed to enjoy great social prestige in the Confucian world, numerous accounts by *sishu* teachers suggested otherwise.[16] Teaching in traditional China was neither financially remunerative nor psychologically gratifying.

There was no accreditation system for the *sishu* in imperial China. The work of a *sishu* was measured either on a very subjective level by the students' parents or on the number of its graduates passing the civil service examination. Yet the *sishu* was so ingrained in the social fabric of traditional China that it persisted even in modern times when new-style schools became part of the state. Despite its inertia built up over two thousand years, the *sishu* enjoyed certain advantages over Western-style schools. First, it was attached to a cultural tradition that was especially entrenched in rural China. Most *sishu* were true neighborhood schools within walking distance from the students' homes. While the first modern schools were relatively expensive and were largely affected by the changing fortunes of the state, most *sishu* were in touch with the local economic conditions and financially efficient. Whereas the curriculum of new schools was unstable in the experimental stage, the *sishu* had a well-established program that, although technically obsolete, still met the needs of many Chinese families.[17] Thus, even though reformers in modern China repeatedly sentenced *sishu* to death, the institution refused to go away and continued to exist into the early 1950s. The government had to soften its opposition to *sishu* and adopt a gradualist approach to transforming them into modern schools.

## SHUYUAN

The *shuyuan* (private academies) originated in the Tang period (618-896) as official publishers and libraries of the imperial government. As such, they provided the imperial government with verified versions of dynastic documents and classics. Over time, they developed into private institutions for higher learning; becoming well-entrenched during the Northern Song (960-1127) period. After the tumultuous Five Dynasties (907-960), when governmental schools were reduced to near extinction, private *shuyuan*, where renowned scholars lectured to youngsters, responded to local needs for advanced learning in southern provinces such as Jiangxi and Fujian. When peace finally returned, it was accompanied by an outpouring of interest in learning. Scholars established private schools in the mountains and forests. Of the 714 known *shuyuan* in the Song period, the overwhelming majority were located in southern China. The most famous were Yuelu, Zuiyang, Haoyang, and Bailudong Shuyuan.

The rise of the *shuyuan* signified a new stage in the development of China's private education. In general *shuyuan* were superior to earlier private schools in at least three aspects. First, most of them had their own campuses which were much larger than those of earlier private schools. The compound of Yingtian Fu Shuyuan (Shuyuan of Yingtian prefecture), for example, claimed 154 studies and the famed Yuelu Shuyuan in Changsha had 5 lecture halls and 52 individual studies. Since the education in the *shuyuan* emphasized self-study, a good library was essential. All *shuyuan* had their own libraries; some, such as Hualin Shuyuan in Zhejiang, possessed over ten thousand books; Heshan Shuyuan in western Sichuan, boasted of one hundred thousand volumes. Such facilities, enviable even to most governmental schools, guaranteed advanced academic pursuits. Second, *shuyuan* perfected their own teaching methods and administrative systems. At a *shuyuan*, a dean (*shanzhang* or *dongzhang*) was both the academic authority and the spiritual leader. He was normally a renowned scholar or a an active or retired official. While presiding over the studies at the *shuyuan*, the dean was assisted by assistant deans (*fu shanzhang*), lecturers (*jiangshu*), and teaching assistants (*zhujiao*). Such structural development was not only unprecedented in China's private education but of great significance for the quality of learning at the *shuyuan*. Finally, *shuyuan* seemed to have more diverse and steady sources of revenue than earlier private schools. While the operation of earlier private schools depended almost solely on students' fees, *shuyuan* collected rent from their land grants (*xuetian*), donations from private sources, and even government subsidies. Land-granting was an effective way for the government to bring the *shuyuan* under its control, but it also helped put the *shuyuan* on a solid financial footing.[18]

Once the Northern Song regime had become entrenched, its rulers allocated vast resources to establish governmental schools in an effort to promote Confucian orthodoxy. At the same time, the government built on the civil service examination system of the Sui and Tang periods as the only channel to recruit talents from the literati for the imperial administration. Under the auspices of the imperial government, schools were established in every prefecture and were directly associated with the civil service examination. The number of private *shuyuan* plummeted as many were taken over by the government while others closed. In the early twelfth century, private *shuyuan* almost totally disappeared.

The collapse of the Northern Song dynasty under foreign invasion and the move of the cultural center southward into the Yangtse valley revived the *shuyuan* during the Southern Song (1127-1279) era. An awareness of national crisis refueled the academic pursuits of Confucian scholars who took refuge south of the Yangtse River. The resurgence of the *shuyuan* coincided with the rise of Neo-Confucianism, an intellectual reform led by the erudite scholar Zhu Xi (1130-1200). As the magistrate of Nankang (in Jiangxi), Zhu Xi rediscovered the remains of the Bailudong Shuyuan (White Deer Cave Academy) and rebuilt it with government funding. Further, he redefined the mission of the *shuyuan* and worked out the Bailudong Shuyuan Rules which combined scholarship with moral cultivation. Just as the Benedictine Rules guided the monastic reform in Medieval Europe, the Bailudong Shuyuan Rules helped promote a wholesome academic atmosphere in *shuyuan* all over China. While most *shuyuan* reflected local needs for education, some of the most famous *shuyuan* attracted students from neighboring provinces as well.

After the Mongol dynasty (1279-1368) during which Confucian learning depreciated, the first few emperors of the Ming dynasty (1368-1644) exercised rigorous ideological control by promoting the formerly suppressed Neo-Confucianism and by restoring the civil service examination. However, because the civil service examination focused on textual study of Confucian classics and since the examination constituted the only ladder of upward mobility, it encouraged conformity rather than creativity, dishonesty rather than academic integrity. In the Song era, an elaborate governmental school system was created under imperial auspices. But quantitative growth did not necessarily result in qualitative improvement. Rather, when governmental schools came to serve the utilitarian purpose of the *keju*, education lost its moral underpinnings. As a result, in some schools, the teachers and students "looked at each other like strangers."[19] To its radical critics, the system helped detach China's intelligentsia from "the people's suffering" and "threatened the country's survival." Deterioration of the civil service examination and the demoralization of the imperial government thus accompanied a spiral of dynastic decline. Honest scholars withdrew from the disintegrating system to work on real scholarship and statecraft.[20]

When, under official pressure, most *shuyuan* were reduced to preparatory schools for the *keju*, the few that remained centers of sincere academic pursuit and critical of the *keju* were subject to political persecution. Responding to the social and political ills in the waning dynasty, these *shuyuan* became seedbeds of new ideas that went beyond mere academic pursuits. Works of scholars such as Wang Yangming (or Wang Shouren, 1472-1528) created an atmosphere of debate that covered a wide spectrum of issues from self-cultivation to the cosmic order. A system of regional public forums developed, many of which attracted hundreds of attendants and spectators. Of the *shuyuan* in the Ming period, Donglin was undoubtedly the most unique and influential. Located on the bank of picturesque Taihu Lake outside the city of Wuxi, it gathered some of the brightest and most outspoken scholars of all times. Facing a moribund regime, Donglin scholars such as Gu Xiancheng and Gao Panlong demonstrated their unusual courage and sense of responsibility by chastising inept officials and immoral court eunuchs. They were true believers in the Confucian philosophy of saving the country through education. Donglin Shuyuan consequently transformed itself from a sheer private academy to a political organization. Because of this, Donglin Shuyuan bore the brunt of the wrath of the eunuch faction in the Ming court. Not only was the academy shut down, but its leading scholars were subjected to horrifying persecution.[21] Under various pretexts, the Ming government altogether launched four inquisitions against the *shuyuan* to impose ideological and political uniformity. Independent-minded Confucian scholars proved too much of a nuisance to the regime.

The Manchus, who conquered China in 1644, were well aware of the Dongling revolt. For almost a century, the Manchu government prohibited the reemergence of private *shuyuan*, even though the new rulers effectively kept the Confucian tradition alive as the ideological buttress for their regime. The regime maintained an elaborate system of governmental schools, largely inherited from its predecessors.[22] There is no doubt that the Manchu rulers promoted education as a means to increase Chinese acceptance of their alien rule and promote general prosperity. Unfortunately, when the Manchus restored the Ming system of education, they also recreated all its weaknesses. The civil service examination, with its emphasis on Neo-Confucian classics, severely crippled intellectual creativity. Moreover, since the school system was integrated into the administrative system, and as a rule, the instructors at governmental schools were bureaucrats, schools lost their autonomy as institutions of learning.[23]

Only in 1733 did the Manchu court grudgingly endorse the *shuyuan* under strict government supervision. The Yongzheng emperor (1723-1735) graciously offered one thousand silver taels to each of the twenty-two model provincial *shuyuan*. As was always the case in China's educational history, the limited resurgence of the *shuyuan* was a product of the dysfunction of governmental schools. Yet because of the repeated persecution of independent-minded scholars by the Manchu regime, the *shuyuan* in the Qing period made only limited advances in scholarship.

Whereas the *shuyuan* was viewed by some as a cure for the intrinsic problems of the governmental school system, it proved unable to totally transcend its cultural environment. Degree seekers forsook governmental schools and came to *shuyuan* to prepare for the civil service examination, thereby compromising the primary goal of the institution.[24] The *shanzhang* of some *shuyuan* likewise followed the tide. They promoted superficial learning of the classics and even encouraged plagiarism. While some *shuyuan* administrations were weakened by the absenteeism of their *shanzhang* and the appointment of instructors by government officials, the practice of enrolling "ghost" students for financial reasons made some *shuyuan* mere hulls of what they had been.[25] Well before the imperial system came to an end, many *shuyuan* had become terribly disoriented.

Governmental control and literary inquisition, however, did not totally eradicate creative learning the *shuyuan's* and prevent them from producing some of the best minds and scholarship in this period. From *shuyuan* emerged farsighted individuals from Gu Yanwu and Yan Ruoju to Dai Zhen and Ruan Yuan. Most of these scholars were original thinkers and critics of the debasement of Neo-Confucianism at *shuyuan* and governmental schools. Yan Yuan (1635-1704), founder of the Zhangnan Shuyuan, broke away from the dominant practice in the *shuyuan* of his time by implementing a highly diverse and highly practical curriculum at Zhangnan. His students not only read Confucian classics, but studied subjects such as mathematics, geography, astronomy, and agriculture as well. Reacting to the thought-strangling effect of the *bagu* (eight-legged) essay in the *keju*, Yan wrote, "As long as the *bagu* dominated our learning, there will be no place for true scholarship; without true scholarship, there will not be effective governance. Consequently, there will not be social progress and economic prosperity. *Bagu* is indeed worse than burning books and burying scholars alive." His motto, "combining learning with practice" (shi xue, shixi, shiyong), thereafter inspired a whole generation of scholars.[26]

The most severe critic of the *keju* system and Neo-Confucian ideology in the mid-Qin period was probably Dai Zhen (1723-1777). Starting his career as a *sishu* teacher and ended as a *shuyuan* master, Dai Zhen believed that education, when properly delivered, held the key to better human beings and better society. The major problem of Neo-Confucianism, Dai argued, was its academic exclusiveness and ideological inflexibility. In a most iconoclastic way, he called the Neo-confucian negation of human desires perverse. His philosophy aimed to reconcile human desires with the cosmic order and his teaching at Jinhua Shuyuan in Zhejiang, aimed to create a synthesis based on genuine understanding of Confucian classics and an eclectic approach to different schools of thinking. His criticism of Neo-Confucian masters such as Zhu Xi, Chen Yi, though controversial, was followed by many scholars and, in fact, became the patent of the famous Anhui School.[27]

With the declining power of the Manchu regime, many *shuyuan* quietly drifted away from ideological orthodoxy and official surveillance. During the late Qing period, some *shuyuan* in Zhejiang and Jiangsu became the podium for new ideas from which reformers such as Zhang Taiyan, Kang Youwei, and Liang Qichao preached social progress and political reform. Yet in the late nineteenth century, the dynastic decline and the onslaught of new ideas made it increasingly difficult for traditional *shuyuan* to survive. During the Reform of 1898, an imperial decree turned all *shuyuan* into schools (*xuetang*) for the so-called new learning. *Shuyuan* in the provincial capitals were designated universities; those at the prefectural level were called middle schools (*zhongxuetang*); and those at the county level were reduced to elementary schools (*xiaoxuetang*).

## AN EVERLASTING LEGACY

For centuries, private schools, especially the *shuyuan*, remained formulators of true scholarship and sources of intellectual creativity. In times of central decline and domestic chaos, they built the bulwark of learning that sustained a fine tradition of academic pursuits. With few exceptions, imperial governments throughout China's history promoted learning by sponsoring the civil service examination and maintaining publicly funded schools at different administrative levels. These governmental schools were intended to conserve the existing knowledge and produce individuals with practical administrative skills. In most cases, however, they stifled rather than stimulated original thinking. Private schools preserved and developed unorthodox learning and maintained the limited independence of China's academia. Through their eclectic approaches, private *shuyuan* enriched the Confucian ideology as well, especially because *shuyuan* leaders were often synthesizers of the Confucian and non-Confucian scholarship.

As a rule, private schools tended to flourish in times of the breakdown of central power and decline of governmental schools. Their strength lay in their flexible programs and their relative academic freedom, which attracted many students of high intellectual caliber who had lost faith in the orthodoxy. During the Ming period, some major *shuyuan* regularly held academic conferences. Scholars from different schools met at these conferences, and their talks often attracted hundreds of listeners. The exchange of views stimulated lively debates and produced great lecturers such as Qian Hongde, Chen Shifang, and Wang Ji. The fact that some speakers at these conferences came from obscure backgrounds suggests the democratic tradition in Chinese education.[28]

Whenever political orthodoxy became entrenched at the beginning of a new regime or when the political establishment felt insecure, private institutions of learning were likely to face literary inquisition. The First Emperor of Qin China, for example, attributed the downfall of the Late Zhou dynasty to the allegedly pernicious influence of Confucian schools and reacted to the challenge of private schools by burning Confucian classics and burying their owners alive. In 267, the government of the Western Jin banned private schools where astrology was taught not only because astrology was so popular but also because it was interwoven with court politics, thereby directly threatening the throne in a time of social unrest. This policy was followed by the government of the Northern

Wei at least twice, first in 440, then in 470. According to an imperial decree in 470, if a private school was found in session, the teacher and his employer's entire family would be executed. Despite the wrath of emperors, private schools never totally went out of existence. Even in the Northern Wei era, private schools revived with a vengeance, only seven years after the 470 ban.

In the Ming and Song periods, the Chinese government made strenuous efforts to incorporate private schools, especially the *shuyuan*, into the orbit of the *keju* system, while at the same time vigorously promoting governmental schools. The Manchu conquerors of China likewise blamed the waning of the Ming regime on the subversive nature of the *shuyuan*. For decades, the Manchu regime kept the *shuyuan* in check while promoting the Confucian orthodoxy in order to establish their credit among the conquered Chinese.

The rise and fall of private schools apparently points to some behavioral patterns of the Chinese state. To its credit, the Chinese government showed continuous interest in education, and the *keju* system was the fulcrum of its power. In times of relative peace and prosperity, education thrived, sometimes at the expense of private schools. The Song dynasty, for example, launched three campaigns to promote education between 1044 and 1102. The result was an elaborate system of governmental schools ranging from the *Zongxue* (school for members of the royal clan) to *xiaoxue* (county schools). Governmental schools not only prepared candidates for the civil service examination but also offered courses in a variety of fields, including medicine, arithmetic, and calligraphy. The Manchu regime perfected the skill of ideological control by attempting to make all *shuyuan* governmental. The regime not only provided scholarships to many *shuyuan*, but also granted their students with academic titles such as *jiansheng* (a student at, or qualified candidate for, the *Guozijian*), *xiucai* (budding talent), and *tongsheng* (qualified candidate). *Shuyuan* curricula consequently became increasingly geared to the civil service examination and focused on textual studies of Confucian and Neo-Confucian classics.[29] The regime did not, however, have the resources or the intention of eliminating private education altogether.

Unfortunately, while governmental schools thrived under a strong central government and in a healthy economy, they usually fell into a downward spiral when the central power disintegrated. In the chaotic interims when the governmental school system collapsed, private schools persisted and helped preserve a fine tradition in education in preparation for the next upsurge in learning. It appears that each surge of private education concurred with the rise of a new school of learning and many of China's greatest thinkers either studied or taught at private schools. In the Spring-Autumn period, private schools thrived during the rivalry of the One Hundred Schools of Thought. Confucius, in particular, collected, studied, and compiled scholars works of the Early Zhou period into what came to be known as the Confucian classics. In the Han period, private education spearheaded the textual learning of pre-Qin classics (*jingxue*), while in the Song and Ming periods, private schools, especially the *shuyuan*, pioneered the so-called Neo-Confucian learning (*lixue*), which later became the sanctified orthodoxy. In his studies at Jishan Shuyuan, Wang Yangming, the most original thinker and innovative educator of Ming China, developed his famous concept of *liangzhi* (man's innate capacity to know good), that added a valuable metaphysical and moral dimension to Neo-Confucian philosophy. In the eighteenth and nineteenth centuries, scholars in the *shuyuan* were among the first to voice concerns about the inadequacy of the Neo-Confucian learning and to advocate educational reform. Scholars such as Gu Yanwu, Huang Zongxi, Hu Wei, and Ran Yuan were active promoters of the so-called practical learning (*shixue*).[30]

Since the Confucian ideology emphasized conformity other than dissension, uniformity other than diversity, private schools, especially at the level of the *shuyuan*, could be dangerous if they attracted unconventional talents and deviated from political orthodoxy. In a culture where social compliance was essential, the government tended to be highly sensitive to any subversive thought. While the *keju* proved extremely effective in keeping China's education under central control, it was nevertheless not immune to human frailty, since it promised political power and financial returns. When the *keju* became dysfunctional, private schools would become disoriented, and some would do things that disturbed the political establishment. During the Song period, the imperial government swore to punish those *shuyuan* that spread political heresy and subversive astrology. However, since the imperial decrees were by and large a preemptive measure, the central government never totally liquidated private academies. The few major campaigns against private schools in the Qin, Jin, and Ming periods tended to be unpopular and short-lived.[31] Moreover, these campaigns seemed to provide additional stimuli for private schools in the ensuing periods.

Despite its ups and downs, the private school remained the mainstay of China's education for over two thousand and five hundred years. The system was, in fact, the vehicle for moral values that sustained Chinese civilization. In a predominantly agrarian society, private schooling demonstrated great vitality because of its low cost and flexible schedule. The intricate interplay between private schools and Chinese society, and between private schools and governmental schools would undergo drastic transformations in modern times, when the entire Chinese civilization was dragged to the brink of annihilation. The revolutionary changes in Chinese society since the nineteenth century posed the most severe test to private schools since their inception. The rise and fall of private schools, in turn, attested to the potency of Chinese culture.

## NOTES

1. In the Zhou period, *zhou* was an administrative unit consisting of twenty-five hunderd households, while *dang*, a unit under *zhou*, consisted of five hundred households.

2. The birth of private education dates back to the dawn of Chinese civilization in the form of *jiaxue* (familiy school) during the era of the Five Emperors (ca. 3,000 B.C.), Mao Lirui & Shen Guanqun ed., *Zhongguo jioyu tongshi* (General history of Chinese education) (Jinan: Shandong Education Press, 1985), vol., 1, pp. 33-34.

3. Namely, the *Book of Poetry* (Shijing), *Book of History* (Shujing or Shangshu), *Book of Etiquette* (Liji), *Book of Music* (Yueji), *Book of Change* (Yijing), and the *History of the States of Lu* (Chunqiu).

4. Fan Ye, *Houhan shu: Rulin zhuan* (Book of later Han: Stories of scholars), see Wu Ni, *Zhongguo gudai sixue fazhan zhu wenti yanjiu* (Studies on private education in pre-modern China) (Beijing: Social Sciences Press, 1996). p. 55.

5. The system started in the short-lived Sui dynasty, 589-618 A.D.

6. In Beijing there were also a number of schools for members of the imperial clan and children of Manchu nobles.

7. Wu Ni, *Zhongguo gudai sixue fazhan*, pp. 162-166.

8. Xiao Jianbin, "Ming-Qing shiqi de *keju* kaoshi zhidu" (The *keju* system in Mong and Qing China), Chen Xuexun ed., *Zhongguo jiaoyushi yanjiu* (Studies in the history of Chinese education) (Shanghai: East China Normal University Press, 1995), pp. 111-184; Hu Chang-tu, "Tradition and Change in Chinese Education," in Hu Changtu ed., Chinese Education under Communism (New York: Bureau of Publication, Teachers College, Columbia University, 1962), p. 15; John Cleverly, *The Schooling of China: Tradition and Modernity* (North Sydney: Allen & Unwin Pty. Ltd., 1985), p. 20.

9. During the Ming period, for example, the Hongwu emperor ordered local governments to establish the *shexue* (community schools or village schools). The endeavor, however, was soon abandoned for financial and administrative reasons. See Wu Ni, *Zhongguo gudai sixue fazhan*, pp. 112-117, 190-191.

10. It was also called alternately *shuguan*, *xueguan*, and *xuefang* and its urban version sometimes called *shixue* (literally township schools).

11. Hu Chang-tu, "Tradition and Changes in Chinese education," pp. 12-13; Evelyn Sakakida Rawski, *Education and Popular Literacy in Ch'ing China* (Ann Arbor: University of Michigan Press, 1979), pp. 24-33.

12. Other common texts used for *mengxue* were: *Yuanshi shifan* (Yuan's model text) by Yuan Cai, the *Three-Character Classic*, the *Hundred Surnames*, the *Si Shu* (Four Confucian classics); *Qianjia shi* (Poetry by a thousand bards), and *Guwen guanzhi* (Best classical prose). See Mao Lirui & Shen Guanqun ed., *Zhongguo jiaoyu tongshi*, vol. 3., pp. 43-53; Wu Ni, *Zhongguo gudai sixue fazhan*, p. 263; Xiao Jianbin, "Ming-Qing shiqi de *mengxue*" (Elementary education in Ming and Qing China), Chen Xuexun ed., *Zhongguo jiaoyushi yanjiu*, pp. 226-229; Rawski, *Education and Popular Literacy*, pp. 47-52.

13. Xiao Jianbin, "Ming-Qing shiqi de *mengxue*," pp. 188-199; Zhou Kai, "Quanyu xiangyang shimin sheli yixue gaoshi" (Governor's notice urging the gentry to establish charity schools), *Neizisongzhai zake* (Essays from Neizisong house), vol. 3, pp. 1-3. See Qu Xingui, *Yapian zhanzheng shiqi jiaoyu* (Education in the Opium War era) (Shanghai: Shanghai Education Press, 1990), pp. 319-320.

14. Li Deli, "Chouyi *yixue* jingjiu shiyi" (Measuers to ensure the continuation of the *yixue*), *Dingying jishi* (Dingying records), vol. 1, pp. 13-17, see Qu xinqui, *Zhongguo jindai jiaoyushi ziliao huibian* (Documents on education in modern China) (Shanghai: Shanghai Education Press, 1990), pp. 322-324; Tang Jian, "Xingli yixueshi" (Notice concerning setting up charity schools), *Tang Quesheng gong ji* (Works of Tang Jian), vol. 5, pp. 16-17, see ibid., pp. 324-325; Jiang Danlin, "*Yixue* tiaogui" (Rules at a *yixue*), *Qiushizhai congshu* (Series of Qiushizhai), vol. 20, pp. 1-3, see ibid., pp. 353-355.

15. He Changling, "Shugui" (Rules at a sishu), *Shugui*, vol. 1, p. 3, see Qu Xingui, *Zhongguo jindai jiaoyushi ziliaohuibian*, p. 358; Rawski, *Education and Popular Literacy*, pp. 44-53.

16. Shu Xincheng, *Wo he jiaoyu* (Education and I) (Taibei: Longwen Press, 1980), vol. 1, pp. 11-19, 29-32; Pu Songlin, "Xuejiu zichao" (A Teachers' self-ridicule), *Pu Songlin ji* (Works of Pu songlin) (Beijing: Zhonghua Shuju, 1962), vol. 2, pp. 1738-1742; anonymous, "*Mengguan shi*" (Song of a *mengguan*), see Qu Xingui, *Zhongguo jindai jiaoyushi ziliao huibian*, pp. 409-410; anonymous, Qingzhan shuku wen" (Bitterness of a teacher), ibid., p. 410; Xiao Jianbin, "Ming-Qing shiqi de *mengxue*," pp. 229-230.

17. Ibid., pp. 14-19, 33-37; Rawski, *Education and Popular Literacy*, pp. 42-44.

18. Wu Ni, *Zhongguo gudai sixue fazhan*, pp. 94-103; Zhang Zhengfan, *Zhongguo shuyuan zhidu kaolue* (A brief study of the *shuyuan* in China) (Nanjing: Jiangsu Education Press, 1985), pp. 6-11.

19. Mao Lirui and Shen Guanqun ed., *Zhongguo jiaoyu tongshi*, vol. 3, pp. 202-203.

20. Tang Chenglie, "Xuexiao pian" (On schools), *Huangchao jingshiwen xubian* (Essays on statecraft), vol. 64, see Qu Xingui, *Zhongguo jindai jiaoyushi ziliao huibian*, pp. 156-157.

21. Chen Qingzhi, *Zhongguo jiaoyushi* (History of Chinese education) (Taibei: Commercial Press, 1968), pp. 436-453.

22. The system consisted of the *Guozijian, Zongxue, Jueloxue, Jingshangxue, Xiangangongxue* at the capital, and *fuxue* (provincial schools), *zhouxue* (prefectural schools) and *xianxue* (county schools). See Li Guilin ed., *Zhongguo jiaoyushi* (History of Chinese education) (Shanghai: Shanghai Education Press, 1989), pp. 204-243.

23. Tang Chenglie, "Xuexiao pian," *Huangchaojingshiwen xubian*, vol. 64, see Qu Xingui ed., *Zhongguo jindai jiaoyushi ziliao huibian*, pp. 156-157; Wang Baoren, "Wueguan lun" (On the official-instructor), *Huangchao jingshiwen xubian*, vol. 65, p. 15, see Qu Xingui ed., *Zhongguo jindai jiaoyushi ziliao huibian*, pp. 160-161; Miu Gen, "Xuetang tongbi ji" (Problems common in governmental schools), *Wenzhang youxi*, see ibid., 164-165.

24. Ge Qiren, "*Shuyuan* yi" (On the *shuyuan*), *Weijingzhai wenji* (Essays from Weijing house) (1850), vol. 1, pp. 3-4, see Qu Xingui ed., *Zhongguo jindai jiaoyushi ziliao huibian*, p. 305.

25. Liang Zhangju, "*Shuyuan* shanzhang" (The dean of a *shuyuan*), *Tuiyan suibi* (Essays from the Tuiyan), vol. 6, p. 17; Dai Junheng, "Tongxiang Shuyuan siyi" (Four comments on the Tongxiang Academy), *Weijing shangguan wenchao*, vol. 1, pp. 16-22, see Qu Xingui ed., *Zhongguo jindai jiaoyushi ziliao huibian*, pp. 306-310.

26. Yan Yuan, *Yan Xizhai xiansheng yanxinglu* (Words and actions of Yan Yuan), See Zhou Dechang, "Yan Yuan-Li Gong xuepai jiaoyu sixiang de lishi diwei he yingxiang" (Education philosophy of the Yan Yuan-Li Gong school: Historical significance and influence), "Mingdai de qingdai de zhongwai wenhua jiaoyu jiaoliu"

(Cultural and educational exchanges between China and the West in the Ming and early Qing periods), Chen Xuexin ed., *Zhongguo jiaoyushi yanjiu*, pp. 283-307, 395-396.

27. Zhou Dechang, "Qiang-Jia xuepai jiaoyu sixiang de lishi diwei he yingxiang" (Educational philosophy of the Qian-Jia school: Historical significance of influence), Chen Xuexun ed., *Zhongguo jiaoyushi yanjiu*, pp. 342-358.

28. Zhang Zhengfan, *Zhongguo shuyuan zhidu kaolue*, p. 81.

29. Wang Fengjie, *Zhongguo jiaoyushi* (History of Chinese education) (Taibei: Zhongzheng Shuju, 1967), pp. 158-159; Wang Jianjun, "Ming-Qing shiqi *shuyuan* de tedian" (Characteristics of the *shuyuan* in the Ming and Qing periods), Chen Xuexun ed., *Zhongguo jiaoyushi yanjiu*, pp. 76-81.

30. Zhou Dechang, "Wang Yangming xuepai jiaoyu sixiang de lishi dewei he yingxiang" (Educational philosophy of the Wang Yangming school: Historical significance and influence), "Jia-Qian xuepai de jiaoyu sixiang," Chen Xuexun ed., *Zhongguo jiaoyushi yanjiu*, pp. 231-282, 347-401.

31. Wang Jianjun, "Ming-Qing shiqi *shuyuan* de tedian," ibid., pp. 69-73; Zhou Dechang, "Jia-Qian xuepai jiaoyu sixiang," pp. 343-344.

# 2

# Private Schools in Early Modern China

Given the unusual success of Chinese education until the nineteenth century, few people thought of changing it. Starting with the mid-nineteenth century, however, a series of events exposed its inadequacy for modern times. China's humiliating encounters with the West, in particular, created an intellectual and social atmosphere in which educational reform was not only possible but necessary for both dynastic and national survival. At the heart of the reformist outcry was the grave concern over China's technological backwardness. Open-minded Confucian officials came to believe that the introduction of Western learning into China was a most viable solution.[1]

## THE DRIVE FOR THE NEW EDUCATION

Educational reform started in the 1860s as a component of the Self-Strengthening Movement and was sponsored by a few high-ranking officials involved in "barbarian affairs" (*yiwu*). It focused on China's need for specialists in such fields as foreign languages and modern technology. After decades of slow progress it gained momentum at the turn of this century, not as a panacea for the Manchu dynasty, but rather as a death knell for China's imperial system.

Under the auspices of reformers such as Li Hongzhang, Zuo Zongtang, and Sheng Xuanhuai, three types of governmental schools were founded between 1862 and 1900: foreign language training institutes, technical schools, and military academies. From the point of view of the Chinese court in Beijing, there was an urgent need to understand Western culture and Westerners. In 1862 the first foreign language school (*Tongwenguan*) was founded in Beijing, under the direct auspices of the Foreign Affairs Office (*Zongli yamen*), for the training of diplomatic personnel. Later, similar schools, such as Guangzhou *Tongwenguan*, Shanghai Foreign Language School (Shanghai *fangyanguan*), and Hubei Self-Strengthening School (Hubei *ziqiang xuetang*) were set up. At these schools, students studied foreign languages in addition to science. In the same period, the government opened a number of technical schools to train much-needed technological personnel. The first one was the Fujian Ship-Building Institute (Fujiang *chuanzheng xuetang*), opened in 1866 by scholar-official Zuo Zongtang, followed by Shanghai Machine-Building School (Shanghai *jiqi xuetang*), Tianjin Telegraph School (Tianjin *dianbao xuetang*), Shanghai Telegraph School (Shanghai *dianbao xuetang*), and Hubei Mining School (Hubei *kuangye xuetang*). In 1881 China's first naval academy, Tianjin Naval Academy (Tianjin *shuishi xuetang*), came into existence, followed by Guangdong Naval Academy (Guangdong *shuishi xuetang*), Tianjin Military Academy (Tianjin *beiwu xuetang*), and Hubei Military Academy, the last of which was sponsored by Zhang Zhidong who, after Li Hongzhang, became the most vigorous champion of China's self-strengthening.[2]

Ambitious as it was, the government's program scored only limited results. To begin with, the reform was aimed not at mass education but at the training of an elite group of technological personnel. The new schools were intended to supplement rather than replace the old school system geared to the civil service examination. Like students from *shuyuan* and other preparatory schools, students from the new schools were expected to pass the tests in Confucian classics to hold government positions. Since the old avenue to officialdom was easier and cheaper, the vast majority of the best and brightest of China's youth kept delving into traditional learning. In the end, several hundred individuals trained in modern science and technology were woefully inadequate for the country's modernization needs.

The inherent inadequacy of the Self-Strengthening Movement, epitomized by China's humiliating defeat in the Sino-Japanese War of 1894-1895, finally convinced some reformers that unless the civil service examination was abandoned, the new education would never get a fair chance. Between 1895 and 1898, reformers called for institutional changes as a remedy for China's chronic weakness. Among the prescribed changes were the abolition of the civil service examination and the implementation of a Western-style school system. In a memorial presented in June 1896, Li Duanfen, Vice-Minister of Justice, laid the blame for China's problems at the door of the *keju* system, saying that the system kept China's best and brightest from going to new schools by offering a greater potential for power and wealth. In order to speed up China's technological progress, Li recommended that foreign languages, literature, arithmetic, astronomy, geography, and world history be added to the curricula of prefectural and county schools. The *shuyuan*, he further suggested, should be renamed *xuetang* (schools) as befitting the new curriculum.[3]

The shock wave sent by the Sino-Japanese War ushered in the haphazard reform of 1898, when reformers such as Kang Youwei and Liang Qichao attempted a comprehensive modernization program. Of the imperial decrees issued between June and September, about a dozen concerned education. The reformers wanted, among other things, to set up colleges and schools in all provinces, prefectures, and cities. The eight-legged essay (*baguwen*), based on Confucian classics was to be replaced in the civil service examination by a topical treatise. However, the Four Books and Five Classics remained the basic texts for all students. The rationale for this change was not without contradiction: "Though technically different, topical treatises and correct interpretations of the classics originate from the same consideration: that a man of learning must be thoroughly familiar with philosophy and history and be competent in practice as well as in theory. He must be a versatile scholar, shying away from sophistry and empty talk. Only then would he not disappoint the government that seeks talents out of the normal avenue."[4]

In the face of imminent national extinction, China could no longer confine Western learning to gunnery and navigational skills but had to incorporate Western philosophy and political science into the curriculum as well. Yet such educational change did not take place in a vacuum; nor was it independent of a myriad of historical forces. While the imperial government adopted a more forward-looking approach to education, the implementation of the new education (*xinxue*) proved to be far beyond its resources. Combined with the social, economic, and political trends at the turn of the century, the introduction of the new education, centered on Western-style schools, became the midwife of an intellectual and political revolution.

Among the founders of new schools were a large number of merchants, many of whom had a gentry background. Since many of the country gentry were also switching their resources to commerce, it became imperative for them or their children to study foreign languages and Western business. It was obviously also in their best interest in the long run to promote education in these fields for Chinese youth so that they could compete with Western merchants and businessmen in China.

Furthermore, patriotic merchants financed education as a reaction to foreign aggression in China. Mu Xiangyue, a textile plant owner in Shanghai who had studied in the United States, opened free elementary schools because he felt deeply ashamed by the foreign control of China's maritime custom service. Yang Sisheng, founder of Pudong Middle School in Shanghai, amassed a great fortune in business. Responding to the call of the government, he set up an elementary school in his own family compound. In a couple of years the school proved a success. Then, against the advice of his family members, Yang contributed his mansion, family shrine, and 190,000 silver taels to set up seven schools, including Pudong Middle School and Pudong Teachers School, leaving only about 10 percent of his fortune to his children.[5]

In the province of Shandong, where the Germans secured privileges from the Chinese government after the Sino-Japanese War, local gentry were incensed by the German effort to impose the German language in all public schools. Educators in the province therefore established the Zhendan Public School (Zhendan *gongxue*) in the city of Qingdao. In the founding bulletin, organizers of the school explained that they set up the school simply because the German occupiers had revealed their villainous ambition by colonizing the eastern half of the province. "The Germans have not only monopolized the mining and railroading in Shandong but dominated our education. Since our nation's survival hangs in the balance, we believe it is the responsibility of every patriotic Chinese to combat the German scheme. We are therefore establishing the Zhendan Public School and sincerely pleading for generous help from our countrymen both at home and abroad."[6]

Out of the newly acquired nationalist sentiment, educators voluntarily offered part-time free schools and evening schools to children from poor families. In 1904 a woman by the name of Hui Xin set up the Zhenwen Girls School. On the day of the opening, she ceremoniously bled her arm when swearing to protect the school, even with her own life if necessary. One year later, the school fell into financial trouble. Hui Xin knocked on the doors of merchants and officials alike and finally secured a promise of funds from the local government. To ensure this financial support, she committed suicide, leaving a will that announced the government's pledge. Her noble but tragic story created widespread responses all over the country. Supporting schools thereafter became a demonstration of patriotism, and the slogan *huijia xingxue* (establishing schools with one's entire family possessions) inspired many well-to-do Chinese.[7]

In this social and intellectual atmosphere, private as well as public schools with private funding were viewed as the vehicle of revolutionary ideas. Naturally, the scholar gentry in the coastal areas took the lead. In 1896, Shanghai gentry scholars Wang Weitai and Zhong Tianwei founded the Yucai Academy (Yucai *shushu*) and Shanghai Sandeng Public School (Shanghai *sandeng gongxue*). Following their example, a Shanxi *juren* by the name of Xing Yanying set up the Congshi Academy (Congshi *shuyuan*); some scholars in Hunan set up the Dongshan Academy (Dongshan *jingshe*); and in Rui'an, Zhejiang province, local gentry opened Xueji School (*Xueji guan*). In 1897, the founding of schools entered into a high tide. Reformers changed the curriculum of the old *shuyuan* and launched a noisy donation campaign which, in many counties, was headed by the magistrates themselves. The scholar-gentry, some of whom were retired officials, also organized academic associations and promoted educational reform in their publications.[8]

## THE GUIMAO SYSTEM AND PRIVATE SCHOOLS

Until 1901, however, China's school system remained by and large in the old groove, and schools at all levels were oriented toward the antiquated *keju* system. In the 1900s, enlightened literati had come to see the civil service examination as just a foot-dragging tradition; even the diehard conservatives could not revitalize the system. Urged by reform-minded officials such as Yuan Shikai, Zhang Zhidong, Sheng Xuanhuai, Liu Kunyi, and Chen Chunxuan, the Manchu court suspended the annual civil service examination at the county level in 1904, and in 1905 it abolished the system altogether to make way for a new school system.

Taking place at a time when the imperial government was tottering on the edge of its grave, the drive for the new education was tied up with the fate of the empire from the very outset. Zhang Zhidong, viceroy of Huguang, wrote "An Exhortation to Learning" (Quanxue pian), which was endorsed by the emperor and widely circulated throughout the country. In this short essay, Zhang stressed the need for education of practical subjects and the development of the skill of adapting traditional thinking to contemporary circumstances. When he wrote that "the strength of Western powers lies in their education," he was voicing the feelings of many of his contemporaries. In fact, all the advocates of reform in the late Qing, from Zheng Guanying and Sheng Xuanhuai to Liang Qichao and Yanfu, saw the establishment of a school system as the remedy for China's chronic illness. At the turn of the century, setting up schools to enlighten the populace became the rallying cry of all reformers.

Although the reform of 1898 became a victim of the power struggle at the top of the Chinese government, its undergirding idea survived the resulting bloody coup. The occupation of Beijing by allied powers in 1900-1901 convinced even the most staunch traditionalists in the court that reform was long overdue. The imperial government picked up the reformers' agenda in the hope of averting the inevitable. The new education thus took off with a vengeance in the darkest hours of the empire. In 1903 the imperial government issued the Guidelines for Educational Affairs (*xuewu gangyao*), drafted by Zhang Baixi, Zhang Zhidong, and Rong Qing. With the guidelines, the Manchu government attempted to make the theretofore scattered and sporadic educational reform into a national enterprise. A Ministry of Learning (*Xuebu*) was organized in December 1905 to coordinate efforts at all levels.

The Guimao Educational System of 1904,[9] as it is often referred to, proved to be a watershed in the history of China's education in modern times. Since Japan had proven its success in modernization, it is not surprising that the 1903 system was by and large a replica of the Japanese schooling system. Based on the guidelines, schools all over China were organized into three major stages and seven levels. Elementary education was composed of kindergarten, and the lower elementary and higher elementary; secondary education consisted in the middle school; and higher education was divided into the preparatory school, specialized college, and university.[10] The new policy was more a symbolic gesture than concrete action by the Manchu regime which, after decades of decay, was quickly falling apart. Nevertheless, it came out at an opportune moment, when the new education was gathering great momentum in Chinese society.

In the Guidelines for Educational Affairs, the imperial government instructed provincial, prefectural, and county governments to open new schools (*xuetang*) and started what can be called a compulsory education program. As part of an eleventh-hour effort to salvage the crumbling dynasty, the new school was not only intended to promote Western science and technology but was also designed to prepare for a constitutional monarchy. Elementary education, the guidelines told government officials and educators alike, constituted the very foundation of a modern nation and was practiced by countries all over the world. At both the elementary and secondary levels, the new school adopted a largely Western curriculum yet included courses aimed at preserving China's cultural heritage. In addition to science and humanity subjects, for example, Confucian classics still occupied hours in the core curriculum.[11]

Following the guidelines, the Ministry of Learning promulgated the Compulsory Education Decree which ordered provincial, prefectural, and county governments to establish the Education-Promotion Office (*quanxuesuo*) and open new schools for children of seven years old and older. The director of the office was put in charge of a school district. He normally collaborated with local gentry in setting up schools and implementing the new curriculum. The merits of an educational administrator were measured by the number of schools established in his territory.[12] If a school-aged child failed to go to school, his father or, in the absence of the father, eldest brother, would be held accountable.

The ailing dynasty, however, was wallowing in a huge financial crisis and never had the resources to match its professed ambition. For example, in 1911 the total government spending of the year was around 300 million silver taels. Educational expenditures made up only 1 percent of the total budget. Even in Sichuan which had the most schools and students in the nation, educational spending of 290,000 silver taels made up only 4 percent of the province's annual expenditures in 1908. Yet in the same year, people in the province squandered nearly one million taels on various religious and superstitious activities. In 1909 China reported 3.7 students per thousand of its population. The comparable number in the United States was 203, in Japan, 112, and in Mexico, 55. Editors of the *Dongfang Zazhi* (Orient Magazine) published such statistics, which were humiliating to the Chinese elite, apparently with a view to stimulating it into concrete efforts in education.[13]

To make up for the lack of funds for education, the central government encouraged charity and the establishment of private schools. The guidelines of 1903 recognized that every province had a very strained budget and that the government alone could not meet the needs of the entire nation. Local governments were therefore told to urge members of the gentry class to donate money for setting up elementary schools. In the Imperially Approved Guidelines for Schools (*Zhouding xuetang zhangcheng*) of 1903, the Manchu court not only called upon the merchant and gentry class to participate in the national drive for new schools but offered incentives such as rewarding investment in education with honorary titles.[14]

Even prior to the guidelines of 1903, a few scholar-gentry had begun to open elementary schools to offer Western learning to children. In 1878 a merchant in Shanghai, by the name of Zhang Huanlun, opened Zhengmeng Academy, which was probably the first new-style elementary school ever set up by a Chinese.[15] Another well-known private school, Nanyang Public School (*Nanyang gongxue*), was founded in 1897. The promulgation of the 1903 educational system set off a drive for new schools; its initial stage involved some of the most forward-looking members of the gentry class. In 1909 the community-funded schools under the auspices of the gentry had become predominant in all provinces except Hubei, where governmental schools took the lead because of the work of Zhang Zhidong.[16]

The explanation for such outpourings of enthusiasm lies in a multitude of factors. First, the abolition of the civil service examination in 1905 signified the demise of traditional learning. Even back in 1901, the change in the content and format of the civil service examination excluded many otherwise eager candidates.[17] The disintegration of the old regime, moreover, called on an increasing number of the scholar- gentry to campaign for the new education. As the ruling elite in traditional Chinese society, these people were imbued with a sense of social responsibility. While most of them were far removed from the struggle between the reformers and conservatives at the top, many were informed enough to be aware of the crisis faced by China. Because political revolution was unthinkable, most of them probably opted for education as both a noble and fashionable endeavor. By patronizing schools, the scholar-gentry expected to preserve their traditional leadership in Chinese society and even obtain greater social prestige and political power. In the capital area, about two dozen private individuals were rewarded for their donations to education, some with government offices. Zhang Zhidong, the renowned reformer in the late Qing era, even received inscriptions from the Emperor and the Empress Dowager for his leadership in the drive for new schools.[18] For those who had been involved in a *sishu* or *shuyuan*, it did not seem to be too sharp a turn to change the school to a *xuetang*, at least in name. Further, advocates of the new education believed that, to revitalize the nation, the Chinese people must open up to the outside world. The success of Japan in modern times offered a viable example. In Hunan and Hubei, local gentry set up the so-called "Learning to Fight Companies," openly associating education with national defense after the Japanese model.

The national drive for the new education was also spearheaded by an increasing number of returned students from overseas, especially Japan.

Although study abroad was experimented with during the Self-Strengthening Movement, it did not gain momentum until the Sino-Japanese War of 1894-1895. In 1896, there were only thirteen Chinese students in Japan. Then the abolition of the *keju* system in 1905 turned a trickle into a flood. In 1906 twelve thousand Chinese were enrolled at dozens of Japanese normal, military, and law schools. Apparently, there was a growing awareness of the inevitability of change and continuing determination among the gentry to maintain their prestige. Between 1905 and 1910, the Chinese government organized officials in charge of education, and gentry involved in education, to visit China's Herculean neighbor. Zhang Zhidong, viceroy of Huguang, sent two delegations to Japan to study the Japanese school system and purchase text books.[19] Chinese students preferred Japan to America or Europe because of the relatively low cost of travel. In addition, Japan's synthesis of Western learning was much easier for the Chinese to digest at second hand.

The movement for Western-style schools was, admittedly, uneven and the participation of the gentry class varied. Not everyone in the gentry class was enlightened, and those pioneered in the new education were motivated by different factors. Yet when the nation called, and the government was unable to assume the responsibility, the gentry proved to be almost the only segment of Chinese society with the resources and expertise to respond effectively. As the elite in rural China, the gentry had long been entrusted with tax-collecting and fund-raising and even the engineering of public works. Setting up new schools only added a new program to their traditional repertoire. In fact, during the 1900s, many of the excises levied on commerce and services were controlled by the local gentry for running new-style schools.[20] It is fair to say that the enlightened gentry constituted the mainstay of the educational reform at the turn of the century.

Many of the new schools under gentry control represented only awkward parodies of their Western model. Over-enthusiasm and a lack of experience, combined with the authoritarian tradition of the ruling class in China, created the opportunity for incidents such as the confiscation of Buddhist temple properties for schools and the exaction of educational funds without adequate consent that incited popular protests. Many of the participants in the new schools were motivated by interests other than national salvation through education. But when well-trained teachers and administrators were lacking, gentry participation was the most desirable start that China's modern education could ever expect. The critics of gentry involvement, for one reason or another, tended to exaggerate the problems.[21] In retrospect, we should give a very positive balance sheet to gentry-scholars as a whole for their contribution to China's infant modern education.

The "New Policies" (*Xinzheng*) implemented between 1901 and 1905 further aroused the zest for Western-style schools. In 1902 seventeen colleges, four normal schools, and three technical schools were established nationwide. This modest beginning, though inviting criticism from reformers such as Liang

Qichao, presaged a new wave of educational reform. In the 1900s and 1910s, scholar-gentry apparently outstripped government officials to be the leaders and sponsors of China's new schools (see Table 1). In Guangdong province alone, 781 new schools were announced between 1904 and 1908. Among the five hundred donors for new schools, 80 percent were from the gentry class. In Sichuan, any person who donated one thousand taels or more was reported to the emperor by the governor-general, and a memorial archway (*paifang*) was built in his honor. Even women's education became a trend in a culture where women had been relegated to an inferior position. In 1907 the Ministry of Learning drew up the Guidelines for Women's Normal Schools. Thereafter private schools for female students were incorporated into the national system.[22]

One of the earlier private schools set up by Chinese in this period was Nankai School in Tianjin. Its founder, Yan Xiu (1860-1929), represented the reformism among the Confucian scholar-gentry. A *jinshi* (advanced scholar) in 1883, Yan became a *hanlin* scholar in 1886. In 1898 he resigned to return to his hometown, Tianjin, where he experimented with the new education. Yan witnessed the occupation of his hometown by Western allied forces during the Boxer Rebellion of 1900. Agonizing over the woes of the country, he became resolved to help China through education: "Survival in today's world requires self-strengthening," he wrote, "Self-strengthening, in turn, takes talents, which could only come out of education."[23] In 1898 Yan Xiu met Zhang Boling, then a retired naval officer, who accepted Yan Xiu's invitation to teach at the latter's family school (*jiaguan*).

Born in Tianjin in 1876, Zhang Boling demonstrated both ambition and talents as a teenager. In 1891 he was admitted into the North Sea Naval Academy (Beiyang *shushi xuetang*), where he was exposed to Western learning and influenced by people like Yan Fu, China's Fukuzawa Yukichi.[24] After graduation, Zhang enlisted in the North Sea Fleet, then the pride of China's young navy. Unfortunately, Zhang's military career came to an abrupt end when the North Sea Fleet was annihilated by the Japanese navy in 1895. At Weihaiwei in Shandong province, Zhang witnessed the transfer of the naval base from the Japanese to the Chinese on one day, only to be delivered to the British on the next. Out of such excruciating humiliation, Zhang decided to commit the rest of his life to educating China's next generation.

In 1904, after two trips to Japan, Yan and Zhang turned Yan's *jiaguan* into a private school, later named Number One Private School of Tianjin. A combination of rigor and innovation at the school attracted an increasing number of students. In two years, Number One Private School faced over-crowding. Luckily, in 1906 it received a land donation south of Tianjin from a local merchant. The swampy property was called Nankaiwa or Nankai Hollow, from which Nankai School derived its famous name. In the meantime, the school entered a new phase of expansion with donations amounting to twenty-six thousand silver taels from a number of patrons. At the new location, Nankai established a reputation as the best private school in north China. In 1911 it was

**Table 1: Percentage of Privately Funded Schools, 1907-1912**

| | | Nantong County | | Jiangsu Province | | National Total | |
|---|---|---|---|---|---|---|---|
| | | Total | Privately Funded (%) | Total | Privately Funded (%) | Total | Privately Funded (%) |
| 1907 | Schools | 56 | 100 | 1,615 | 72 | 35,787 | 67 |
| | Pupils | 1,732 | 100 | 55,779 | | 1,006,743 | |
| 1908 | Schools | 64 | 100 | 1,870 | 79 | 42,424 | 70 |
| | Pupils | 2,203 | 100 | 66,215 | | 1,278,242 | |
| 1909 | Schools | 74 | 100 | 2,135 | 80 | 101,382 | 72 |
| | Pupils | 3,058 | 100 | 82,166 | | 1,573,740 | |
| 1912 | Schools | 194 | 20 | 5,343 | 18 | 87,272 | |
| | Pupils | 7,892 | 19 | 236,351 | 18 | 2,933,387 | |

Note: The apparent drop in the percentage of private schools in 1912 results from a change in the definition of public schools by which a large number of privately funded schools were classified as public. For details, see Marianne Bastid, *Educational Reform in Early Twentieth-Century China*, pp. 68-69.

joined by two governmental schools, Tianjin Keji School and Changlu Middle School, thereby acquiring an additional fund of eight thousand silver taels per year. In the Republican period, Nankai would become the pride of China's modern education.[25]

Because of its autonomous or semiautonomous status and the very nature of the new education, a private school could also turn into a center of political agitation, not unlike the *shuyuan* in imperial China. The Tongmenghui (Revolutionary Alliance) under Sun Yat-sen, largely employed new schools for its bases. Members of the organization not only joined the teaching staff of existing new schools, but also founded their own schools as well. In the winter of 1901-1902, Cai Yuanpei, a member of the Tongmenghui, together with his comrades Jiang Guanyun and Huang Zongyang, set up the Patriotic Women's School (*Aiguo nuxue*) in his residence in Shanghai; the founders' wives and daughters were in the first class. The school vowed to repudiate traditional restrictions on women and promote gender equality. In its bylaws, the school set as its goal to elevate women's intellect, morals, health, and patriotic feelings.[26] Topics discussed at the school included the French Revolution and Russian anarchists and, to prepare its students for revolutionary conspiracy, the chemistry teacher even taught the female students how to make bombs. In 1905, revolutionaries inaugurated the Datong School in Shaoxin, Zhejiang province. Qiu Jin, a female revolutionary of the Joan-of-Arc type, was put in charge of the school's general affairs. During an abortive uprising, quite a few of Datong's students, together with Qiu Jin, were arrested and put to death by the Qing government.[27]

The government was naturally concerned with the potentially subversive nature of private education and took precautions against its undesirable effects. In the Guidelines for Educational Affairs, the state prohibited the teaching of Western political science because, while Western science had practical applications, Western politics was "abstract rhetoric" (*kongtan*). Private schools were also forbidden to offer military training without official permission. Ultimately, students were required to focus on practical skills in order to serve the nation; they were not permitted to criticize government policies.[28]

The discrepancy between the government's over-ambitious goals in education and its fiscal limitations, plus the public's interest in education, resulted in a rapid growth of private and locally funded public schools. Before 1905 governmental schools dominated the new education. By 1909, in contrast, the number of privately-funded schools was more than twice the number of public schools. In some areas, all new schools were privately funded as a result of the promotion and participation of local gentry. At the same time, the old educational administration betrayed an increasing inability to handle new schools. Thus local governments gradually transferred school administrations to private individuals, especially the well-educated scholar-gentry.[29] This shift further weakened the tie between education and the government, allowing a more dynamic and relatively independent school system to emerge in China.

The development of the new education required changes in the traditional private schools as well. As early as the 1870s, farsighted educators began to modify the curricula in some *sishu* and *shuyuan* by instilling Western learning into their classrooms. From the point of view of the government, China's hundreds of thousands of *sishu* were natural candidates for implementing the new curricula. For educators at the *sishu* and *shuyuan*, remolding their programs was the right thing to do to save both the nation and their own careers. As the viceroy of Huguang, Zhang Zhidong began to reform the curricula at Lianghu Shuyuan. His example was eagerly followed by others. During the Reform of 1898, the central government instructed local functionaries to help the better *sishu* and *shuyuan* to develop into schools. Unfortunately, because of the opposition of the Empress Dowager, the government failed to follow through on this initiative. During her exile in Xi'an in 1901, however, the Empress Dowager herself decided to adopt what her opponents had proposed. Between 1901 and 1905, all *shuyuan* were turned into new schools, at least in name.

Compared with the change in name, the change in substance proved to be much tougher. In 1906 educators in Shanghai took up the challenge of remolding the *sishu* in the Yangtse delta. In the bylaws of the Sishu Reform Society (Sishu gailianghu*i*), promoters found inspiration in Fukuzawa Yukichi, the greatest educational reformer of Meiji Japan and his Keio-Gijuku School, which eventually grew into Keio University. "Given the financial conditions of the country and the educational level of its people, China was not only short of money but also short of teachers to develop the new education in a nation-wide scale." Rather than abolish millions of *sishu*, the government and educators should reform the existing school system according to Shanghai educators. The reformers urged their colleagues in *sishu* to adopt the new pedagogy, giving up the traditional rote learning for a more interactive approach even to the study of the Confucian classics which remained the basic texts. In some localities, two or more *sishu* merged into one to improve teaching efficiency and increase the diversity of subjects. Knowing that most *sishu* teachers did not have the requisite expertise in science, the Sishu Reform Society urged the establishment of teachers training schools, which would prepare young teachers to handle such subjects as mathematics, geography, science, and physical education. To monitor the quality of instructions at *sishu*, students of member schools were to take uniform exams twice a year. Although most *sishu* were still considered inferior to new schools, a *sishu* graduate who passed government-sponsored exams would qualify for governmental schools at the higher level.[30] Such stopgap measures nicely bridged the gap between *sishu* and new schools.

In 1910 the Ministry of Learning formulated Guidelines for the Reform of the *Sishu* and instructed local governments to conduct a general survey of the conditions in these schools. The guidelines set criteria for all *sishu* teachers and programs. According to the guidelines, Education-Promotion Offices were to administer qualifying exams for graduates of all *sishu* to monitor their progress and quality. Although the document targeted the inferior *sishu*, it did not specify how to deal with schools that failed to meet the criteria.[31]

The reform of the *sishu* and *shuyuan* was a mammoth task that would take decades. But the effort to upgrade the hundreds of thousands of *sishu* into the national program proved to be a worthy enterprise. The reform of the *sishu* received official support from the very outset. Officials in most cases apparently took the reform as part of their routine. Thus reforming the *sishu* and founding schools became related and coordinated efforts of both the government and local gentry. The best of these schools had acquired the necessary conditions for the transformation. Some, such as Jukui Shuyuan in Jiangjing, Sichuan, would become models for others.

## EARLY MISSION SCHOOLS

A peculiar phenomenon in China's modern education was the significant number of schools set up by Western missionaries. Missionary education in China dates back to 1818, when British missionaries opened schools in Malacca for the children of overseas Chinese. The second half of the nineteenth century witnessed a steady rise in the number of mission schools due to a growing interest of missionaries in education and a general advancement of Western powers in China. In many ways, mission schools were a catalyst for the educational reform in modern China.

The earliest mission schools were set up largely because of the Chinese indifference to the Christian Gospel. For example, it took the American Methodist mission in Guangzhou (Canton) ten years to make the first Chinese convert. It soon became obvious to Westerners that proselytizing had little effect on a people who were extremely proud of their cultural heritage. Eager to make converts, both Protestants and Catholics set up schools and made them vehicles of the Judeo-Christian civilization and a means of overcoming the resistance of the Confucian tradition. Missionaries had to teach their would-be Chinese allies Western languages so that the latter could understand the Bible, or they had to take up the challenge to master the unmanageable Chinese characters. Mission schools also served as training centers for Western workers and teachers who had just arrived in the field.

Starting in the 1840s, mission schools came under the protection of a series of "unequal treaties" between the Chinese government and the Western powers. The Sino-U.S. Treaty of Wangxia (Wang-hea) in 1844 provided, for instance, that citizens of the United States be allowed to establish their churches. The Sino-French Treaty of Huangpu (Whampoa) later that year acknowledged the privileges of French nationals to propagate Catholicism, a principle applied to all powers in China with the most-favored-nation status. The Treaty of Tianjin (Tientsin) in 1858, signed by China, Britain, and France, formally recognized the right of Westerners to conduct evangelical activities in China's interior.

Shortly after its inception, Christian education became an integral component of the missionary enterprise in China. Enormous amounts of human and material resources were allocated to dozens of Christian colleges and hundreds of mission schools in the central kingdom. In 1845 American Presbyterians set up Ningbo Boys' School. In 1851 St. John's Academy in Shanghai, the embryo of St. John's University, was founded by American Episcopalians as a school for Chinese boys.[32] In 1866 American Episcopalian missionaries set up Dengzhou (Tengchow) Boys' School (Wenhui guan), and in 1894, English Baptist missionaries began Qingzhou (Tsingchow) Boys' Boarding School (Guangde shuyuan) in Qingzhou. Dengzhou and Qingzhou were later consolidated into one school, which eventually became Qilu (Cheeloo) University. Mission schools multiplied after the Treaty of Tianjin. The First General Conference of Protestant Missionaries in 1877 reported twenty Protestant mission schools with 231 students.

The pace of Christian education picked up further around the turn of the century in the explosion of missions known as the Christian Occupation of China. In 1899 there were 1,296 Protestant missions in the Celestial Empire. By 1914, the number had more than quadrupled. By 1906, there were over 2,000 elementary schools and 400 middle schools run by Western missions.[33] On the eve of the Republican Revolution of 1911, Western missionaries operated 3,145 schools in the country. Protestant mission schools enrolled 138,937 students in 1912. Catholic and Orthodox mission schools had a student body of 50,000 to 100,000. In Southern Manchuria, the Japanese ran 28 schools with a total enrollment of 5,551 students.

A prominent trend in missionary education was the dramatic growth of Christian higher education in the late nineteenth and early twentieth centuries. After 1890, Protestant missions concentrated their resources on founding and operating colleges. While being an outgrowth of the general missionary education in China, the expansion of Christian colleges also suggested the need of Western missionaries to produce Chinese leaders for the missionary movement. To many Western missionaries, the Chinese intelligentsia's identifying with the missionary enterprise was of crucial importance for Christianity's fate in a largely secular culture.[34] Among the colleges set up by Protestant missions in China were Suzhou College (Soochow College or Dongwu Daxue) (1901) in Suzhou; Boone (Wenhua) College (1903) in Wuhan; Canton Christian College (1903) in Guangzhou (Canton); North China Union College (1904) in Beijing; Aurora (Zhengdan) University (1903) in Shanghai; West China Union University (1910) in Chengdu; the University of Nanking (1910) in Nanjing; and Hangzhou (Hangchow) Presbyterian College (1911) in Hangzhou.[35] The growing popularity of Christian colleges stemmed in part from the educational reform in general and the abolition of the civil service examination in 1905 in particular. As an increasing number of aspiring youth turned to Western-style education, mission schools began to seek both qualitative and quantitative improvements.

Early Christian education was divided along national and denominational lines, and few Christian colleges possessed the commensurate strength and quality of higher education. Most of them were more like secondary or preparatory schools. At the turn of the century, however, mission societies began to break sectarian boundaries to pool their resources together in setting up and running Christian colleges. Shandong Christian College, the predecessor of Qilu University, was a cooperative effort of American Presbyterian and English Baptist missions. When the school was renamed Qilu University in 1931, it was supported by five American missions, five English missions, and one Canadian mission. The University of Nanjing (*Jinling daxue*), which combined Nanjing University, Nanjing Christian College, and Presbyterian Academy, was jointly sponsored by American Presbyterian and Methodist missions. West China Union University in Chengdu was proposed in 1905 by American, English, and Canadian missionaries and came into operation in 1910.

The proliferation of mission schools spoke of Westerners' recognition of the role of education in the missionary enterprise. Mission schools proved the most effective and efficient tool to Christianize the Chinese empire, even though at the elementary and secondary levels, missionaries had to concede to their students' need for traditional Chinese learning. Overall, "the mere act of the gathering of younger members together and providing them with an education is the wisest and best contribution that one could make."[36] The success of Western missionaries in education was also made possible by the intellectual climate of the late Qing period, when opened-minded Chinese elite adopted a more positive attitude toward Western learning. In fact, reformers like Wang Tao and Sun Yat-sen embraced Christianity partly because they believed that the trinity of industry, Christianity, and democracy explained the enormous success of the West and were therefore the best remedies for their beleaguered country.[37] With the prosperity of the treaty ports, an increasing number of Chinese were willing to send their children to mission schools where English was the medium of instruction because they realized that a command of the English language would give the youngsters more opportunities in the business world on the China coast.

Almost from the very beginning, Christian colleges in China tried to establish ties with Western universities for academic as well as administrative purposes. Upon its birth in 1902, Suzhou (Soochow) University registered in Texas. St. John's University in Shanghai had a license from the District of Columbia, and Jinling (Ginling) College in Nanjing functioned as a branch campus of the State University of New York. Enlisting the support of Western institutions of higher education helped elevate instructional quality at mission colleges in China; it also helped promote the schools, because a diploma from a Christian college in China carried additional weight and might well be the gateway to an advanced degree in the West.

Until the 1900s, Christian education in China was funded almost exclusively from home missions. Since Chinese families of good standing showed little interest in an alien heterodox faith, missionary stations had to exhort children from poor Chinese families to attend Bible classes and bribe them with free schooling. While the management of middle schools was handled by missionaries in the field, the administration of a mission college was more complex. In most cases, the administration of a mission college was divided into two levels. A board of trustees in a Western country would make fundamental policies for the school and conduct fundraising; the day-to-day administration was left in the hands of a board of managers (*Guanli weiyuanhui*), which was often headed by a president appointed by the board of trustees. Compared with their Chinese counterparts, which came under the authority of the government from their inceptions, mission schools boasted considerable autonomy. Christian colleges, such as the Beijing Union Medical College and Xiangya (Hsiang-Ya) Medical College, were also financially healthier than Chinese colleges because, through the China Medical Board, they were fueled by such powerful institutions as the Rockfeller Foundation.[38]

Although some of the earliest mission schools had to provide free education and scholarships to attract Chinese students, they became quickly entrenched in the Chinese educational system because of their excellent facilities and programs as the springboard of study abroad. Starting in the 1910s, it became increasingly fashionable for affluent Chinese families to send their children to mission schools. The source of mission schools' revenue changed accordingly. By 1930 tuition from students had surpassed overseas funding to become the largest source of income of most Christian schools.[39] Thus, mission schools were not only an ally of Chinese private schools but also a strong competitor in many ways.

For decades, mission schools, especially Christian colleges, enjoyed privileges under the protection of the "unequal treaties." The Chinese government might not be happy with what Western mission schools were doing, but there was little it could do to stop them. Education authorities of the Chinese government, including the Ministry of Education and provincial education administrations had no say in the operation of mission schools nor did they realize the importance of the issue of educational sovereignty. In September 1906, when the Manchu dynasty was on its death bed, the Ministry of Learning (*xuebu*) even waived the registration requirement for foreign schools. "All countries differed from one another in their customs and cultural heritage and the education of one country does not necessarily fit the situation of another. In the drive for educational reform, it is the responsibility of people all over the country to set up schools for our people. As to the schools opened by foreigners in the interior, the imperially approved regulations had no specific restrictions. Thus while those already in existence are allowed to continue their operation, new ones in the future need not register."[40] To later patriots, this dispensation was tantamount to relinquishing educational sovereignty.

Many new schools in the early twentieth century, especially those under official auspices, were haphazardly organized. Some existed only in name and did not have the resources needed to fulfill the curriculum required by the central government. Private schools, especially those with adequate funding, were thus a valuable addition to the infant public school system. Those which claimed a national repute, such as Nankai in Tianjin and Mingde in Changsha, Hunan province, were marked by strong teaching staffs, a curriculum that combined traditional subjects and Western learning, and sufficient homemade and imported equipment. While many enrolled students from well-to-do families, scholarships to students from poor families were not uncommon.

From 1895 to 1911, the Manchu regime made several attempts to avert its inevitable collapse. The educational system adopted in 1903 was only part of the eleventh-hour reform. Though seemingly forward looking, the reform indicated the imperial government's belated recognition of the need to save itself through a modern educational system. However, the imperial government was lacking both in experience and determination. Thus although the call for a new education was answered by the merchant and gentry class, the government did not have the resources to accomplish its objective. Nor did it develop the mechanisms necessary to ensure orderly growth of China's modern school system. The result was uneven progress in the transition from traditional *sishu* and *shuyuan* to the new-style, largely Western school system. Private schools, including mission schools, were most likely to succeed in major cities, especially the treaty ports. In the hinterland, modern private schools had a slow start; yet their modest beginnings represented a truly revolutionary departure from a time-honored tradition.

## NOTES

1. Feng Guifen, one of the earliest advocates of Western learning in Qing China, urged prompt action to obtain Western knowledge in his treatises such as "On the Seeking of Western Knowledge," "On the Manufacturing of Modern Weapons," and "On the Establishment of a Foreign Language School in Shanghai."

2. Hu Chang-tu, "Tradition and Change in Chinese Education," in Hu Chang-tu ed., *Chinese Education under Communism* (New York: Bureau of Publication, Teachers College, Columbia University, 1962), p. 18.

3. Donghua xulu, Guangxu era (Shanghai, 1909), vol. 134, p. 1, see Knight Biggerstaff, *The Earliest Modern Government Schools in China* (Port Washington, N.Y.: Kennikat Press, 1961), p. 88; Douglas R. Reynolds, *China, 1989-1912: The Xinzheng Revolution and Japan* (Cambridge, Mass.: Council on east Asian Studies, Harvard University, 1993), pp. 148-150. As early as the 1880s, a debate over reforming the civil service examination system occurred in the central court. Superficial as it was, the debate at least touched the need for Western learning.

4. Mao Lirui and Shen Guanqun ed., *Zhongguo jiaoyu tongshi* (General history of Chinese education) (Jinan: Shadong Education Press, 1985), pp. 254-270.

5. Jiang Weiqiao, "Jinshi xingxue san weiren" (Three giant promoters of education in modern times), see Shu Xincheng ed., *Jindai zhongguo jiaoyu shiliao* (Sources on the history of education in modern China) (Shanghai: Shanghai Shudian, 1928), pp. 233-234.

6. Unfortunately, the school was shut down by the German viceroy in Shandong the next year. See Luo Xiaoqiong, "Wan qing xiangsheng tuidong xie de xingxue rechao" (School-funding wave by the scholar gentry in the late Qing period), *Jiaoyushi yanjiu* (Studies in the history of education), 3 (March 1994): 24.

7. The wife of the Minister of Industry pledged all her family possessions to local schools in her will. In Jiangyin a widow donated her husband's legacy of two hundred *mu* land to local schools. See I. B. Lewis, *The Education of Girls in China* (TCC, New York, 1919), p. 27.

8. Evelyn Sakakida Rawski, *Education and Popular Literacy in Ch'ing China* (Ann Arbor: University of Michigan Press, 1979), p. 24-28.

9. *Gui* and *mao* are the Chinese characters representing the year 1904 in the Chinese lunar calendar.

10. Wang Fengjie, *Zhongguo jiaoyushi* (History of Chinese education) (Taibei: Zhengzhong Press, 1976), p. 289; Chen Qingzhi, *Zhongguo jiaoyushi* (History of Chinese Education) (Taibei: Commercial Press, 1958), pp. 586-596; *Cihai* (Ocean of words: A Chinese dictionary) (Shanghai: Shanghai dcitionary Press, 1979), p. 1610.

11. Zhang Baixi, Zhang Zhidong, & Rong Qing, "Xuewu gangyao" (Guidelines for educational affairs), see Shu Xincheng ed., *Jindai zhongguo jiaoyu shiliao*, vol. 2, p. 11; Chen Qingzhi, *Zhongguo jiaoyushi*, pp. 590-591.

12. Ministry of Learning (*Xuebu*), "Zhouding quanxuesuo zhangcheng" (Imperially approved guidelines for the education-promotion office), see Shu Xincheng ed., *Jindai zhongguo jiaoyu shiliao*, vol. 2, p. 131, 133.

13. "Sichuan Should Reduce Waste to Develop Beneficial Endeavors," Sichuan guanbao (Shichuan provincial government bulletin), vol. 20, 1910; "Letter from Lin Wanli," *Dongfang Zazhi* (Orient magazine), November 18, 1908. The statistics do not include the students at the traditional *sishu*. See Rawski, *Education and Popular Literacy*, pp. 1-4.

14. Zhang Baixin, Zhang Zhidong & Rong Qing, "Xuewu gangyao," p. 11; Ministry of Learning, "Ten Regulations Concerning Compulsory Education," see Shu Xincheng ed., *Jindai zhongguo jiaoyu shiliao*, vol. 2, pp. 148-149; also see *Zhongguo ribao* (China daily), April 3, 1907.

15. Luo Xiaoqiong, "School-Funding Wave by the Scholar Gentry in the Late Qing Period": 21.

16. Xiong Ming'an, *Zhonghua Minguo jiaoyushi* (History of education in republican China) (Chongqing: Chongqing Press, 1990), pp. 374-375; Sally Borthwick, *Education and Social Change in China: The Beginnings of the Modern Era* (Stanford: Hoover Institution Press, 1983), pp. 93-94.

17. As early as 1898, reformersin Beijing secured an edict from the Guangxu emperor to close private academies (*shuyuan*) all over the country to clear the way for Western-style schools. "Lun Zhongguo xuetang chengdu huanjin zhi yuanyin" (On the slow growth of the new schools in China), *Dongfang zazhi*, no. 6 (1904), Education section, pp. 126-127; Borthwick, *Education and Social Change*, p. 95.

18. Luo Xiaoqiong, "School-Funding Wave by the Scholar Gentry in the late Qing Period": 23; Zhou Junyi, "Zhang Zhidong yu yangwu jiaoyu" (Zhang Zhidong and the Self-Strengthening education), *Jiamusi shiyuan xuebao* (Journal of Jiamusi Teachers College), 2 (February 1992): 25-28; William Ayers, *Chang Chi-tung and Education Reform in China* (Cambridge, Mass.: Harvard University Press, 1971), pp. 196-244.

19. Zhang Baixi, Zhang Zhidong & Rong Qing, "Xuewu gangyao," p. 10; John K. Fairbank, Edwin Reischauer & Albert M. Craig, *East Asia: Tradition and*

*Transformation* (Boston: Houghton Mifflin Co., 1973), p. 729; Reynolds, *China, 1898-1912*, pp. 41-49, 134-135.

20. Chang Yufa, *Zhongguo xiandai hua de quyu yanjiu: Shangdong sheng, 1860-1916* (Modernization in China, 1860-1916: A regional study of social, political, and economic change in Shandong province), pp. 458-459; Marianne Bastid, *Educational Reform in Early Twentieth-Century China* (Trans. Paul J. Bailey) (Ann Arbor: University of Michigan Press, 1988), pp. 29-44, 89-92.

21. "Lun xuetang zhi fubai" (On the corruption in schools), *Dongfang zazhi*, no. 9 (1907), Education section, p. 33; Wang Di, "Educational Reform and Social Change in Sichuan, 1902-1911," paper presented at the 44th Annual Meeting of the Association for Asian Studies (April, 1993), p. 9; Sang Bing, "Qing mo xingxue rechao yu shehui bianqian" (Drive for new schools and social transformation in the late Qing period), *Lishi yanjiu* (Historical studies), 202 (June 1986): 13-16; Luo xiaoqiong, "Wan qing xiangsheng tuidong xia de xingxue rechao": 21-25.

22. Wang Di, "Education Reform and Social Change in Sichuan," p. 9; Di er ci zhongguo jiaoyu nianjian (Second yearbook on Chinese education) (Shanghai: commercial Press, 1948), p. 118; John Cleverley, *The Schooling of China: Tradition and Modernity in Chinese Education* (North Sydney: Allen & Unwin Pty. Ltd., 1991), pp. 26-27.

23. Yang Zhixing, Ji Wenyu & Li Xing, "Yan Xiu jiaoyu sixiang yu Nankai zaoqi tese" (Yan Xiu's educational philosophy and some characteristics of early Nankai School), *Jiaoyushi yanjiu* (Studies in the history of education), 3 (March 1994): 27.

24. Fukuzawa Yukichi (1835-1901) was the most influential advocate of Western-style education in Meiji Japan.

25. Yang Zhixing, Ji Wenyu & Li Xing, Yan Xiu jiaoyu sixiang yu Nankai zaoqi tese": 26-29; Zheng Zhiguang & Yang Guangwei, *Zhang Boling zhuan* (A biography of Zhang Boling) (Tianjin: Tianjin People's Press, 1989), pp. 12-14.

26. Hao Chang, "Intellectual Change and the Reform Movement, 1890-1898," in John K. Fairbank & Kwang-ching Liu ed., *Cambridge History of China* (New York: Cambridge University Press, 1978), vol. 11, late Ch'ing, 1800-1911, Part II, pp. 291, 329-331; Chuzo Ichko, "Political and Institutional Refomr," ibid., pp. 376-382; Zhu Youxian ed., *Zhongguo jindai xuezhi shiliao* (historical documents on the educational system in modern China) (Shanghai: East China Normal University Press, 1983), Part II, vol. 2, pp. 612-613.

27. Zheng Dengyun ed., *Zhongguo jindai jiaoyushi* (History of education in modern China) (Shanghai: East China Normal University Press, 1994), pp. 176-179.

28. Zhang Baixi, Zhang Zhidong & Rong Qing, "Xuewu gangyao," p. 18.

29. Guanban xuetang gaigui shenshi banli" (Turn governmental schools under the operation of local gentry), *Danggongbao*, December 15, 1906.

30. "Sishu-Reform Society Constitution," in Shu Xincheng ed., *Jindai zhongguo jiaoyu shiliao*, vol. 2, pp. 149-156.

31. Zhu Youxian ed., *Zhongguo jindai xuezhi siliao*, pp. 311-313; also see Hu Yan, "Zhongguo jinxiandai sili xuexiao,: in Zhang Zhiyi ed., *Sili minban xuexiao de lilun yu shijian* (Theory and practice of private and *minban* schools) (Beijing: Chinese Workers Press, 1994), pp. 29-30.

32. Kenneth S Latourette, *A History of Christian Missions in China* (New York: The MacMillan Company, 1929), p. 267.

33. Ibid., p. 606; for details, also see Paul Cohen, "Christian Missions and Their Impact to 1900," in John K. Fairbank & Kwang-ching Liu ed., *Cambridge History of China*, vol. 10, Late Ch'ing, 1800-1911, pp. 576-581.

34. Shi Jinghuan, "Jindai xifang chuanjiaoshi zaihua jiaoyu huodong de zhuanyehua (Professionalism in the Western missionaries' educational activities in modern China), *Lishi yanjiu*, 6 (June 1989): 35; also see Arthur J. Brown, *Report on a Second visit to China, Japan, and Korea, 1909, with a Discussion of Some Problems of Mission Work* (New York, 1910), pp. 184-185.

35. See Jessie Gregory Lutz, *China and the Christian Colleges, 1850-1950* (Ithaca: Cornell University Press, 1971), pp. 531-533.

36. Evelyn S. Rawski, "Elementary Education in the Mission Enterprise," in John K. Fairbank ed., *The Missionary Enterprise in China and America* (Cambridge, Mass.: Harvard University Press, 1974), p. 137.

37. John K. Fairbank, *China: A New History* (Cambridge, Mass.: Harvard University Press, 1992), p. 224.

38. Lutz, *China and the Christian Colleges*, pp. 146-158.

39. Hu Yan, "Zhongguo jinxiandai *sili* xuexiao," p. 15.

40. *Di er ci zhongguo jiaoyu nianjian*, vol. 2, p. 118.

# 3

# Non-Governmental Schools
# in the Nationalist Era

The collapse of the imperial government in China was followed by an era of utter confusion. After a short experiment with constitutionalism between 1912 and 1915, the republican government fell prey to factionalism. In the absence of a strong central government, militarism swelled in the provinces. Not until 1929 was order restored by the rise of the Nationalist Party (Guomindang or GMD). Reorganized with Soviet assistance and the cooperation of the Chinese Communist Party (CCP), the GMD adopted the organizational principle of democratic centralism and built a partisan military. Its victory in 1929, however, was not without a price. In addition to splitting with the more radical communist party, it also alienated the Soviets; the ensuing bloody civil war reinforced the autocratic nature of the Nanjing government. Worse still, the difficult progress toward peace and prosperity was violently interrupted by the Japanese invasion of Manchuria in 1931 and the all-out war against Japan in 1937 through 1945. The resulting tragedies fed a popular desire for a strong central government, which was not especially conducive to a strong private educational system.

## PRIVATE SCHOOLS IN THE EARLY REPUBLIC

Unification under a single government created a basis for change which, however shaky, promised orderly reforms, which covered a wide range of issues, from the status of women and marriage to city sewer systems. The decade between 1928 and 1937 witnessed an economic boom in the cities spearheaded by a burgeoning industry and commerce. With both domestic and foreign investment, China's industry grew at a phenomenal annual rate of 13.4

percent between 1912 and 1920, and 8.7 percent between 1923 and 1936. In the midst of economic growth, a civil society emerged, which was increasingly conscious of its interests and power. Even though the status quo stubbornly held ground, an urban culture began to demonstrate its tremendous vitality. In the vast countryside, remnants of the past were also on the way out, although at a much slower pace.

Accompanying the economic growth was a cultural ferment, in which a young and sometimes restless China eagerly sought its identity in a time of disorientation. Some twenty thousand Chinese students who returned home from Japan and Western countries were very vocal on both the national and the local scene, although they were only a small group against the country's population of 400 million. These students were not only imbued with the sense of mission characteristic of the Confucian literati, but also equipped with modern ideas ranging from constitutionalism to Marxism. Through a variety of public forums, civic organizations, academic associations, and especially through the modern press, China's new intelligentsia catered to the public while imbibing Western culture. The lack of an effective central government, and the continuous danger of national extinction, produced a fertile ground for propagating change. In the face of adversities, the Chinese intelligentsia demonstrated more enthusiasm and creativity than it had ever shown before.

Representatives of the New Culture often adopted an iconoclastic approach to the Confucian tradition, viewing it as the ultimate culprit for China's disastrous experiences in modern times. At the same time, they eagerly improvised in their foolhardy effort to change the "national character" of the Chinese people. Dr. Hu Shi, a disciple of the American philosopher John Dewey of Columbia University, called for direct communications between the educated elite and the largely illiterate masses while advocating the use of the vernacular speech as a vehicle for new ideas. An educator himself, he marketed his philosophy of instrumentalism which, among other things, aimed to direct education toward social reform. He invited his American mentor, Dr. John Dewey, to China for a two-year lecture tour. Apprehensive of the growing radicalism among intellectuals, including his former ally Chen Duxiu, who championed a proletarian revolution, Hu Shi desperately cautioned his countrymen against any rash actions. Well aware of the daunting task of overhauling Chinese society and culture, he propagated a gradualist approach to combating China's backwardness, pinning his hope on the education of China's youth.

Radicals, in contrast, chanted the battle song in their fight against what they saw as a moribund social order. They envisioned a new society that was "honest, progressive, positive, free, equal, creative, beautiful, peaceful, cooperative, productive, and happy." Such a new society would rein in the aggressive and possessive military and financial overlords. By the same token, the radicals urged Chinese youth to jettison the obsolete elements in traditional culture and morality. They aimed to create among the youth a respect for experimental science as the precondition for social progress and a weapon in repudiating superstition and impractical thinking. Frustrated by the holy alliance between Western powers and their Chinese agents, some radical Chinese intellectuals turned to Marxism. For Chen Duxiu and Li Dazhao, two of the apostles of Marxism in China, the country would achieve rebirth only when the passive masses were mobilized into an armed rebellion against the remnants of the *ancien regime*.

The search for modern nationhood and economic prosperity created the first golden age of education in modern China. From 1912 through 1929, the Beijing government demonstrated great interest in the nation's school system. Leading the drive for better education in the early republican period was Cai Yuanpei, the Minister of Education. A *hanlin* scholar in the late Qing and student of German philosophy, Cai was one of the early republic's most vocal advocate of the new education and most effective leaders in educational reform. Under Cai's leadership, important changes were introduced into China's school system. In July 1912, the First Conference on National Education was convened in Beijing. At the conference, the development and reform of education was described as the precondition for the nation's rejuvenation and the first step toward creating a new citizenry. The new education was expected to cover five fields: military training, practical skills, moral cultivation, esthetic education, and world outlook. Conspicuously missing in the new agenda was loyalty to the emperor and reverence of Confucius. A new schooling system was promoted between 1912 and 1913, based on a series of decrees from the Ministry of Education. The new system was characterized by, among other things, a democratic spirit on matters such as equal opportunity for both genders. The government encouraged the development of private education at all levels as a valuable addition to governmental schools.[1]

In 1912 and 1913, the Beijing government promulgated Regulations Concerning Public and Private Schools and Regulations Concerning Private Universities. These documents affirmed the interest of private citizens in setting up all kinds of schools except those for teachers' training. They also laid out the criteria for private schools and stipulated the proper application and registration procedures. Like its predecessor, the Beijing regime twice called for donations to education nationwide and publicized detailed rules for providing rewards for generous donors.[2] In 1915, the government published the Guidelines for Private Colleges with a view to promoting investment in China's infant higher education. In 1917 the Ministry of Education formulated a new version of the guidelines that included more specific criteria for approval procedure, accreditation and teacher supervision, and summarized the legal responsibilities of the founding agent. The government was apparently attempting to exercise control over ideology and quality of private education, which was growing rapidly and sometimes recklessly.[3] One has to recognize the highly volatile political atmosphere of the early republic to appreciate the government's forward-looking attitude. For one thing, in his effort to restore the monarchy,

Yuan Shikai, the first president of the Chinese republic, began to promote a conservative policy in education by reverting to Confucian ideology. This contradictory policy would have inflicted severe damage to the new education if Yuan had not died in 1916.

The relatively liberal policy of the Beijing government released the pent-up energy of the Chinese elite. Private higher education made the most impressive progress. In the first decade of the republic, private colleges outnumbered governmental ones. Nationwide, most private colleges focused on technical and vocational training. This practical orientation reflected their limited resources and China's need for economic growth. Another peculiar phenomenon of private higher education was the large number of post-secondary schools for professional training (*zhuanke xuexiao*), many of which were schools of law and political science (*fazheng zhuanke xuexiao*). The concept of professional training originated in the late Qing era, but the focus on law and public service apparently stemmed from the extensive cultural borrowing and experimentation with the constitutional government of the early republic.[4]

In 1922 while trying to open up more sources of revenue to finance China's school system, the Beijing government implemented a reform that loosened governmental control over higher education. This "benevolent neglect" triggered another wave of private colleges. In the summer of 1924, for example, thirteen private colleges were created in Beijing and eight in Shanghai. Many of these new colleges did not register with the government and some were speculative schemes. This sporadic growth of private colleges drew almost immediate criticism in news media.[5] In 1925 the Ministry of Education in Beijing, responding to the unchecked proliferation of private colleges, put together the Recognition Criteria for Private Colleges, which required private colleges to meet the same standards as governmental colleges. To be recognized by the Ministry of Education, a private college had to have its own campus and possess fixed assets worth at least fifty thousand yuan. All freshmen had to pass exams given by the ministry.[6] In October the Beijing government ordered private colleges all over the country shut down, an event that has not been explained to this day. Luckily the government had neither the authority nor the resources to carry it out. In like manner, the Nationalist regime in Guangzhou responded to the surge of private schools with the Regulations Concerning Private Schools and Regulations Concerning Private School Boards. At the heart of these regulations was the resolve of the government to assert its authority to regulate private education and, with regard to Christian schools, to effect a transfer of power from foreigners to Chinese and prohibit compulsory religious education and activities.[7]

In comparison, the growth rate of private middle and elementary schools fell far behind that of public schools. In 1916 there were fifty-one registered private middle schools, making up only 14.6 percent of the nation's middle schools. These schools enrolled 7,647 students, accounting for 12.5 percent of the nation's middle school students. Starting in 1922, the balance began to tilt toward the private sector. Between 1922 and 1925, the number of private schools increased by over 400 percent to make up 41.2 percent of the nation's schools.[8] Student population of private secondary schools constituted 39.5 percent of the nation's student body. The dramatic growth in private secondary schools stemmed from a change in the organization of the school system. First, the length of secondary education increased from four years to six years; second, junior middle schools could be now established and run separately from senior middle schools. As a result, private investors put their resources into setting up junior middle schools in many localities to meet the shortages in the governmental school system.

The growth of private education in the early republic is a fascinating story that has not been seriously studied. It took place in an era of social and cultural experimentation when central authority was eclipsed by local power. China's modern education faced some enormous obstacles, one of which was the dogfight between the warlords. These regional satraps were understandably more concerned with their own survival than with learning. Only a few, like Yan Xishan in Shanxi and Chen Jiongming in Guangdong, showed interest in education. On the whole, the politics of the Beijing government was an extension of the militarism in the provinces. The limited growth of private schools, rather than erecting a monument to the government's foresight, revealed its weaknesses.

It also seems that private schools demonstrated a greater degree of instability than governmental schools partly as a growing pain due to rapid expansion. Some common problems plaguing private schools included inadequate funding, unqualified teaching staff, poor student performance, inflated academic reporting, and a lack of discipline. In 1913, for example, the Ministry of Education dispatched inspectors to Jiangsu, Zhejiang, and Anhui provinces. The shocking findings of the inspectors resulted in the forced closing of a number of schools, including private Nanjing University and the Jingling Institute of Political Science and Law. Since then it has been a permanent challenge to the Chinese government to maintain the quality of private schools without discouraging public interest in them.

## THE NANJING GOVERNMENT AND PRIVATE EDUCATION

Since its very inception, the Nationalist government demonstrated much foresight and determination in promoting education as an integral part of its domestic agenda. While still in Guangzhou, its Education Administration Committee (Jiaoyu xingzheng weiyuanhui) formulated regulations concerning the founding and running of private schools, a largely symbolic gesture to assert its position and authority. In October 1926, the Education Administration Committee published the Private School Regulations and the Private School Boards Regulations. These regulations required private schools to establish a board of trustees and to hire only Chinese chief administrators. The decrees also prohibited the opening and closing of private schools without the government's approval.[9]

During the Northern Expedition, the Nationalist government formulated its educational objectives under the Three People's Principles: "The education in the Republic of China, based on the Three People's Principles, is intended to enrich the people's social life, and to improve the standards of living, thereby achieving the nation's salvation. It will serve the cause of national independence, democracy, and economy, and strive for world peace."[10] Shortly after its inauguration in Nanjing, the Nationalist government implemented a compulsory education program. To assume leadership, the government centralized educational administration and standardized the curricula in public elementary and secondary schools. In 1928 the Nationalist government renamed its Education Administration (Daxueyuan) the Ministry of Education (*Jiaoyubu*), which soon reorganized the school system built on the structure created by the Education Administration Committee of the Guangzhou regime in 1922. Despite continued financial difficulties, a system of new education took shape, with national universities such as Qinghua at the top of the pyramid and citizen schools (*Guomin xuexiao*) at the bottom.

Between 1928 and 1937, education in China enjoyed a precious interval of almost uninterrupted growth. The so-called "Nationalist Decade" witnessed economic growth, social progress, and relative tranquillity under partial national unification. Within its limits, the Nanjing government did a remarkable job in promoting education both in the public and the private sectors. It promulgated a series of laws and regulations, including the Elementary Education Law, the Secondary Education Law, and the Higher Education Law. This legislation was designed to develop the country's school system and make it an essential component of the Nationalists' nation-building program. The focus on public education presumed that modern nationhood depended on the cultivation of an educated citizenry and it was the state's unshakable obligation to popularize learning. In 1929 the government produced the Middle School Law, the Teachers Education Law, the Vocational Education Law, and the University Organization Law. In 1933 further regulations provided a comprehensive program for the country's basic education.

In the same period, Chinese education experienced a transition from the earlier Japanese model to the American model, partly because of the return of students from the West, especially the United States, and partly because of China's deteriorating relationship with Japan. Though small in number, Western-educated scholars nevertheless formed the core of leadership in the academic field. These people pushed China's educational reform toward a new frontier. The involvement of Americans, from educators to philanthropic institutions such as the Rockefeller Foundation, further stimulated this trend. With the growing American influence, the intellectual leadership of Liang

Qichao and Cai Yuanpei was replaced by that of American-educated scholars such as Hu Shi and Jiang Mengling.

Private education likewise thrived due to favorable socioeconomic conditions and the government's generally positive attitude toward private schools. All the major educational legislation by the GMD government contained sections or articles on the private sector and, overall, the government encouraged the founding of private schools for most fields of learning with the exception of teachers' training, which the government wanted to keep under central control.

Hardly had it become entrenched in Nanjing, when the Nationalist regime in December 1927 published through the Ministry of Education (Zhonghua Minguo Daxueyuan) the Private Colleges and Vocational Schools Founding Ordinance and the Private Secondary and Elementary Schools Founding Ordinance. In the former, the regime made it mandatory for all newly established private colleges and post-secondary technical schools to register at the Ministry of Education and required a three-year provisional period before private colleges and post-secondary technical schools could be officially recognized. Private secondary and elementary schools also had to register, the former at the provincial education bureaus and the latter at the prefectural education offices. With a view to defending and, in some cases, regaining educational sovereignty, the ordinances prohibited foreigners from being the chief administrators of private schools at any level. The Ministry of Education also required at least one-third of the faculty of private colleges or post-secondary technical schools to be full-time teachers, while at the secondary and elementary levels, full-time teachers had to make up two-thirds of the teaching staff. In February 1928 the Nanjing government upgraded its decrees concerning private schools in Guangzhou into the Regulations Concerning Private Schools and the Regulations Regarding Private School Boards. These decrees established the legal status of private schools with a view to incorporating them into a national system of schooling.[11]

After the successful Northern Expedition, when the GMD regime established itself as the only legitimate government in China, it faced a rapid growing number of private schools. Therefore the government issued the Private Schools Ordinance of 1929. Based on earlier decrees, the new ordinance consisted of five chapters and thirty-eight articles, covering almost every aspect of the founding and operation of private schools. Although the ordinance was revised three times, first in 1933, and then in 1943 and 1947, it remained fundamentally supportive of the efforts of the individuals and institutions involved in private education. A prominent feature of the ordinance was the will of the state to take some control of the seemingly anarchical situation and to prevent instructional activities contrary to official ideology. Reacting to the many schools that were either poorly managed or suspected of anti-government tendencies, the ordinance authorized educational offices at all levels of the government to shut them down.

Although the Nationalist government was primarily interested in developing a public school system and gave private schools little financial assistance, private education nevertheless grew by leaps and bounds. In 1927, for example, there were 18 registered and 12 unrecognized private colleges in full operation compared to 34 governmental colleges. The general drive for higher education proved contagious. Even warlords such as Zhang Zuolin contracted the enthusiasm. In 1930 he launched the Northeastern University in Fengtian. In 1936 the year before the all-out Japanese aggression against China, the number of private colleges reached 53, up by 83 percent from the number a decade earlier. The student population of private colleges had grown to 20,664, accounting for 49 percent of the nation's college students. Private middle schools increased in number as well (see Table 2). In 1936, 1,200 private middle

**Table 2: Private Middle Schools, 1912-1945**

| Year | Private Schools | | | | Total of Private & Public Schools | Percentage of Private Schools |
|------|-------|--------|--------|------------|---------|---------|
|      | Total | Middle | Normal | Vocational |         |         |
| 1912 | 54    | —      | —      | —          | 373     | 14.5    |
| 1913 | 46    | —      | —      | —          | 406     | 11.3    |
| 1914 | 64    | —      | —      | —          | 452     | 14.2    |
| 1915 | 59    | —      | —      | —          | 444     | 13.3    |
| 1916 | 51    | —      | —      | —          | 350     | 14.6    |
| 1925 | 283   | —      | —      | —          | 687     | 41.2    |
| 1928 | 363   | —      | —      | —          | 954     | 38.1    |
| 1929 | 430   | —      | —      | —          | 1,225   | 35.1    |
| 1930 | 856   | —      | —      | —          | 1,874   | 45.7    |
| 1931 | 968   | 855    | 36     | 77         | 3,026   | 32.0    |
| 1932 | 984   | 868    | 36     | 80         | 3,043   | 32.3    |
| 1933 | 1,030 | 895    | 32     | 103        | 3,125   | 33.0    |
| 1934 | 1,079 | 929    | 32     | 118        | 3,140   | 34.4    |
| 1936 | 1,200 | 981    | 27     | 192        | 3,264   | 36.8    |
| 1938 | 618   | 523    | 10     | 85         | 1,814   | 34.1    |
| 1939 | 904   | 788    | 14     | 102        | 2,278   | 39.7    |
| 1940 | 997   | 875    | 15     | 107        | 2,606   | 38.3    |
| 1941 | 1,041 | 916    | 11     | 114        | 2,812   | 37.0    |
| 1942 | 1,261 | 1,116  | 17     | 128        | 3,187   | 39.6    |
| 1943 | 1,368 | 1,215  | 16     | 137        | 3,455   | 39.6    |
| 1944 | 1,471 | 1,304  | 16     | 151        | 3,745   | 39.3    |
| 1945 | 2,152 | 1,937  | 10     | 205        | 5,073   | 42.4    |

Source: *Di er ci zhongguo jiaoyu nianjian*, vol. 2, pp. 122-123.

schools enrolled 274,801 students, while 2,070 public middle schools enrolled 352,600 students. Even though private schools' percentage of the total of the country's secondary schools declined from 43 percent in 1926 to 37 percent in 1936, their absolute number increased almost tenfold from 1916 to 1936 (see Table 3).

**Table 3: Middle School Student Population, 1912-1945**

| Year | Total | Private | | | Public & Private | Percentage of Private School Students |
| | | Middle Schools | Normal Schools | Vocational Schools | | |
| --- | --- | --- | --- | --- | --- | --- |
| 1912 | 6,672 | — | — | — | 52,100 | 12.8 |
| 1913 | 6,313 | — | — | — | 57,980 | 10.9 |
| 1914 | 8,373 | — | — | — | 67,254 | 12.4 |
| 1915 | 8,622 | — | — | — | 69,770 | 12.4 |
| 1916 | 7,647 | — | — | — | 60,924 | 12.6 |
| 1925 | 51,285 | — | — | — | 129,978 | 39.5 |
| 1928 | 68,149 | — | — | — | 188,700 | 36.1 |
| 1929 | 97,464 | — | — | — | 248,668 | 39.2 |
| 1930 | 173,234 | — | — | — | 396,948 | 43.6 |
| 1931 | 202,172 | 181,560 | 6,586 | 14,026 | 536,848 | 37.7 |
| 1932 | 206,809 | 185,648 | 7,618 | 13,543 | 547,207 | 37.8 |
| 1933 | 212,633 | 189,456 | 7,143 | 16,034 | 559,320 | 38.0 |
| 1934 | 217,596 | 193,562 | 6,761 | 17,273 | 541,479 | 40.2 |
| 1936 | 274,801 | 246,033 | 6,292 | 22,476 | 627,246 | 43.8 |
| 1938 | 165,710 | 155,688 | 1,519 | 8,503 | 477,585 | 34.7 |
| 1939 | 250,096 | 233,516 | 1,709 | 14,871 | 622,803 | 40.2 |
| 1940 | 306,260 | 287,600 | 986 | 17,674 | 768,533 | 39.8 |
| 1941 | 326,712 | 307,493 | 686 | 18,533 | 846,552 | 38.6 |
| 1942 | 404,594 | 380,134 | 2,053 | 22,407 | 1,001,734 | 40.4 |
| 1943 | 438,547 | 411,364 | 1,937 | 25,246 | 1,101,087 | 39.8 |
| 1944 | 450,801 | 421,045 | 1,893 | 27,963 | 1,163,113 | 38.4 |
| 1945 | 612,116 | 581,052 | 1,736 | 29,328 | 1,566,393 | 39.1 |

Note: Students in unregistered private schools were not counted.
Source: *Di er ci zhongguo jiaoyu nianjian*, vol. 2, pp. 123-124.

This phenomenal growth mirrored the government's favorable policy toward education in general on the one hand and the discrepancy between the government's will and abilities on the other. Although they were the government's favored children, public schools often suffered from insufficient and sporadic funding. In 1935, for example, the projected educational expenditure was only 49 million yuan, or 4.8 percent of the nation's annual budget. In some localities, delays in educational funding were not uncommon.

Whenever this happened, public schools were severely affected. A good indicator was the decrease in governmental universities from 76 in 1925 to 55 in 1936. Private schools, though sometimes treated as illegitimate children by the government, fared better as they were part of an expanding market and remained self-reliant. They were exempt from the vacillations in the government's educational budget. This was especially true in major cities such as Beijing, Tianjin, and Shanghai. In Shanghai, for example, there were 550 private elementary schools in 1936, accounting for 74.1 percent of the city's total. In 1948 Shanghai had 151 private middle schools which enrolled 75,743 students, representing 59 percent of the total number of schools and 84 percent of the city's middle school student body. In 1947 Shanghai claimed 24 private colleges, approximately a third of the country's total. Even during the Japanese war, when Shanghai was under Japanese occupation, the city still experienced a continuous expansion in private education. Most of the 53 private schools established between 1937 and 1945 were in foreign concessions beyond Japanese control.[12]

This rapid growth in private schools indicated such favorable conditions as a booming economy, a concentration of the educated population, and especially a growing middle class in the major cities. These cities were often treaty ports, where Western influence was strong and where expanding commerce, industry, and communications demanded a great pool of talents. The multi-level private educational system in the metropolis answered this need with its flexible programs and financial innovations. Private schools in major cities, moreover, trained thousands of students from inland provinces, contributing to the modernization of the entire country.[13]

In the vast countryside, the situation proved to be much more immutable. After two decades of severe criticism for its backwardness, the *sishu* miraculously lingered on, even though in 1924 the Beijing government ordered provincial governments to abolish them altogether to open the way for new Western-style schools. Under the circumstances in the early republic, no political or social authority could force the *sishu* into extinction. In fact, in the 1920s, they still far outnumbered the new schools, both private and public, and enrolled at least as many students as did the new schools nationwide. The crucial support for *sishu* came from millions of farmers. To them, new schools seemed unfamiliar and were too expensive, and the subjects taught at these schools were impractical and even culturally monstrous. In contrast, *sishu* provided the farmers' children with the knowledge and skills necessary for survival in the countryside. Thus many farmers defied the government's authority and ignored the propaganda of reformers by keeping their children at *sishu*.[14]

Although for many of the modern-minded Chinese elite, the continuous existence of *sishu* was an embarrassment, abolition of all *sishu* was simply out of the question. The government therefore had to adopt a gradualist approach to reforming the *sishu*. Moderate reformers realized that, rather than being an obstacle to the new education, the *sishu* could become part of the compulsory education program. The thousands of *sishu* all over the country were complements to public schools rather than opponents. For example, in Shanxi education progressed rapidly in part due to the contribution of the reformed *sishu*. Given its resources, the government could help reform the *sishu* by providing training programs and seminars for *sishu* teachers. The educational administration could assist the *sishu* with their curriculum design and supervise their operations.[15]

In September 1930 the municipal education administration of Shanghai implemented a qualifying examination for all *sishu* teachers based on the core curriculum of the public school system. Those who passed the examination were allowed to continue their teaching but had to renew their licenses every two years. Those who failed were ordered to quit teaching by the end of the year.[16] In Jiangsu province, the government crafted and implemented the Administrative Measures Concerning the Sishu. In addition to requiring all *sishu* to follow pertinent educational legislation, the provincial bureau of education urged local governments to organize a Sishu Administrative Committee (*Sishu guanli weiyuanhui*) in every school district. This semiofficial organization was supposed to supervise and guide the operation and reform of the *sishu*. To ensure that the *sishu* complemented rather than competed with the public school system, the measures prohibited them from operating near governmental schools.[17] For *sishu* teachers, the provincial education authority formulated certification criteria apparently intended to replace old *sishu* teachers with graduates of normal schools, a very sensible policy indeed given the circumstances at the time.

Reform of the *sishu* continued and in the mid-1930s spread to provinces such as Shandong and Hubei. In both provinces, the educational authority produced comprehensive programs for improving the *sishu*. The Ministry of Education quickly endorsed these programs.[18] The experiences of these provinces were crystallized in the Measures for Reforming the Sishu by the Ministry of Education, which came out in June 1937, on the eve of the all-out Japanese aggression. The document set rules for *sishu* all over the country, including compliance with policies and regulations of the central government. It also required a *sishu* to have well-trained staff; spacious, well-lit, and well-vented classrooms; auxiliary facilities such as sports fields; and officially approved texts. *Sishu* were to serve a complementary rather than a competitive role with public schools.[19] The national government wanted to see the total transformation of all *sishu* but never had the time and resources to achieve this. Until 1949, the *sishu*, reformed or otherwise, remained a significant component of China's educational system.

## STRIVE FOR EXCELLENCE

In general, the quality of a private school reflected the vision and ability of its founder. The best private schools thrived under dedicated and talented leadership. Although each successful school had its own unique quality and experience, Nankai University in Tianjin, Mingde School in Changsha, and Jukui in Jiangjin, Sichuan seemed to best exemplify the accomplishment of China's private education.

For decades, Nankai remained a symbol of China's aspiration to modern nationhood and excellence in education. After the republican revolution, Nankai entered into a stage of steady expansion, even though the school was not totally immune to the political and social disturbances common in this period. In 1912 the school enrolled 260 students, mostly from local gentry families. In 1924 Nankai Middle School had 1,554 students from twenty-four provinces and two countries.[20]

As is the case with most private schools, tuition constituted the majority of Nankai's revenue. Understandably, most of Nankai's students came from well-to-do families. Yet part of the success of both Nankai Middle School and Nankai University lay in their ability to open up new sources of revenue while increasing recruitment. From its early years, Nankai Middle School received assistance from industrial and commercial enterprises, from political leaders and from local gentry. Chinese leaders from Zhang Xueliang, the Manchurian warlord, to the GMD general Fu Zuoyi were among the benefactors of Nankai. Fu Zuoyi used his position as the commander-in-chief of the local garrison in Tianjin to give Nankai over one hundred acres of land that provided the school with an annual income of twenty-five thousand yuan. Starting with the 1920s, Americans came on the scene. The Rockefeller Foundation gave Nankai University $225,487 between 1923 and 1932.[21]

The reputation of Nankai was no accident. It was hard-earned by a well-designed, rigorous program emphasizing math, science, and the English language at the secondary level, by the devotion and skill of its staff, and by the superb performance of its students. The challenge of Nankai started at the entrance examination which covered Chinese, arithmetic, and English. Those who passed the examination had to survive six years of rigorous programs. Over the years, Nankai developed an almost relentless policy on grading, promotion, retention, and graduation. Every course took great effort to pass, every test was closely monitored, and cheating was severely punished. The use of English in all courses, with a few exceptions such as Chinese literature, was a novelty. But this practice forced many students to spend much of their spare time struggling with the language. In the fight for survival, casualties were predictably high. For instance, the class of 1918 began with 360 students. Four years later, only about 70 graduated. At the end of the 1924 school year, as many as 142 students failed to advance into higher grades.[22]

Academic rigor alone did not explain Nankai's success. From its early years, Nankai sought to cultivate well-rounded individuals. To achieve this goal, moral education figured prominently in the curriculum. For years, Zhang Boling himself undertook the unenviable job of teaching ethics. A patriot with an intense sense of mission and a superb orator who had a knack of embodying principles in plain and humorous language, Zhang believed that Nankai needed, above all, a unique soul before it could give its students good values. Acutely aware of the weakness of the Chinese nation, he made *yungong yunneng*, that is, public service and ability, the motto of Nankai. Zhang explained, "Only *gong* can combat selfishness and disunity...and only *neng* can overcome the ignorance and feebleness of our people and enable us to serve the public." At Nankai, students were expected to develop five qualities: ambition, honesty, diligence, modesty, and sincerity. This was no easy job for, among other obstacles, a large proportion of students were, in Zhang's words, "profligate children" of rich families. A Christian convert himself, Zhang Boling was a bona fide missionary for educational excellence, and he made patriotism the overarching theme of his weekly lectures and speeches.[23] Under his leadership, Nankai turned patriotism into good academic performance and a team spirit that permeated the campus.

Classroom work at Nankai was balanced by a variety of extra-curricular activities, ranging from the YMCA and Boy Scouts to drama. For years, Nankai Theater put on plays, some of which written by teachers and students, that carried intense social messages. The skills of Nankai actors and actresses won praise from both amateurs and professionals. In Hu Shi's words, these plays were among the best in China's modern theater.[24] Especially impressive was Nankai's sports program, which won numerous prizes and awards. For years, the school boasted the best basketball and baseball teams in north China, and some of its athletes represented the nation at international games.[25] These honors bore witness to a program that involved all students and staff, a program that reflected Zhang Boling's philosophy that a strong nation required a healthy populace. The sports program also promoted camaraderie and sportsmanship among the students which, in turn, contributed to a wholesome campus atmosphere.[26]

The blueprint of Nankai University was drawn up during World War I. The school was inaugurated in early 1919 after Zhang Boling and Yan Xiu returned from a field survey of higher education in the United States and after they had solicited eighty thousand silver dollars from various sources. When the school opened, it taught humanities, science, and business. Among the first group of freshmen was Zhou Enlai, a graduate of Nankai Middle School who would become a staunch communist and the most versatile diplomat modern China has ever produced. From 1922 on, Nankai University received financial support from the Beijing government and donations from the Rockefeller Foundation. In 1923 the university moved to Balitai in the suburb of Tianjin, where it remains today. In 1925 Nankai University was formally recognized by the Beijing government. Thereafter Nankai experienced a period of steady growth. In 1930 it had a school of humanities, a school of science, and a school of business. On the eve of the Japanese War in 1937, Nankai offered bachelor's degrees in twelve majors and had 429 students, which made it then the largest private college run by Chinese.

In its embryonic stage, Nankai University displayed the strong influence of American education as many professors at Nankai had studied at American universities. Its real maturity occurred in the late 1920s, when the school formulated its own core curriculum, which was geared to China's social and economic needs. Its professors rewrote their lecture notes, and some compiled texts based on firsthand research. The School of Economics, for example, carried out a series of reform under Dr. He Lian, a dedicated teacher and innovative administrator. He Lian convinced his colleagues that the success of the school depended on its ability to adapt Western theories to China's economic reality and to respond to the country's need for talent. Students conducted extensive fieldwork as part of their academic program. Indeed, in China's new higher education, Nankai served the role of a trailblazer in more than one field. Many Nankai scholars had their studies published in Chinese and foreign academic journals. Some scholars, such as the mathematician Ke Zhao and the historian Jiang Tingfu, were world-renowned in their own fields.[27] The Western nexus of Nankai also brought a continuous flow of visiting scholars from America and Europe, including the American philosopher, John Dewey. The influx of new information helped keep Nankai scholars abreast of the latest developments in their own fields.

Also holding the key to Nankai's near miracle were thrift, efficiency, well-defined rules, and democracy in management that involved both the faculty and students.[28] Like other good private schools, Nankai derived its success from the character and ability of its founders. Without overemphasizing the role of a single person, it would be nevertheless proper to attribute the success story of Nankai to the devotion, personal charisma, and exemplary role of Zhang Boling. At once a visionary and doer, his career consisted of overcoming one obstacle after another and his unending optimism inspired both the faculty and students, especially in times of adversity. As it received only limited funding from the government, Nankai's budget was constantly in the red, and Zhang Boling's principal focus was to keep Nankai's head above the water. He believed that, to establish its legitimacy, any Chinese government had to show interest in education. He understood well the charitable side of human nature and the deep-seated interest in education among many well-to-do Chinese. Thus he supplicated donations from all possible sources, and he had the persuasive skills to move the most unlikely donors.[29] A believer in thrift, Zhang lived the life of a puritan. He even set his own salary lower than that of some professors. It fair to say that, to a great extent, the Nankai spirit was just an emanation of Zhang Boling's personality.

Although Nankai University had a relatively lower revenue than public colleges of comparable size, and Nankai faculty's salaries were lower than those at governmental universities, first class scholars like Li Ji, Jiang Tingfu, and He Lian came and stayed at Nankai. The school also attracted young and aspiring scholars because of its wholesome academic climate and family atmosphere. At Nankai professors enjoyed a considerable degree of academic freedom and were trusted to develop their own fields. The administration took serious measures to encourage the participation of students as well as teachers. *Nankai Weekly*, for example, provided a vent for even the most caustic criticism of the school's administration. On the other hand, being a private institution and independent of the government, Nankai was also relatively free from the massive fluctuations suffered by governmental schools in the era of warlordism.[30]

Amoy (Xiamen) University in the southeast, in comparison, thrived in the first decade almost exclusively on the generosity of its founder-benefactor Chen Jiageng, a native of Jimei, in Fujian province. In 1890 Chen Jiageng quit school to assist his father in Singapore. In 1904, after the failure of his father's business, he started his own business and in four years was prospering on his natural rubber plantation. A patriot, Chen took on the responsibility of helping his mother country develop education. In 1912 he founded Jimei Elementary School, a project later followed by a middle school, a normal school, and a business school. In 1918 Chen suffered appendicitis. Expecting to die soon, he drew up his will in which he donated all his property—two million silver dollars—to the Jimei schools. After he recovered, Chen not only kept this will but also set in motion a plan to build a university. Xiamen (Amoy) University, which opened in April 1921, would become the first college supported by overseas Chinese.[31]

Even though his own business experienced ups and downs and his initial efforts to find allies among wealthy overseas Chinese went almost nowhere, Chen bullheadedly underwrote the operation of Xiamen University with his entire fortune. At its height during the New Culture Era, the school's faculty claimed some of the most famous names in China: Lin Yutang, the famed writer, philosopher, and linguist; Lu Xun, probably the greatest writer in modern China; and Zhang Yi, an Oxford Ph.D. in Western philosophy. In 1928 Amoy University was formally recognized by the Ministry of Learning under Cai Yuanpei and in 1930 the university offered degrees in twenty-one majors and was composed of   five schools: the School of Humanities, the School of Science, the School of Law, the School of Business, and the School of Education.[32]

Fudan University in Shanghai likewise took intense pride in its academic independence and liberal atmosphere. The school was the product of a student rebellion against the religious policies at the Catholic Zhendan (Aurora) University. For three decades between 1919 and 1949, Fudan University remained an important center of student activism in East China. With little connection to the political and financial establishment, Fudan depended on the dedication of its administration and faculty for survival. Its journalism and business majors won wide acclaim, and many of its graduates became leaders in these fields.[33] Like Nankai in Tianjin, Fudan's success could be explained by the energy and dedication of its founders such as Ma Xiangbo who combined the best of Confucian and Christian traditions: the Chinese sense of loyalty, and the Western faith in science.[34]

Though every private school was unique, the most successful seemed to share some common attributes. As institutions of education, private schools succeeded, first and foremost, because of the accomplishments of their students. Although private and public schools employed much the same mechanisms to ensure learning excellence, private schools probably traveled the extra miles in enforcing them to get results. Records of some well-run private schools showed that high standards were applied from matriculation to graduation. Quality instruction was accompanied by rigorous exams and rules concerning admission, promotion, retention, and graduation. In these schools, English was emphasized, sometimes at the cost of other subjects.[35]

The need to survive combined with a strong belief in reform promoted rigorous and innovative programs in many private schools. In addition to the core curriculum dictated by the Ministry of Education, the better private schools offered a variety of elective courses ranging from astronomy and drama to law and photography. Private colleges remained on the cutting edge of educational reform by responding to the needs of society. In the early 1920s, when the country was entering an economic boom, Nankai and Fudan were the first to offer programs in business. Most private colleges tended to offer courses in areas that were cost-efficient. In 1937 private colleges had more students in humanities, law, and business than did public colleges.

Private schools distinguished themselves from most public schools by their rich extracurricular activities for students, including lectures by established celebrities, special interest groups, service clubs, and intramural sports. Some private schools owned radio stations that broadcast on a regular schedule. In their effort to cultivate well-rounded individuals, the best private schools always put a premium on the physical fitness of their students and accordingly promoted sports. As a rule, those private schools with the most impressive extracurricular programs were boarding schools, where it was much easier for the students to get organized.

Like private colleges, many private middle and elementary schools pioneered in educational reform. When the Dalton Laboratory Plan[36] was introduced into China, for example, some private schools were the first to embrace the novel approach. In 1922 it was first practiced in the China Public School (*Zhongguo gongxue*), a private school in Wusong near Shanghai, and later, in the private Yiwen Middle School in Beijing, which made a name for itself by implementing this method.[37] Under the Dalton Plan, learning in school was combined with practice and instruction was tailored to meet the specific needs of each individual student. Obviously, this approach was practical only in schools with a favorable teacher-student ratio.

Financial independence from the government enabled private schools to resist the pressure from the ruling party to offer courses exclusively for ideological indoctrination and to sidestep government regulations, thereby attracting more students. Relatively free of official control, private schools displayed greater flexibility than public schools in a variety of matters such as student admission and teacher recruitment. Yucai School, founded by the reformer-educator Tao Xingzhi, not only refused to maintain a political education department but spared its students from such rituals as singing the national anthem and raising the flag, which were common at public schools. The school even discarded the officially sanctified texts and offered some unorthodox courses.[38]

In a time of confusion, some private schools turned into breeding grounds for radical ideas. Hunan Self-Study University (*Hunan zixiu daxue*), organized by Mao Zedong and his friends in Changsha, Hunan province, was intended to "combine the best of modern and traditional schools while avoiding the defects of both." Specifically, the "university" would carry the new wine of modern education in the old bottle of a *shuyuan*. While emphasizing self-study, the school had an overambitious program encompassing Chinese literature, Western literature, English, ethics, psychology, education, history, sociology, journalism, law, political science, economics, plus several academic societies. Though much of the students' activities were limited to abstract rhetoric on social and political issues, the school's dubious nature soon caught the government's attention. Less than four months after its birth, the "university" was shut down by the governor of Hunan for its "erroneous learning and threat to social stability."[39] In Shanghai, Dalu University, Huanan University, and Jianhua High School were shut down in 1929 by police, who found Communist propaganda materials on their campuses.[40] At Societal University near Chongqing, the core curriculum evolved around four themes: character, knowledge, organizational skill, and technology. The school targeted adult students and emphasized self-study and practice. Due to its leftist orientation and its founder Tao Xingzhi's well-known connection with the Communists, the university was closed by the government in March 1947.

In its vigorous growth, China's new education seemed to raise more questions than it answered. Pundits observed a gulf between the reality at the new schools and what they claimed to be. Problems tended to be especially acute in some private schools. Critics pointed out that many private colleges were in fact at the level of middle schools and many middle schools were performing at the level of elementary schools.[41] Even some of the most reputable schools such as Fudan in Shanghai, had to make do with facilities that were dilapidated by Western standards.[42] There is no denying that many private schools were hastily set up, and many of their founders were motivated by profit.

Consequently, the Ministry of Education had to take administrative measures to enforce standards in private schools. Responding to a proliferation of private schools in the cities, a notice by the Ministry of Education in 1929 admonished parents not to sent their children to unapproved private schools because they were inferior in quality and illegal.[43] In April 1929 the Far Eastern University in Shanghai was closed by the city's education bureau for poor administration, followed by private Qingdao University. Other closed private schools included Shanghai Fine Arts Academy, Xinmin (New People) University, Jianshe (Reconstruction) University, Huaguo University, Guangming (Light) University, Wenfa (Humanities and Law) College, and Dongya (East Asia) University, under such charges as rule violations, poor facilities, and possession of "reactionary materials and books."[44]

In a society where personal connections counted and where the rule of law was yet to be realized, much could be and had to be achieved through extralegal channels. Government regulations in fact often created the need for bribery. An increasing number of private schools therefore put government officials on their payroll by appointing them to school boards, hoping that these people would help them circumvent government restrictions and pass the inspection by the education administration. This practice besmirched the image of private schools and raised questions about the government's moral integrity. In an attempt to keep up the morale of the school system and its own employees, the Ministry of Education prohibited government officials from serving on the boards of private schools.

The Nationalist government provided financial assistance to private schools, primarily to the better ones as a reward for their superior performance. Overall, however, government aid figured insignificantly in the growth of private schools. As a result, most private schools allocated a greater proportion of their revenue to teachers' salaries than to maintenance and expansion. For the same reason, private schools had to spend a greater proportion of their revenues on teachers' salaries, which were in general lower than those at public schools. In 1931, for example, the average monthly salary of professors at private colleges was 124.3 yuan, 40 yuan less than the average salary at national universities and 90 yuan less than that at provincial public colleges.[45] On average, there was not a significant difference between the expenditure per student of private schools and that of public schools. For example, in 1936, the year before the all-out Japanese aggression against China, private secondary schools spent an average of 84 yuan per student while public schools spent an average of 87 yuan.[46] Yet there was an enormous gap between mission schools and private schools run by Chinese, and between the elite private schools and those that could barely make ends meet. In 1925, for example, the expenditure per student of Peking Union Medical College amounted to 27,345 yuan, whereas Peking North China University reported only a meager expenditure per student of 15 yuan. Even Fudan University in Shanghai spent only 181 yuan on each student.[47]

Variations in revenue made it difficult for many private schools to maintain a stable first class staff. In the 1930s and 1940s, when the nation's economic problems became malignant, many private schools experienced financial difficulties. when Chen Jiageng's business entered into a spiral of decline in the late 1920s, Xiamen (Amoy) University became short of funds. As a result, some of its best teachers resigned.[48] Even though other overseas Chinese came to the rescue of Xiamen University and the government provided emergency funding, the school had to downsize and streamline in order to stay alive. Its employees launched several donation campaigns to save the school from collapse. Eventually, Chen Jiageng sought governmental takeover of Xiamen University, which materialized in July 1937.[49] The short and glorious life of private Xiamen University demonstrated at once the strength and vulnerability of a private school. Exclusive dependence on the success and largess of a single business enterprise and the good will of a single person was in the end inadvisable.

## PRIVATE SCHOOLS IN WORLD WAR II

The Japanese aggression from 1937 through 1945 took a heavy toll on China's education. During the war, the total loss of private colleges amounted to over 44 million yuan. While the best universities and colleges received limited government assistance in evacuating coastal cities and moving to western China, most middle schools were left on their own. Only the most determined and financially better-off schools managed to escape the juggernaut of the Japanese military. Both student enrollment and faculty dropped dramatically from 1937 through 1939.[50] Of the 1,200 private middle schools in 1936, only 618 remained in 1938. In the same period, the student population of private middle schools declined by 40 percent from 274,801 to 165,710, and the number of private school teachers declined by 52 percent. Private college faculties were reduced by 31 percent, from 4,800 to 3,300 (see Table 4). Some important private institutions like Northeastern University and Xiamen University gave up their private status so that they could receive government support after being dislodged by the Japanese.[51]

Fudan University in Shanghai met with the same fate. After the Japanese occupation of Shanghai, Fudan relocated to a new campus at Xiaba near Chongqing, China's wartime capital. Most of its four thousand students were refugees from the lower Yangtse valley, who were unable to afford tuition. As the school's revenue went below 10 percent of its prewar level, it faced a total shutdown and the only way to save it was to turn to the public coffers. An emergency meeting of the school's board of trustees and influential alumni in September 1940 agreed to seek help from the Chongqing government; this ended the school's independent status.[52] In retrospect, the appeal to the state was a necessary evil entailed by wartime exigencies. At least the government takeover kept the schools from going out of business.

Schools that remained in Japanese occupied areas had to deal with the occupiers and their collaborators, while those that relocated to Free China had to fight for survival in a new environment and struggle with the malaise during the

**Table 4: College Student Population, 1936-1946**

| Year | Private | Private & Public | Percentage of |
|------|---------|------------------|---------------|
| 1936 | 20,664 | 41,922 | 49.3 |
| 1937 | 12,880 | 31,188 | 41.3 |
| 1938 | 15,546 | 36,180 | 43.0 |
| 1939 | 17,910 | 44,422 | 40.3 |
| 1940 | 22,034 | 52,376 | 42.1 |
| 1941 | 24,742 | 59,457 | 41.6 |
| 1942 | 22,223 | 64,097 | 34.7 |
| 1943 | 24,624 | 73,669 | 33.4 |
| 1944 | 25,919 | 78,909 | 32.8 |
| 1945 | 27,816 | 83,498 | 33.3 |
| 1946 | 40,581 | 129,336 | 31.4 |

Note: Students in unregistered private colleges are not counted.
Source: *Di er ci zhongguo jiaoyu nianjian*, vol. 2, p. 120.

stalemate between 1940 and 1944. In 1941, the fortune of Free China hit bottom when a spiraling inflation reduced the life of thousands of salaried people to the subsistence level. Government officials and military officers resorted to a variety of schemes to make ends meet. Colleges and schools alike suffered severe financial problems that produced unrest among professors, school teachers, and students. Private schools, depleted of funding, contracted all kinds of ills. Many of them could barely pay staff salaries. Library acquisitions and purchase of instructional materials were out of the question. Some of the best teachers left private middle schools to teach in public schools or took up another trade that could help them save their children from malnutrition or starvation. Student morale likewise plummeted. Facing the unrest on campuses, the Chongqing government ordered schools to discipline their staffs and students. In a circulated document, the Ministry of Education told the students to "focus on their study and respect their teachers...and not to interfere with the government's decisions."[53]

Even though the Chongqing government rendered moral as well as financial support to private schools during the Japanese war, educational expenditure never exceeded 4 percent of the government's strained budget.[54] Thus what happened in this period was a miracle almost contrary to common sense: instead of decreasing in number, private schools multiplied. According to government statistics, private colleges grew from the prewar figure of 52 to 64 in 1946. Private middle schools increased from 523 in 1938 to 1,937 in 1945; their enrollment rose from 155,688 in 1938 to 581,052 in 1945 (see Table 5). The number of private elementary schools in 1945 was slightly smaller than the prewar figure, however, one reason being that many of the best private element-

**Table 5: Private Elementary Schools, 1931-1945**

| Year | Private Elementary Schools | Total of Private And Public Elementary Schools | Percentage of Private Elementary Schools |
|---|---|---|---|
| 1931 | 60,871 | 259,863 | 23.4 |
| 1932 | 65,429 | 263,432 | 24.8 |
| 1933 | 45,591 | 259,095 | 17.6 |
| 1934 | 46,648 | 260,665 | 17.9 |
| 1935 | 45,248 | 291,452 | 15.5 |
| 1936 | 45,550 | 320,080 | 14.2 |
| 1937 | 39,565 | 229,911 | 17.2 |
| 1938 | 33,406 | 217,394 | 15.4 |
| 1939 | 33,697 | 218,758 | 15.4 |
| 1940 | 23,368 | 220,213 | 10.6 |
| 1941 | 18,537 | 224,709 | 8.3 |
| 1942 | 14,270 | 258,280 | 5.5 |
| 1943 | 7,452 | 273,443 | 2.7 |
| 1944 | 12,390 | 254,370 | 4.9 |
| 1945 | 15,279 | 269,937 | 5.7 |

Note: All numbers include kindergarten.
Source: *Di er ci zhongguo jiaoyu nianjian* (Second yearbook on China's education). vol. 2, p. 126.

ary schools were renamed citizen schools (*guomin xuexiao*) due to the government's program of compulsory education. During the war, many private schools, especially those in areas where no good public schools existed, were turned into *guomin xuexiao* by the government. Considering the devastation of the war, and the Japanese occupation of all major cities in eastern China, the growth of private schools was indeed impressive.[55] Only the will of the Chinese people to carry on their cultural heritage can adequately explain this phenomenon (see Table 6).

At the same time, the convergence of educational institutions brought an unprecedented renaissance to culturally underdeveloped provinces such as Sichuan and Yunnan. Nankai University, for example, arrived in Kunming in Yunnan province in early 1938. There it joined with Qinghua and Beijing University to form the National Southwest Associated University or Lianda. Lianda not only preserved the best of China's higher education but also testified to the fortitude of Chinese educators. Three of the country's best schools worked together and benefited from the attendant cross-fertilization in both academic affairs and administration.[56]

**Table 6: Private Elementary School Student Population, 1931-1945**

| Year | Private Elementary School Students | Total of Elementary Students | Percentage of Private Elementary Students |
|------|------|------|------|
| 1931 | 2,743,572 | 11,720,596 | 23.4 |
| 1932 | 2,967,594 | 12,232,066 | 24.3 |
| 1933 | 2,407,515 | 12,383,479 | 19.4 |
| 1934 | 2,660,912 | 13,188,133 | 20.2 |
| 1935 | 1,658,714 | 15,110,199 | 11.0 |
| 1936 | 1,757,644 | 18,364,958 | 9.6 |
| 1937 | 1,780,701 | 18,990,050 | 9.4 |
| 1938 | 1,868,421 | 12,281,837 | 15.2 |
| 1939 | 1,865,958 | 12,669,976 | 14.7 |
| 1940 | 1,621,909 | 13,545,837 | 12.0 |
| 1941 | 1,259,957 | 15,058,051 | 8.4 |
| 1942 | 1,066,820 | 17,721,103 | 6.0 |
| 1943 | 699,030 | 18,601,239 | 3.8 |
| 1944 | 1,037,314 | 17,221,814 | 6.0 |
| 1945 | 1,594,469 | 21,831,998 | 7.3 |

Note: All numbers include kindergarten.
Source: *Di er ci zhongguo jiaoyu jianjian*, vol. 2, p. 126.

In 1938, Nankai Middle School reopened in Chongqing on the basis of Nanyu Middle School, which had been established by Zhang Boling in 1936 when he realized the vulnerability of Tianjin. By the time Nanyu was renamed Nankai Middle School in December 1938, its enrollment had reached fifteen hundred. Thereafter, Nankai Middle School prospered under the special patronage of Jiang Jieshi (Chiang Kai-shek), exercising great influence in Sichuan.

The end of World War II witnessed renewed hope for education. The Nationalist government intended to make education the number one priority in its program of national reconstruction. At the National Conference on Postwar Educational Reconstruction, Generalissimo Jiang Jieshi told officials and educators that only by making education the top priority on its agenda could China achieve the goal of modernization.[57] The new constitution of 1947 reaffirmed Jiang's pledge. Article 164 provided that 15 percent of the central government's budget would be spent on education, science, technological development, and cultural affairs. At the provincial level, such spending was to be no less than 25 percent of the government's budget, and at the county and municipal level, no less than 35 percent.[58]

Optimism translated into a robust growth for education despite the cloud of civil strife. In 1947 Nationalist China had 67 private colleges, 2,422 private middle schools and 17,140 private elementary schools.[59] To prevent the uncontrolled proliferation of private schools, the Nanjing government in 1947 set a minimum funding capital for schools and later adjusted this figure several times to keep up with inflation.

On the whole, however, the civil war between 1946 and 1949 made it impossible for the government to implement its blueprint for postwar education. In 1948 and 1949, education was paralyzed when government forces collapsed at the front. Runaway inflation brought many private schools to the brink of total shutdown. Even in the face of an imminent fiasco, the GMD government appropriated 12.5 billion yuan to help 112 private colleges. But this was little more than a symbolic gesture given the crumbling condition of the regime.

## PRIVATE VOCATIONAL SCHOOLS

Vocational education received special attention in China since the beginning of the Self-Strengthening Movement. The Guimao System of 1904, for example, envisioned vocational training as an integral part of China's new educational system. In the 1910s and 1920s, reform-minded intellectuals advocated vocational education as a powerful remedy for China's lack of skilled workers and the inadequacies of formal education. In 1917 forty-eight reformers, including Huang Yanpei, Cai Yuanpei, Ma Xiangbo, and Wu Tingfang, initiated the Zhonghua Vocational Education Society (*Zhonghua zhiye jiaoyu she*). This organization thereafter became the most vocal advocate and effective promoter of vocational education in China. In 1918 it established the first Zhonghua Vocational School in Shanghai, where students took highly practical courses such as metalwork, carpentry, and ceramics. In 1921 there were 700 vocational schools nationwide, 27 of which were for girls and women. In the 1920s the Zhonghua Society expanded its work into rural areas, since rural development held the ultimate key to China's modernization. It set up a number of outposts in Shanxi, Zhejiang, and Jiangsu aimed at technological advancement as well as social progress.[60] In 1926 the number of vocational schools reached a record high of 1,695, indicating the great potential of vocational education.

The Nationalist government recognized the nation's need for vocational and technical education from the outset. A national conference on education in 1928 asked high schools nationwide to develop programs in agriculture, industry, business, and home economics. In 1930 the Nationalist government reiterated the need for practical skills at all levels of formal education. Beginning in 1931 education authorities tried to steer private schools toward vocational training and in December 1932 the Nanjing government institutionalized its support of vocational education in the Vocational School Law and related regulations.

Through this legislation, the government encouraged private citizens and enterprises to open vocational schools and provided incentives such as subsidies. The government established secondary vocational and post-secondary technical schools that emphasized agriculture and basic industries such as mining, metallurgy, textiles, chemistry, and telecommunications. In comparison, private technical schools tended to focus on the humanities and social sciences. Of the thirty post-secondary technical schools in 1932, ten were private, specializing in such fields as law, fine arts, and library science.[61] In general, vocational education, especially at the secondary level was localized. In urban areas, various vocational schools appeared in the early 1930s because of the cities' booming economies and swelling populations. In Nanjing, the capital, twenty-three vocational schools were created to answer the needs of governmental and business endeavors. At these schools a variety of courses were offered, including Chinese, English, mathematics, engineering, and typing.[62]

After the government retreated to the fastness of Sichuan, the enthusiasm for technical and vocational training regained momentum. In 1938 the Ministry of Education drew up the Guidelines for Vocational Schools at the County and Municipal Levels. Local governments were asked to take the initiative in meeting the needs of their own areas. Yet because of the governments' financial difficulties, a significant share of the responsibility for school support was left to private agents. In Chongqing and other major cities in Free China, day and night schools of all kinds mushroomed from 1939 through 1941. Many of these schools were remedial, some were suspected of spreading ideas incongruent with government policy. In the Wartime Regulations on Remedial Schools, the government threatened to shut down any remedial school whose curriculum ran counter to the Three People's Principles.[63]

Zhonghua Vocational Education Society continued to play an active role in the drive for technical and vocational training. The society operated extensively in the southwestern provinces of Sichuan, Yunnan, and Guangxi. On the whole, vocational education survived the traumatizing effect of World War II. After World War II, the total number of post-secondary technical schools rose to 68, of which 26 were private, specializing in such fields as business, dentistry, and industry.[64] Of the 494 secondary vocational schools in 1936, 192 were private. In 1945 the total number of vocational schools rose to 576, of which 205 were nongovernmental.[65]

The somewhat chaotic growth of vocational education reflected the government's priority for developing the skilled labor necessary for postwar reconstruction. Even though the Nationalist regime committed itself to a very aggressive educational strategy, private resources had to be tapped to meet the needs of a myriad of trades. An incomplete governmental survey in 1947 indicated that nearly seven hundred vocational schools existed nationwide; over three hundred of these schools were nongovernmental. In major cities such as Shanghai, Tianjin, and Chongqing, private vocational schools showed enormous vitality, outnumbering governmental vocational schools.[66] In July 1947 the government revised its regulations concerning vocational schools, making it easier to set up private schools for vocational training. The new rules not only recognized the schools established prior to and during World War II but encouraged the use of facilities such as hospitals, factories, and farms. In addition, the Ministry of Education postponed the deadline for registration from 1947 to 1949, a decision that bespoke the cost of the civil strife.

On the whole, private education in Nationalist China was a logical extension of the drive for new education in the late Qing period between 1895 and 1911. Like its predecessor in late imperial China, the Nationalist government was seldom free from financial exigencies due to both external and internal problems. As the public school system was never large enough to answer the needs of the nation and fulfill the ambition of the government, private education continued to grow as a supplement to governmental schools and a challenge to the Nationalist regime. Thus even though both the Beijing government between 1912 and 1928, and the Nanjing government between 1927 and 1949, played a role in education, governmental leadership was not the only explanation for the vicissitudes of private schools in this period.

The development of the new education in Nationalist China was uneven. In addition to a shortage of qualified teaching staff, most new schools did not have the needed facilities to fulfill their mission. In the vast countryside where the majority of China's school-aged children lived, the new education had barely started. Zhu Jiahua, the Minister of Education, regretted the miserable situation in a published report and insisted that only a continuous and vigorous readjustment could ameliorate the problem. Private schools certainly did not create this problem. Yet they did not provide a solution, either. In some cases, however, the gap between the elite private schools and the average public and private schools magnified the problem. This would contribute to their demise after the Communists seized power.

## NOTES

1. *Di san ci zhongguo jiaoyu nianjian* (Third yearbook on Chinese education) (Taibei: Zhengzhong Shuju, 1957), vol. 2, p. 101; Xiong Ming'an, *Zhonghua minguo jiaoyu shi* (History of education in nationalist China) (Chongqing: Chongqing Press, 1990), pp. 24-25; Song Enrong ed., *Jindai zhongguo jiaoyu gaige* (Educational reform in modern China) (Beijing: Educational Science Press, 1994), p. 197; Mao Lirui & Shen Guanqun ed., *Zhongguo jiaoyu tongshi* (General history of Chinese education) (Jinan: Shandong Education Press, 1988), vol. 4, pp. 349-360.

2. *Di er ci zhongguo jiaoyu nianjian* (Second yearbook on Chinese education) (Shanghai: Commercial Press, 1948), vol. 15, pp. 90-96.

3. Xiong Ming'an, *Zhonghua minguo jiaoyu shi*, pp. 377-378.

4. Unfortunately, many of these schools had neither adequate funding nor qualified faculty. Of the 36 post-secondary technical schools established in 1912, 15 had gone out of business by 1929. See *Di yi ci zhongguo jiaoyu nianjian* (First yearbook on Chinese education) (Shanghai: Kaiming Shudian Press, 1934) vol. 3, pp. 148-189; Xiong Ming'an, *Zhonghua minguo jiaoyu shi*, p. 376.

5. Ibid., pp. 19-20; Central Institute for Educational Research, *Zhongguo xiandai jiaoyu dashiji* (Major educational events in modern China) (Beijing: Educational Science Press, 1988), p. 89.

6. "Minguo shisi nian zhongguo jiaoyu zhinan" (Guide to Chinese education in 1925). See Central Institute for Education Research, *Zhongguo xiandai jiaoyu dashiji*, p. 102.

7. *Daxueyuan gongbao* (Ministry of learning news bulletin), vol. 1, no. 1 (1926); Central Institute for Educational Research, *Zhongguo xiandai jiaoyu dashiji*, pp. 157-158.

8. *Di er ci zhongguo jiaoyu nianjian*, vol. 2, pp. 122-123.

9. *Daxueyuan gongbao*, vol. 1, no. 1 (1926).

10. See Hu Yan, "Zhongguo jin xian dai sili xuexiao" (Private schools in modern China), in Zhang Zhiyi ed., *Sili minban xuexiao de lilun yu shijian* (Theory and practice of private and *minban* schools) (Beijing: Chinese Workers Press, 1994), pp. 21-22.

11. *Daxueyuan gongbao*, no. 1 & 2, 1927, no. 3, 1928; Xiong Ming'an, *Zhonghua minguo jiaoyu shi*, p. 378.

12. Yuan Mingxuan, "Shanghai shi jiefang qianhou de sili xuexiao" (Private schools in Shanghai before and after the liberation), in Zhang Zhiyi ed., *Sili minban xuexiao de lilun yu shijian*, pp. 80-82.

13. Ibid., p. 82.

14. Mao Zedong, "Hunan nongmin yundong kaocha baogao" (Report on the peasant movement in Hunan province), In Mao Zedong, *Mao Zedong xuanji* (Selected works of Mao Zedong) (Beijing: People's Press, 1991), vol. 1, pp. 39-40.

15. Rui Lianggong, "Sishu wenti" (On the issue of the Sishu), *Zhonghua jiaoyu jie*, vol. 16, no. 4, see Central Institute for Educational Research, *Zhongguo xiandai jiaoyu dashiji*, p. 123.

16. *Minguo ribao* (Republican daily), 16 December, 1930.

17. *Di yi ci zhongguo jiaoyu nianjian*, vol. 2, pp. 166-170.

18. *Jiaoyubu gongbao* (Ministry of education bulletin), vol. 8, no. 21, 22 (1936).

19. Ministry of Education, "Sili xuexiao guicheng" (Regulations on private schools), *Jiaoyubu gongbao*, no. 9, 1929; Ministry of Education, *Di er ci zhongguo jiaoyu nianjian*, vol. 2, Chapter 6, pp. 126-127; Ministry of Education, "Xiuzheng sili xuexiao guicheng" (Revised regulations on private schools), *Di yi ci zhongguo jiaoyu nianjian*, vol. 2, pp. 65-68.

20. *History of Nankai University* Committee, *Nankai daxue xiaoshi* (History of Nankai University) (Tianjin: Nankai University Press, 1989), p. 27

21. Ibid., pp. 111-118.

22. Ibid., pp. 32-35; 172-173.

23. Zheng Zhiguang & Yang Guangwei, *Zhang Boling zhuan* (A biography of Zhang Boling) (Tianjin: Tianjin People's Press, 1989), pp. 37-40.

24. Zhang Yuan, "Cong xiaoshi kan Nankai" (To view Nankai through some little things), in Nankai Middle School, *Tianjin shi Nankai zhongxue jianxiao jiushi zhounian jinian zhuankan* (Ninetieth anniversary of Nankai middle school) (Tianjin, 1994), pp. 18-20; *Xin Qingnian* (New youth), vol. 6, no. 3, March 15, 1919.

25. He Fengshan, "Huainian Yali" (Yali remembered), in *Yali Zhongxue jianxiao bashi zhounian jiniance* (Eightieth anniversary of the founding of Yali middle school: 1906-1986) (Changsha, 1986), pp. 30-36; Hu Dongsheng, "Wushi nian hou hua dangnian" (Reflections on Nankai fifty years ago), in Nankai Middle School, *Tianjin shi Nankai zhongxue jianxiao jiushi zhounian jinian zhuankan*, pp. 15, 17, 60-62 ; He Jin, "Beijing No. 25 Middle School," in Wei Yiqiao ed., *Zhongguo mingxiao* (Famous schools in China) (Shenyang: Liaoning University Press, 1992), p. 38.

26. *History of Nankai University* Committee, *Nankai daxue xiaoshi*, pp. 46-72.

27. Ibid., pp. 97-101, 164-167, 183-186.

28. Ibid., pp. 14-21.

29. Zheng Zhiguang & Yang Guangwei, *Zhang Boling zhuan*, pp. 31-40.

30. *History of Nankai University* Committee, *Nankai daxue xiaoshi*, pp. 121-3; Hong Yonghong ed., *Xiamen daxue xiaoshi* (History of Xiamen University) (Xiamen: Xiamen University Press, 1992), pp. 61-77, 113-122; *Di er ci zhongguo jiaoyu nianjian*, vol. 14, p. 6.

31. Hong Yonghong ed., *Xiamen daxue xiaoshi*, pp. 1-5, 14.

32. Ibid., pp. 37-39, 65-72, 94-97; Zheng Dengyun, *Zhongguo jindai jiaoyu shi* (History of education in modern China) (Shanghai: East China Normal University Press, 1994), p. 281.

33. Chen Changbo, "Guoli fudan daxue zhi" (Brief history of Fudan University), *Fudan Tongxun* (Fudan news bulletin), vol. 30 (1975), pp. 8-11; Wu Nanxian, "Qishi nian lai fudan lixiao techu de chuantong jingshen" (Fudan's unique spiritual heritage in the past seventy years), *Fudan Tongxun*, vol. 30 (1975): 6-7.

34. Ma Xiangbo was an ex-official and Christian convert. To set up Fudan University, he gave up a huge inheritance of three thousand *mu* (approximately five hundred acres) of land and forty thousand silver dollars.

35. Zhu Youxian, *Zhongguo jindai xuezhi shiliao* (Historical documents on the educational system in modern China) (Shanghai: East China Normal University Press, 1990), p. 170; He Fengshan, "Huainian Yali," p. 31; He Jin, "Beijing No. 25 Middle School," in Wei Yiqiao ed., *Zhongguo mingxiao*, pp. 37-38.

36. A teaching system initiated by Helen Parkhurst at Dalton High School in Dalton, Massachusetts in the early 1920s, see Paul R. Mort & William S. Vincent, Introduction to American Education. (New York: McGraw-hill Book Co. Inc., 1954), p. 377.

37. Song Enrong ed., *Jindai zhongguo jiaoyu gaige* (Educational reform in modern China) (Beijing: Educational Science Press, 1994), pp. 190-192; Mao Lirui and Shen Guanqun ed., *Zhongguo jiaoyu tongshi* (General history of Chinese education) (Jinan: Shandong Education Press, 1988), p. 28; Mei Ruli, "woguo jindai sili xuexiao" (Private schools in our country's recent history), *Zhong xiao xue guanli* (School administration), 4 (April 1994): 15-16; Shu Xincheng, *Wo he jiaoyu* (Education and I) (Taibei: Longwen Press, 1980), vol. 1, pp. 163-165, 180-182; 201-208.

38. Shu Xincheng, *Wo he jiaoyu*, vol. 1, pp. 115, 136, 165-166; *History of Nankai University* Committee, *Nankai daxue xiaoshi*, pp. 136-138; Xuan Hong, "Beijing jiefang qianhou de sili xuexiao" (Private schools in Beijing before and after 1949), in Zhang Zhiyi ed., *Sili minban xuexiao de lilun yu shijian*, pp. 62-65; Huang Yaojun, "Chongqing Yucai School," in Wei Yiqiao ed., *Zhongguo mingxiao*, pp. 552-553.

39. Mao Zedong, "Hunan zixiu daxue" (Hunan self-study university), see Angus W. McDonald, Jr., *The Urban Origins of Rural Revolution: Elite and the Masses in Hunan province, China, 1911-1927* (Berkeley and Los Angeles: University of California Press, 1978), pp. 116-120.

40. *Shibao* (Time), May 10, 1929.

41. See Chen Qingzhi, *Zhongguo jiaoyu shi* (History of Chinese education) (Taibei: Commercial Press, 1968), p. 685; also, Hu Yan, "Zhongguo jin xian dai sili xuexiao," in Zhang Zhiyi ed., *Sili minban xuexiao de lilun yu shijian*, p. 24.

42. Chen Changbo, "Guoli fudan daxue zhi" (Brief history of Fudan University), *Fudan Tongxun* (Fudan news bulletin), 30 (1975): 8-11.

43. Ministry of Education, *Jiaoyubu gongbao*, vol. 1, no. 6 (1929).

44. Ministry of Education, *Jiaoyubu gongbao*, vol. 2, no. 8, 9, 10 (1929).

45. It has been argued, however, that lives of teachers at private schools were less subject to the problems of the government.

46. *Di er ci Zhongguo jiaoyu nianjian*, vol. 14, pp. 37, 43.

47. *Di yi ci zhongguo jiaoyu nianjian*, vol. 4, p. 16.

48. Hong Yonghong ed., *Xiamen daxue xiaoshi*, pp. 79-80.

49. Ibid., pp. 113-127, 151-155.

50. E-Tu Zen Sun, "The Growth of the Academic Community, 1912-1949," John Fairbank ed., *Cambridge History of China*, vol., 13, p. 413.

51. *Di er ci zhongguo jiaoyu nianjian*, vol. 14, pp. 33, 37, 41, vol. 5, pp. 136, 152.

52. Wu Naxian, "Muxiao gaigui guoli zhi xiaoshi wenxian" (How did sili Fudan university turn into a national university), *Fudan tongxun* (Fudan news bulletin), 30 (1975): 22-24; Chen Changbo, "Guoli fudan daxue zhi" (Brief history of national Fudan University), Ibid., pp. 10-11.

53. Ministry of Education, *Jiaoyubu gongbao*, vol. 13, no. 19, 20 (1941); also see, "Changjiu daxue jiaoyu" (Save our higher education), *Dagongbao*, September 23, 24, 1941.

54. *Di san ci zhongguo jiaoyu nianjian*, vol. 15, appendix 3, "Statistics," p. 74.

55. *Di er ci zhongguo jiaoyu nianjian*, vol. 14, pp. 33-34, 37-38; Xiong Ming'an, *Zhonghua minguo jiaoyu shi*, pp. 376-377.

56. *History of Nankai University* Committee, *Nankai daxue xiaoshi*, pp. 228-274.

57. *Di er ci zhongguo jiaoyu nianjian*, vol. 1, Chapter 3, pp. 13-14.

58. Xiong Ming'an, *Zhonghua minguo jiaoyu shi*, pp. 319-320.

59. Ibid., pp. 376-377, 392-393.

60. Zheng Dengyun, *Zhongguo jindai jiaoyu shi*, pp. 416-419.

61. Ministry of Education, "Jiaoyubu buzhu gong si li youliang zhiye xuexiao banfa" (Measures for rewarding good public and private vocational schools), July 1, 1936; Central Institute for Educational Research, *Zhongguo xiandai jiaoyu dashiji*, p. 347; *Di er ci zhongguo jiaoyu nianjian*, vol. 8, "Zhiye jiaoyu" (Vocational education), pp. 1-2.

62. *Zhonghua jiaoyu jie* (Chinese education), vol. 19, no. 2.

63. Ministry of Education, *Jiaoyubu gongbao*, vol. 13, no. 17, 18 (1941).

64. *Di er ci zhongguo jiaoyu nianjian*, vol. 8, pp. 15-16.

65. Ibid., pp. 33-34.

66. *Di er ci zhongguo jiaoyu nianjian*, vol. 3, pp. 31-62.

# 4

# Ups and Downs of
# Mission Schools

Like other private schools, mission schools made great strides in the early years
of the Chinese republic. The expansion of mission education stemmed first of all
from the growing interest in China of both Catholic and Protestant missionary
societies and a beneficial shift of focus from proselytizing to education. It
coincided with a growing Chinese acceptance of Western learning as a result of
the intellectual revolution in China in the first three decades of the twentieth
century. The growth of mission education was further facilitated by the efforts
of the Nanjing government to modernize the country. Even the Japanese
invasion between 1931 and 1945 did not arrest the growth of mission schools.
Rather, while slowing down mission education in some areas, the Sino-Japanese
War of 1937-1945 helped create a vast framework of cooperation between
missionary societies and their Chinese hosts. Needless to say, the search for a
common ground was difficult for both missionaries and the Chinese. Yet on the
whole, mission schools not only became the center of Western missionary
enterprise in China but formed a bridge between Chinese nationalism and the
West.

## EXPANSION

Following the Boxer Rebellion of 1900, mission stations and mission
schools multiplied. In 1888 the Protestants were running 1,296 stations in
China. By 1914, the number had more than quadrupled. In the 1900s, almost
every mission station ran some type of school; and of the 693 Protestant mission

stations, 306 had higher primary schools, and 141 had middle schools. In the meantime, mission schools attracted a growing number of Chinese students as a result of their improvements in instructional quality. In the early 1920s, Protestant missions were operating 6,599 elementary schools with a total student body of 184,481, and 291 middle schools with a total student body of 15,213. Catholic missions likewise experienced significant progress at this time. In 1920 Catholic missions in China were running 3,518 boys' schools with an enrollment of 83,757 and 2,615 girls' schools with an enrollment of 53,283 students.[1]

The most impressive progress of Christian education, however, was in higher education. Between 1910 and 1937, sixteen Christian colleges came into being, thirteen of them were sponsored by Protestants; three (Aurora College for Women in Shanghai, Catholic University in Beijing, and Tianjin College of Industry and Commerce) were by Catholic missions. Of the Protestant colleges, Jinling (Ginling) College was founded in 1913 and opened in 1915; another, West China Union University, was inaugurated in 1910. Most of these colleges, however, were built either on earlier educational institutions or resulted from the amalgamation of several institutions. Fujian Union College (1916), for example, was formed by joining Fuzhou Anglo-Chinese College, St. Mark's Anglo-Chinese College, and Fuzhou College. Suzhou (Soochow) University (1911) combined Suzhou (Soochow) University (1901) and Shanghai Anglo-Chinese College (1882); the University of Nanjing (1910) grew out of Union Christian College, which in turn, was founded on the basis of Nanjing University (1888), Nanjing (Nanking) Christian College (1880s), and the Presbyterian Academy (1880s). Qilu (Cheeloo) University, renamed from Shandong Christian University in 1931, was in fact a merger of Shandong Christian University and the North China Union Medical College for Women (1908). Huazhong (Central China) University (1924) was created from the merger of Boone University (1909), Wesley College (1885), and Griffith College (1899).[2]

These amalgamations reflected the missionary societies' recognition of the central position of education and the need for international as well as interdenominational cooperation. At various occasions, such as the centenary conference of Protestant mission in China in 1907, delegates from different societies expressed a strong desire to cross national and sectarian lines. The creation of the National Christian Council in 1922 reinforced the trend toward collaboration. The need for coordination became all the more urgent because of the competition from Chinese governmental schools, especially the national universities heavily funded by Nanjing. By pooling their resources together, missionary societies reduced wasteful rivalries and created better centers of higher learning. In fact, most Christian colleges in this period were sponsored by several missionary societies. The North China Educational Union, for example, pulled together American Congregationalists, English Congregationalists, and American Presbyterians to maintain Gordon Memorial Theological College and Lockhard Medical College in Beijing, and North China

Union College in Dengzhou (Tungchow). Qilu (Cheeloo) University was supported by more than a dozen missionary societies, while Hangzhou Presbyterian College was sponsored jointly by the American Northern Presbyterians and the Southern Presbyterians.[3] West China Union University combined the efforts of American, British, and Canadian missionary societies.

The expansion of Christian schools, especially Christian colleges, also indicated the growing popularity of China missions in the West. Under the general goal of saving China by Christian faith, home societies eagerly sent money and personnel into the field. The Student Volunteer Movement, inaugurated in 1888 in the United States, brought fresh blood into the missionary enterprise. Many student volunteers taught at mission schools during their service in China.

As revenues increased and the qualities of education steadily improved, enrollment in Christian schools rose dramatically. By 1925 enrollment in Christian colleges had reached 3,500. At the same time, there were 26,000 students in 333 Christian middle schools and more than a quarter of a million pupils in over 7,000 mission primary schools.[4] In 1947 Christian colleges had a total enrollment of 12,654, twice the number of a decade earlier. Overall, Christian colleges enrolled about 12 percent of China's college student body. Most Christian colleges were small; the largest—Yanjing (Yenching) University in Beijing and St. John's University in Shanghai—had no more than 500 hundred students. The mere number of students, however, does not adequately reflect the significance of these colleges.

Mission schools could be viewed two ways. From the point of view of radical Chinese nationalists, they were tools of Western cultural imperialism because they disseminated values of the Judeo-Christian culture among the Chinese people. Even for the medical missionaries, who offered medical treatment to Christian and non-Christian patients alike, evangelical concerns were always paramount. Because of this emphasis, Christian schools spearheaded the Western effort to break the integrity of Chinese culture and challenged the sovereignty of the Chinese state.

On the other hand, mission schools made undeniable contributions to China's modernization, not only in technological terms, but in social and political terms as well. Christian colleges answered the need of Chinese youth for Western learning and pioneered instruction in practical fields such as medicine, nursing, agriculture, sociology, economics, and law. Although their facilities did not meet Western standards and the qualities of their faculties left much to be desired, Christian colleges were nevertheless small oasis of modern learning in a vast desert of scientific illiteracy. Many graduates from these schools became leaders in their own fields. Despite the small number of Christian colleges, they formed a bridge between China's burgeoning professionalism and the Western world and served as models for China's new schools.[5]

In a period of social and political transition, mission schools often provided the yeast of change. They were among the first schools to enroll girls as well as boys, thereby championing the emancipation of Chinese women. Earlier Christian schools for overseas Chinese girls were set up in places such as Malacca, Macao, and Singapore.[6] Before the Chinese government recognized women's need for modern education, missionary enterprises had moved forward to establish the first schools for women. In 1844, the British Society for Promoting Female Education in the East founded Miss Aldersey's School, the first school for Chinese girls, in Ningbo, followed by others such as Bridgman Girls' School in Beijing (1864), and Shanghai Chinese-Western School for Girls (1890). In 1905, Protestant missionaries were teaching 7,168 girls in their primary schools and 2,761 female students in their secondary schools.[7]

In addition to a number of girls' schools run by missionaries, some women's colleges were established by Western missions as well. In 1908, North China Union Medical College for Women was opened by American Presbyterians, Congregationalists, and English Congregationalists. Huanan (Hwa Nan) College in Fuzhou (Foochow) evolved from earlier boarding schools for girls and remained committed to women's education throughout the 1920s and 1930s. Jinling (Ginling) College in Nanjing, which was opened in 1915, enrolled 137 women in 1925. Of the three Catholic universities in China, two (Aurora, or Zhendan University in Shanghai and Catholic, or Furen University in Beijing) had a women's college. By offering subjects ranging from education to medicine, Christian colleges opened up the professions from which they had been barred to Chinese women.

Overall, female students represented a much greater proportion of the student body at Christian schools than at non-Christian schools, public and private. The first Chinese schools for girls did not emerge until the 1890s; Beijing University enrolled the first batch of female students in 1920. In most cases, the Chinese government's early efforts to educate women were limited to the elementary and middle school levels.[8] At these schools, courses for female students were designed to promote the virtue of domesticity and teach basic literacy. The emancipation of women remained a paper ideal for years.

In many respects, missionary schools spearheaded the revolution in China's education. Academically, they were the first to introduce relatively comprehensive programs in science and technology. Like Matteo Ricci in the seventeenth century, both Catholic and Protestant mission schools were instrumental in spreading Western science and technology, although their initial intention was different. "Secular missionaries" such as John Fryer (1839-1928) introduced hundreds of Western texts into the curriculum of Chinese schools. In addition to a general program in science and humanities, most mission colleges also developed their specialties. The University of Nanjing and Lingnan University in Guangzhou built strong programs in agronomy and pest control. Soochow  University led in the field of law, while St. John's and Zhijiang

(Hangchow) University each boasted of a business department. Yenching University in Beijing pioneered in journalism and sociology.[9]

In the field of medicine, missionaries made an equally indelible imprint. As early as 1837, Westerners were training Chinese in modern medicine. In 1896 St. John's University opened the first department of medical education in China. In 1905 China's first medical college, the North China Union Medical College, was founded by American Episcopalian missionaries with the support of the Rockefeller Foundation. For almost a century, the college remained the best medical school in China. West China Union University in Chengdu, Sichuan, contributed much to social progress in an otherwise underdeveloped region of China.

## PROBLEMS OF MISSION SCHOOLS

In spite of all their positive attributes, mission schools also had their grave problems, some of which were not of their own making but inherent in the very nature of Christian evangelism. Others were circumstantial, arising from both internal and external conditions. These problems prevented mission schools from taking root in Chinese society and meeting their full potential.

As outposts of Christianity in China, instructions at early mission schools focused on proselytizing. As far as their home societies were concerned, the purpose of a mission school was, first and foremost, evangelistic, not educational. In the selection of teachers and appropriation of resources, academic quality was often secondary. A still greater handicap proved to be a lack of training in the Chinese language among Christian educators. Largely because of the prevalent arrogance among the missionaries and the short duration of most teaching assignments, few foreign teachers at mission schools had obtained a Chinese proficiency that would have allowed them to work effectively with their Chinese students and colleagues. As a result, Christian schools relied on Western languages, especially English, as the media of instruction. In many cases, however, this policy prevented Christian schools, especially colleges, from recruiting otherwise promising students who were not proficient in English or simply resented the attitude of Western missionaries.[10]

Such lopsided emphasis on foreign languages proved to be disadvantageous. Even the Chinese students of mission schools were not properly trained in their native culture; some would find it difficult to work with their own people. Since most mission schools were located in the treaty ports and major cities, their graduates were especially ignorant about rural China. Academically, mission schools were pioneers in spreading modern science and technology, yet they were slow in addressing the urgent problems facing the Chinese people and in shaping their programs to practical use. For example, graduates of Peking Union Medical College and the Dental School of Western China Union University were so dependent on modern medical facilities that they could barely function in a Chinese village. Such problems limited access to the benefits provided by Christian medical schools.[11]

On the other hand, the Chinese intelligentsia obtained from the West an enormous ideological arsenal against the missionaries. For example, political and social activists of the New Culture era (1915-1925) found it easy to condemn mission schools in the name of nationalism, science, and democracy. Mission schools were by-products of Western encroachment in China; their administrations excluded Chinese faculty from decision-making and ignored the will of their students in curriculum design. Further, when Darwinism gained wide currency among China's educated elite, religious practice could be easily labeled superstition. In Beijing, scholars organized the Grand Anti-Religious Alliance (Fei zongjiao datongmeng), which claimed a diverse membership ranging from Communists and anarchists to ultranationalists. Even Western-educated liberals, such as Cai Yuanpei and Hu Shi, were unhappy about the policies of the missionary establishment and sympathized with radical students who demanded the closing or takeover of all mission schools. In the spirit of the Enlightenment, the Chinese elite in general favored the separation of church and state and advocated state regulation of all educational institutions.

As an integral aspect of Western penetration into China, the expansion of mission education was accompanied by the rise of Chinese nationalism. Thus Christian education faced a dilemma almost from the very outset. To justify its existence, mission education had to maintain its religious nature. By doing so, however, it antagonized the Chinese people. The surge of Chinese nationalism made it impossible for most Christian schools to adhere to their original missions. Yet if they accommodated to Chinese nationalism, mission schools would face the danger of losing their unique identity and, if they thoroughly sinified, they would sacrifice their right to exist, as far as their sponsoring organizations were concerned.

Despite missionary efforts to communicate with the Chinese populace, a huge gulf always existed between mission schools and the Chinese society at large. In an era of nationalist awakening, Chinese became increasingly alert to the growing influence of missionaries. Yet the curricula at Christian schools mostly ignored Chinese intelligentsia's concern about national sovereignty and China's cultural heritage. Mandatory religious activities angered even the Chinese students at mission schools. At the same time, missionaries remained insensitive to the feelings of the Chinese people, since evangelism itself presumed the superiority of the West over China. The Protestants, in particular, were none too subtle when reporting on their success in China: "About three-fourths of China is now claimed by Protestant forces, and seven provinces report no unclaimed areas whatever.... All of the cities with populations of 50,000 or more are occupied except eighteen."[12] Though apparently inflated, these figures nevertheless provoked Chinese patriots and confirmed their fear of a Western scheme for conquering China both physically and spiritually. In addition, starting with the 1920s, many mission schools increasingly catered to only a small segment of Chinese society. When their enrollment increased, mission schools raised their tuition. Yet in so doing, they began to shut out their traditional clientele and gained the reputation of being "aristocratic schools."

## CHALLENGE OF CHINESE NATIONALISM

However great their contributions to China's modernization, mission schools were never universally welcomed in China. First, they functioned in a culture which, until the early twentieth century, had remained fundamentally impervious to all alien cultures. Second, given China's vast population and their small capacity, mission schools were only tiny enclaves of modern learning in a land of mass illiteracy. Geographically, their enrollment was limited to coastal areas, especially a few major cities; and socially, their clientele was confined to Chinese Christians and well-to-do Chinese families. To China's *laobaixing* (common people), missionaries were but some soft-spoken *yangguizi* (foreign devils). To zealous patriots, mission schools were warts of colonialism because of their immunities to Chinese law and autonomy from the Chinese state. Thus they became prominent and easy targets for Chinese nationalism in the twentieth century and would soon be swept out of revolutionary China.

The anti-Christian movement was not new to China, even though it suffered a major setback in the aftermath of the Boxer Rebellion of 1900. In the 1920s anti-Christian movement gained new momentum as a result of both domestic and international situations. The chief driving forces of the movement were the surging nationalism during the New Culture Movement and the Nationalists' campaigns for national unification.

Chinese nationalism came to a climax in 1919 after the May 4 Incident in which Beijing students protested against the Western powers' sellout of former German holdings in Shandong to Japan. In this eruption of anger, there was an unprecedented awareness of national sovereignty not only in the cry of student demonstrators in Beijing but in the support they received from a wide spectrum of the Chinese public. The chambers of commerce in Beijing, Shanghai, and Tianjin, for example, endorsed the student movement, while calling for a boycott of Japanese goods. The policy of Western powers in China, and the very existence of unequal treaties, further fed Chinese antagonism toward missionary settlements and Christian education. In the nationwide "rights-recovery campaigns," the issue of educational rights came to the fore.

In the heavily charged political atmosphere following the May 4 Incident, student strikes took place on the campuses of Christian schools nationwide. Although the faculties and administrations of some Christian schools initially endorsed student activism on their campuses, they soon became concerned about order and increasingly impatient with the seemingly endless disruptions in education. In June and December 1919, students at St. John's University in Shanghai went on strike twice. Both times, an unsympathetic faculty and administration were reluctant to sanction the students' action, causing a fissure between the student body and the school's staff. Undaunted, students continued to hold frequent meetings and even carried their message to farmers near the school. In April 1920, when the students prepared for the third strike in a year, the administration refused to yield. As a result, the school was paralyzed for three weeks. In another instance, students at Hangzhou Christian College took to the streets several times in 1919. When the administration forbade their strike in the fall, seventy students walked out of the school; half of them never returned.[13] Qilu University in Shandong and Jinling College in Nanjing experienced similar disruptions. Authorities of both schools refused to endorse the students' political activism.[14]

Functioning in a diplomatic framework defined by the unequal treaties, missionaries were naturally slow to recognize the legitimacy of student activism. As the anti-Western movement moved forward, mission school faculties and administrations became increasing ambivalent and even antagonistic toward Chinese nationalism. This reaction betrayed an uneasiness among missionaries about their dubious status—despite all their charitable work, mission schools remained outposts of Western expansionism in China.

Simmering anti-Christian sentiments boiled over in 1922 during the Conference of the World's Student Christian Federation in Beijing. For the first time, educational rights became the rallying point of Chinese protests. During the conference, patriotic students in Shanghai proclaimed the Alliance of Non-Christian Students (*Fei jidujiao xuesheng tongmeng*), which was echoed in Beijing where some influential intellectuals initiated the "Beijing Non-Religion Alliance" (*Beijing fei zongjiao da tongmeng*). Leading intellectuals such as Hu Shi, Ding Wenjiang, and Tao Menghe argued that education should serve as a vehicle for scientific ideas rather than an instrument of religion and that missionaries should not engage in education. Cai Yuanpei, the famed chancellor of Beijing University, called for the separation of education and religion. In the absence of a church, he argued, good morals could be cultivated through aesthetic education.[15] This view had profound echoes among the Chinese people. *Young China* magazine, founded by the anti-imperialist Young China Association, released three special issues on the topic of religion. Contributors to these issues fired a vehement volley at Christian education.

In 1924 the Young China Association, the All China Students Federation, the Association for Educational Progress, and the All China Teachers Federation voiced their opposition to Christian education as well. Communist organs such as *Guide Weekly* (Xiangdao zhoubao) were equally fiery in comparing missionary enterprise with colonization. They called on the Beijing regime to follow the example of the Turkish government, which had shut down all schools run by Americans.[16] In their writings, radicals from the Communists to anarchists parroted Karl Marx in calling religion the opiate of the people. "In recent years many students have come back from America to spread this ill-smelling murderous superstition among our young people. And they have dared to hold in Peking, at Tsing Hua (Qinghua) University a conference of the World's Student Christian Federation. All you misled young people had better wake up and oppose this federation which is only the toy dog of capitalism."[17] At the same time, there was a noticeable tendency among the educated elite to approach the masses, in an earnest effort to arouse their political consciousness and patriotic feelings. Both the Nationalists and the Communists made strenuous efforts to tap the heretofore dormant nationalism among the common people. "Down with the imperialist powers" was the battle cry of the new populism.

Chinese nationalism surged again during the May 30 Movement of 1925. The so-called May 30 Massacre started as a boycott of Japanese goods. After the Sikh police Shanghai's British concession killed one Chinese worker and wounded some, the boycott snowballed into a barrage on all foreign powers in China. In the ensuing nationwide protest, patriots pointed to the evil of extraterritoriality and the helplessness of the Chinese government. While a few foreign teachers in Christian schools such as Yanjing openly condemned the atrocities of the British and even called for the abolition of all foreign privileges in China, Chinese students at Christian schools were incensed at the general lukewarm sympathy and even indifference of their foreign faculties.[18] In Beijing, Tianjin, Hunan, Hubei, Fujian, and Jiangxi, students withdrew from Christian schools en masse. In Changsha all mission schools were attacked by angry students and their supporters. Students in Chinese schools put great pressure on their fellow students at Christian schools to join their protest and even threatened them with violence if they refused.[19] Students at St. John's University were enraged when its American president, Hawks Pott, allegedly insulted the Chinese national flag. When the administration closed the school, more than half of the students vowed never to return. With some Chinese professors, these students established Guanghua (Bright China) University.[20] At Lingnan University in Guangzhou, angry students, who vowed to expel all "imperialists" from the faculty, successfully forced Alexander Baxter, vice-president of the school, to resign.[21]

The Chinese elite had long been suspicious of the intentions of mission schools and resented the religious components of their curricula. In the outcry for national sovereignty, mission schools came to be seen easily as instruments of the cultural imperialism of Western powers, and their religious programs, whether regular courses or Sunday morning services, as tools of spiritual enslavement. In Hubei alone, over two thousand students walked out of their mission schools, leaving some totally empty.[22] In Hunan, the administration of Yali (Yale in China) College hastily closed the school for the summer to prevent student protests from evolving into violence. In Fengtian, schools run by the Japanese were targeted by the Educational Rights Recovery Committee. The committee called a boycott of all Japanese schools in the province and asked the provincial education bureau to dissolve all of them. Under pressure, the bureau issued an order to close all schools in the province that were run by foreigners.[23]

The crux of the matter was China's educational sovereignty. As early as 1923 nationalistic Chinese began to explicitly talk about educational rights. China's educated elite seemed to have come to a consensus that the rebirth of China was contingent on the creation of a new citizenry imbued with a sense of national identity. The internationalist nature of Christian missions was apparently working at cross-purposes with Chinese nationalism. Politically sensitive Chinese Christians were also unhappy because, until 1925, no Christian college had a Chinese president, and their boards, consisting mostly of foreigners, usually exercised remote control from home country headquarters. Such administrative setups hardly demonstrated the missionaries' professed concern for China's well-being.

The Chinese government moved quickly to take advantage of the anti-Christian movement. In 1924 the Ministry of Education of the Beijing government enjoined mission middle schools to register with the government so their diplomas would be recognized by Chinese colleges.[24] In November 1925 the ministry formally published the Regulations Concerning the Founding of Foreign-Financed Schools, which required founders and sponsors of Christian schools to follow the same application procedures and meet the same criteria as other private schools. Furthermore, it asked the schools to prefix the term "private" (sili) to their names. According to the regulations, principals of Christian schools should be Chinese or, if a foreign principal was already in office, a Chinese vice-principal should be appointed. The document also stipulated that the majority of the board of managers of a mission school had to be Chinese citizens. Christian schools should be operated, and their curricula designed, according to the guidelines from the Ministry of Education. The schools were prohibited from requiring their students to take any religious courses. Christian colleges were likewise required to acknowledge that their purpose was to "impart higher and deeper knowledge, and to nurture scholars and great personalities in order to meet the needs of the nation."[25] These regulations demonstrated the Chinese government's resolve to assert its sovereign power against the "soft belly" of Western imperialism. They amounted to a denial of the peculiar nature and purpose of mission schools. In February 1925, in a special issue devoted to educational rights recovery, Chinese Education magazine carried articles by famous scholars such as Cai Yuanpei, Shu Xincheng, and Zhou Taixuan. In their articles, these people repeated the argument that Chinese education should be controlled by the Chinese. Cai Yuanpei, in particular, reiterated his belief that Chinese education must be separated from religion. This issue of Chinese Education contained the most comprehensive exposition of the nationalist position on education.[26]

Although founded by an avowed Christian, the Guomindang cashed in on the anti-foreign tide to its best advantage. The Second Congress of the GMD in Guangzhou passed the Resolution on the Youth Movement, which called on all anti-Christian forces, including students in mission schools, to form a grand anti-imperialist united front. The party swore to recover educational rights in areas under its control.[27] Like the Beijing government, the GMD regime in Guangzhou enjoined mission schools not to require their students to take courses in religion or to coerce them to take part in religious services. Mission schools teachers were not to engage in religious propaganda. In elementary schools operated by missionary organizations no religious services or activities were to be held. With regard to the administration of mission schools, the Guangzhou regime went one step further than the Beijing government, by making it mandatory for these schools to have a Chinese chief administrator and a board with a Chinese chairperson and a Chinese majority.[28] Although even Chinese Christian students complained about the political myopia of missionary leadership, it nevertheless took the missionary establishment five long years to face the issue seriously. At the First College Conference at Jinling College in 1924, and the second one in 1926, Western Christian educators grudgingly recognized the indispensable role of their Chinese colleagues and began to anticipate the eventual transfer of authority into Chinese hands.[29]

The recognition and willingness to work with Chinese nationalism were also expressed at the Conference on Christian Education in China, held in New York City on April 6, 1925. Facing "the most serious and widespread criticism" in the history of Christian education, the conference established the rationale and strategy for the continued existence of Christian schools in China. It endorsed the view of some earlier Chinese Christian educators that only by becoming "more Chinese, more efficient, and more Christian" could Christian education successfully fulfill its mission.[30] Many missionaries realized that social gospel in the form of education and medicine was much more effective than proselytizing in spreading Christian influence in China and that there was no contradiction between serving China and being a good Christian.

The Northern Expedition in 1926 through 1929 provided an additional impetus to the zeal of Chinese nationalism. The victorious march of the revolutionary army of the Guangzhou regime brought anti-imperialist agitation into the middle and lower Yangtse valley, where Western interests were heavily concentrated. While the primary target of the expedition was the warlords in central and north China, missionaries and foreigners in general often faced harassment. Church and school properties were subject to pillaging or outright confiscation. In October 1926 Hunan became the focal point of the anti-missionary movement. All mission schools in Changsha were attacked by angry mobs, even though Jiang Jieshi, commander-in-chief of the revolutionary army, had made conciliatory gestures to Western powers in China. In March 1927, after entering Nanjing, GMD troops launched a "reign of terror" against foreigners during which John E. Williams, vice-president of the University of Nanjing, was shot by looting soldiers. To avoid similar tragedies, foreign staff and faculty of Jinling College were evacuated to Shanghai. The next year, Miss Wu Yifang, a Chinese graduate of Jinling, was appointed the new president of Jinling to replace Mrs. Lawrence Thurston who had led Jinling since 1913.[31] By the summer of 1927, a large number of Westerners, including teachers of mission schools had withdrawn from the interior. By the end of 1927, three thousand missionaries had left China.[32]

In Guangzhou revolutionaries seized control of Lingnan University run by American Presbyterians, in January 1927. After the takeover, the old board of managers was pushed aside. A new board was organized, composed of thirteen Chinese and five foreigners. Zhong Rongguang was appointed president of the school. St. John's, Aurora, Suzhou University, and Jinling College followed suit later that year. At Qilu University, a Chinese Dean, Li Tianlu, was promoted to the position of vice-president in 1927, and in 1928 the school's board of trustees ratified the board of managers' recommendation to make Li president of the Christian university.[33] The provincial government of Zhejiang issued a decree in June 1927 that required all schools run by foreigners to turn over their administrations to Chinese citizens. Foreigners were prohibited from holding top positions or even sitting on the boards of managers. Once registered with the government, these schools would be treated as private schools.[34] Under the aegis of the provincial committee of the GMD in Hunan, over 120 organizations, including the Teachers Association, formed an Anti-Cultural Imperialism Alliance, which committed itself specifically to fighting mission schools.[35] The China Christian Education Association, realizing the benefit of compromise and the impracticality of continued confrontation, urged mission schools to comply with government rules and recruit more Chinese staffs. In 1927 Qilu, Yanjing, the University of Nanjing, Suzhou, Shanghai, Yali, Huazhong, and West China Union University redesignated their religious courses as electives. By the end of 1928, Chinese were in key administrative positions at most Christian colleges in eastern and southern China. Lingnan university had a Chinese president and vice-president.[36]

While Christian colleges stumbled through the storm of Chinese nationalism, Christian elementary and middle schools were hardest hit of all. Under the principle of educational sovereignty, the Nationalist regime refused to register any elementary or middle schools that taught religion or held religious services. Many mission schools were therefore turned over to Chinese private groups. Others were abandoned when governmental schools were opened nearby. Curiously, the decline in the number of mission middle schools was accompanied by a rise in their enrollment. Between 1925 and 1936 the number of mission middle school students doubled, partly because of the deficiencies of the governmental schools and partly because of the registration of mission schools with the Chinese government.[37]

In 1929, when the Nationalists nominally unified China, Zhijiang University in Hangzhou, Zhejiang; Qilu University in Jinan, Shandong; and Tongwen Academy in Jiujiang, Jiangxi, were also reorganized.[38] At Qilu University, students organized an Alliance for Educational Rights Recovery and launched a general strike in November 1929. The alliance petitioned the president of the university to reorganize the board of trustees and replace the board of managers with a university council. In addition, it asked the school to remove all religious courses from the catalog. Miraculously, the university administration met all the demands of the students and was able to resume operations. The university's first Chinese president, Li Tianlu, resigned under pressure, apparently because of his pro-Western sympathies and lack of nationalist credentials.[39] In their nationalist propaganda, the students equated Christian education with cultural imperialism, saying that "Cheeloo, a cooperative undertaking of thirteen missions, is the headquarters of the imperialists of (sic) North China. The influence of this institution in destroying Chinese intellectual life is more dangerous than big Krupp guns pointed at our chests. Now that we are awake we solemnly vow to eliminate this obstacle to China's progress."[40] Such words summed up the argument of Christian education's radical opponents.

## NANJING GOVERNMENT AND CHRISTIAN EDUCATION

Once entrenched in Nanjing, however, the Nationalist government began to distance itself from student activism. As the ruling party, the GMD had to behave more responsibly to maintain an amicable relationship with the West. At the same time, it needed to distinguish itself from the radicalism of its erstwhile Communist ally which, for philosophical and political reasons, unequivocally advocated the total abolition of mission education. The GMD's policy between 1929 and 1931 thus focused on controlling mission schools and turning them into part of the national educational program. Through a series of ordinances, the government laid down the basic rules for foreign schools as well as for private schools in general. The mission schools, after witnessing the "emotional base of Chinese nationalism" during the chaos of 1925 through 1928, were eager to come to terms with the Chinese government.[41] They knew they had to convince the Chinese that there was a common ground between Christian schools and Chinese nationalism.

Facing a situation of political disunity due to challenges from within and without, Nanjing was resolved to rally the entire nation behind it. Like its predecessors, the Nationalist regime strove to build an ideological basis for political control. In a period of "political tutelage," the party took up the responsibility of preparing the Chinese people for the implementation of a constitutional government. Organizational and propaganda departments of the ruling party accordingly extended their tentacles into schools with a view to inculcating the younger generation with the party doctrine. In 1931 Jiang Jieshi attributed the slow progress of education to a lack of faith among the teachers. While the hope of the country's future lay in education, he believed it was imperative that all teachers embrace the Three People's Principles, the official philosophy of the GMD.[42] Mission schools were not exempt from this drive for party ascendancy. Despite the displeasure of foreign missionaries, local education administrations appointed political instructors to mission schools. The political instructors reported any political deviations from official policies to the relevant government agencies.[43]

The educational rights movement culminated with legislation by the Nanjing government in 1929. Initially, the new regime seemed to be resolved to do away with all Christian schools, which was indicated by the Methods Concerning the Abolition of Private Schools Run by Religious Organizations. Confronted with resistance from foreign missionaries and pressure from Western diplomats, the government softened its stance by asking foreign schools to register as private schools and to meet pertinent requirements. As a conciliatory measure, the government recognized religious freedom and the privilege of Westerners to proselytize in China. However, it prohibited institutions run for evangelical purposes from assuming any name that might be mistaken for that of a regular school. The government argued that foreign schools were equivalent to academic associations and should be treated accordingly. This subtle distinction was intended to tighten the noose on Christian schools without antagonizing Western powers. Most mission schools complied, but some did so only on the surface. They changed their names but remained quintessentially Christian schools and continued their evangelical mission. Nanjing was incensed by such duplicity. The Ministry of Education put further constraints on mission schools by prohibiting them from recruiting Chinese under eighteen, or they had to comply with government regulations on all private schools.[44] In September 1929 and November 1930, the Ministry of Education reiterated its position of forbidding religious teaching at mission schools. Under government supervision, mission schools had to remove all pictures with religious motifs from their school buildings and religious materials from their libraries. Christian colleges and high schools were allowed to maintain such materials as references for elective courses.[45] Between 1929 and 1931, most mission schools fulfilled the requirements from the Ministry of Education, thereby extricating themselves from the hellish crucible of Chinese nationalism.

Such compliance required a radical change in the nature and role of mission schools in China. With few exceptions, mission schools yielded to the Chinese government in dropping activities such as mandatory Sunday services. To be accepted by the Chinese people and their government, mission schools had to meet the needs of their hosts and respect the Chinese people's nationalist aspirations. Such recognition and the resulting sinification of mission schools helped pacify Chinese patriots and create a working relationship between the schools and the Chinese government in the 1930s. Moreover, the Japanese aggression in Manchuria and North China helped deflect pressure from mission schools, and the suspicion of Communist agitation among students, especially in events like the December 9 Movement in 1935, also pushed Nanjing to oppose student activism.

In the hinterland, the movement proceeded relatively smoothly without much resistance from the missionary establishment. In the treaty ports where foreign enclaves existed as states within a state, things were not so easy. In

1930, for example, among the 1,227 private schools in Shanghai, about half were in foreign concessions, and most were under foreign control. In its struggle to recover educational rights in China's largest treaty port, the municipal education administration sought the assistance of the GMD and such organizations as the Chinese Taxpayers Association, which operated in the city's foreign concessions. Nanjing hesitated for good reasons. Before the abolition of foreign privileges in China, the government had little recourse in international law to take over foreign schools in the treaty ports. In June the Executive *Yuan* instructed the Ministry of Education to work with the Foreign Ministry in dealing with the issue. It made clear its interest in recovering educational sovereignty in the foreign concessions. However, since the matter concerned foreign relations, the government balked in fear of possible diplomatic repercussions.[46]

Teachers in private schools in the foreign concessions were not passive. In 1932 teachers in elementary and secondary schools in the French Concession in Shanghai formed a professional association. In a so-called "fund-request campaign," the association demanded the French Bureau of Public Service earmark at least 20 percent of its annual budget for the education of Chinese children in the French concession. The campaign received much news coverage and moral support from the city's Board of Educators and the Chinese Taxpayers Association. In April 1933 the concession's education authority ordered the closing of nine private schools, including a girls' school. The move prompted immediate protest from the French Concession Private School Association. The association held rallies and sent petitions to the city government requesting intervention. Faced with widespread opposition, the French authorities backed off. In a few days, all the shut-down schools reopened.[47]

In a measured attempt to assert authority in education, the Chinese government continued to limit the domain of Christian missions. As the country's economic situation improved, the government vigorously promoted a compulsory education program through the "citizen schools" (*guomin xuexiao*). In 1933 Western missions were forbidden to run elementary schools for Chinese children.[48] Overall, the number of missionaries declined between 1929 and 1937, but the decline did not arrest the growth of mission schools, as many transferred their administration into the hands of Chinese Christian educators. The foundation for this transfer of leadership, however, was laid in the turbulent years of the 1910s and 1920s.

The readjustment of the 1930s led to the closing of some institutions and merger of some small schools which often meant reducing the number of female students and even a decline in the quality of scholarship. Yet missionary education as a whole persisted in most areas with the teaching staff intact. The union of some small and poorly equipped schools was not only necessary but ultimately beneficial for these schools and their clientele. The main differences were "the cutting off of scholarships which had been provided for promising young people in the church constituency and a weakened program of religious activities as the schools were registered." [49] Overall, the registration of mission schools with the Chinese government indicated that Western missionaries were learning to adapt to the historical situation.


## SEARCH FOR A COMMON GROUND

Out of the trial of the 1920s, many Christian educators in China seemed to have come to the revelation that Christian education could not achieve its goals unless it forged an alliance with Chinese nationalism. It became crystal clear to many that, without the sympathy of the Chinese government, the missionary movement could hardly get anywhere. This belief was clearly indicated in the words of Dr. E. W. Wallace, Secretary of the China Christian Education Association: "Christian schools must at whatever cost maintain their Christian character, for that is the justification for their continued existence. That character, however, does not depend upon the maintenance of any particular form or method of religious education, but rather upon the personal influence of Christian teachers and the general atmosphere of the school, expressing itself in many and varied ways." [50]

The mission schools' concern to come to terms with Chinese nationalism and the Chinese government was reinforced by Japan's all-out aggression against China in July 1937. Western powers, especially the United States, became concerned about the Japanese expansion in East Asia. Between 1938 and 1941, the Roosevelt administration shifted from its obstinate neutrality to a more resolute stand against the Japanese aggression. Throughout the Japanese War, mission schools proved an important ally of the Chinese government in the latter's struggle for survival. The alliance between China and the Western democracies opened up a new phase in the history of mission education characterized by a willingness of mission schools to readjust their goals to serve China's cause of national salvation.

The fate of Christian colleges demonstrated the significance of the reconciliation. By 1937 there were more than 11,000 graduates of Christian colleges and universities. Approximately 41 percent of the graduates were engaged in education, 11 percent were religious workers, 13 percent were in medicine, 11 percent in commerce and industry, and 6 percent in public service. When the war broke out in 1937, there were 8,898 students in the thirteen Christian colleges. The number dropped to about 4,000 in 1938. But in 1942, it rose to 9,009. [51]

From 1937 through 1941, some prominent mission schools, such as Suzhou, Qilu, and Yanjing University stayed behind the Japanese lines and continued their operation to serve the needs of the local Chinese by flying Western flags. The associated Christian Colleges in Shanghai became the largest center of Christian education in China, with a total enrollment of over three thousand in

1940.[52] The faculty of Yanjing University, for example, stayed in Beiping at first, but the school was shut down by the Japanese after Pearl Harbor. The Western faculty, including twenty-two Americans, were detained by the Japanese. While most of them were repatriated by the end of 1943, a few stayed until the end of World War II.[53]

The teachers and students of some mission schools, such as Jinling College, Qilu Medical College, Suzhou Department of Biology and the University of Nanjing, took the two-thousand-mile trek to Western China. Many settled in Chengdu, the capital of Sichuan province. The alumni of Yanjing University set up a new branch of the school in Chengdu also, after its Beiping campus ceased to function under the Japanese occupation. Those in Free China decided to shift their resources to the reconstruction of China's interior.[54] After the outbreak of the Pacific War, the Chongqing government softened its attitude toward mission schools by allowing Western missions to establish and operate middle and high schools in Free China. Elementary schools run by foreigners were legitimate as long as they only enrolled foreign students.[55]

During the Sino-U.S. honeymoon after Pearl Harbor, the Chinese government helped the mission schools in the area under its control, creating in fact a golden age for such mission schools as West China Union University (WCUU). The Ministry of Education gave grants to various programs especially those in the department of agriculture which aimed to improve farming technology and living conditions of the people in Free China. The provincial government of Sichuan welcomed mission schools to relocate to Sichuan, seeing this as an opportunity to improve local education and the economy.[56] With the support of the Chinese government, scholars of WCUU took up the mission of popularizing science and education among the local people. Researchers at WCUU, working in conjunction with the West China Border Research Society, carried out extensive investigation of the natural resources, economic conditions, and societies of Sichuan and Tibet. In early 1944 when a famine struck Henan in central China, the school sent medical personnel to the province.[57]

The war transformed Christian education in many ways. The composition of the student population of mission schools changed due to the relocation. Prior to the war, mission schools drew most of their students from Christian Chinese families and Christian colleges, in turn, received their students primarily from the feeder mission schools. Relocated to an area where mission education had barely started and during a period of war, the migrant Christian colleges from the coast recruited their students increasingly from non-Christian families.[58] This trend added to the sinification of mission schools and helped elevate educational levels in the interior provinces, especially in Sichuan.

During World War II, the faculty and students of mission schools became genuinely interested in China's social and political conditions. Many participated enthusiastically in social work and political propaganda to create national consciousness among the masses of Free China. Students and teachers of West China Union University, for example, visited villages and slums to teach people how to improve personal hygiene and public sanitation. Other mission schools engaged in similar programs during the war. Female students from Jinling College set up a rural center and through service projects they helped improve life in rural Sichuan while learning first-hand about the countryside. Fujian Christian College, Lingnan University, and the University of Nanjing engaged in a variety of programs including organization of farmers' credit cooperatives and improvement of rice nursery technology.[59] Between 1943 and 1945, when the Nationalist government recruited soldiers from among the students, many mission school students answered the call. Some became interpreters under the command of General Joseph Stilwell. Female students from Jinling College worked at the American air base near Chengdu as typists, telephone operators, and accountants.[60]

## THE TRIAL OF CIVIL WAR

Following the Japanese surrender, many exiled mission schools returned to their old locations. As the nation tried to rebuild its education upon the rubbles of the war, most mission educators expected a quick return to normalcy. All hopes were dashed by the outbreak of the civil war, however. Like schools in general, mission schools were hurt by the runaway inflation starting in late 1947. Even though mission schools received money from the West, much of the value of the money was lost when it was changed into Chinese currency at an artificial rate set by the Chinese government.[61] To maintain operations, some mission schools had to increase tuition, a policy that put additional strains on the students.

Between 1946 and 1948, when the government was fighting for its life at the front, it also faced a challenge to its legitimacy from the students. In a nationwide wave of anti-civil-war and anti-hunger demonstrations, students at mission schools struck for adequate rice subsidies and called for an end to civil strife.[62] In June 1946 students in Shanghai organized the Striving for Peace Student Federation that involved the students of most Christian colleges and middle schools in the Yangtse Delta.[63] St. John's University and Soochow University, where Communist influence was strong, were two centers of the peace movement. In their desperate effort to end the civil war, students of mission schools demonstrated increasing sympathy with the underdog Communists. At the same time, they became increasingly critical of the United States, for its support to the GMD was in effect perpetuating the civil war in China. Anti-American feelings received a shot in the arm when two U.S. Marine soldiers raped a Beijing University student on Christmas Eve in 1946. In the protest following the incident, students of mission schools joined students of other schools in calling for the immediate withdrawal of all U.S. troops from

China.[64] Throughout the anti-American protests in 1946 and 1947, mission school students were as active as the general student population, if not more so.

Frustrated by the students' opposition, the Nationalist government resorted to a policy of coercion accompanied by campus raids and arrests. The government's drastic measures and determination to carry on the campaign against the Communists to the end convinced many students that nothing less than a revolution could bring about a national rebirth. At the same time, the students continued to plead for respect and legal protection of their civil rights. With the support of its subsidiary organizations, the All China Students Federation continued its defiant attitude toward the government and criticism of U.S. involvement in the Chinese civil war. Then in 1948, when the U.S. government revealed its plan to rebuild Japan, many Chinese were angered by what they saw as the ethnocentric nature of U.S. foreign policy. When Ambassador John Leighton Stuart warned the students about the dire consequences of their protests of U.S. policy, he was vehemently denounced by his colleagues at Yanjing, and a new wave of demonstrations began. YMCA and Student Christian Movement leaders called Stuart's statement an act of coercion and interference. This event dealt a deadly blow to the already strained relations between the United States and Chinese students and faculty at mission schools and prepared the students psychologically for the upcoming Communist victory. When the Communists finally came, the activists of Christian schools had no qualms about joining the victors in their southward drive to conquer the rest of the country. Years of disillusionment led many students hope for a new era under a Communist government. Few realized that the Communist movement sealed the fate of mission education in China; or if they did, they were not concerned.

The implications of the rise and fall of mission education in China were manifold. The aggressive missionary enterprises in China occurred under peculiar circumstances. They were part of the general advancement of Western civilization in the Orient. The movement reached its zenith in the first two decades of the twentieth century when the fate of China seemed to hit bottom. China's deplorable situation created the illusion that it was ready to be taken over by Western culture. The dramatic story of mission education mirrored, in John K. Fairbank's words, "the abysmal degree of China's backwardness at the time."[65] Yet the slogan to "Save China by Christianity," proved to be no more than a romantic dream, and the very premises of the missionary movement contained the seeds of its demise. For in the crusade to save Chinese souls, missionaries fostered values and knowledge that fueled Chinese nationalism and brought to China Western learning that eventually became part of China's cultural rejuvenation. In the final analysis, Western technology was strong enough to batter the Chinese empire, but Western culture did not have the capacity to engulf the Chinese nation. Given the enormous odds against missionary enterprises, Christian education in China was foredoomed.

Critics of mission schools were quick to point out their inadequacies, such as their relative isolation from Chinese society and their slow response to the needs of the host country. But criticism should not obscure the fact that mission schools represented the best the West could offer to the Chinese people in their struggle for modern nationhood. In 1947, for example, Christian colleges enrolled twelve thousand students and in most years, they were training 15 to 20 percent of the college students in China.[66] Even though the demise of Christian education in mainland China disappointed Westerners, the efforts of Christian schools in China were not all in vain. Like Buddhism since the early Middle Ages, Christian education has made an indelible imprint on Chinese society and culture. It is a great triumph for an alien religion to become a dimension, however small, of a civilization with a recorded history that dates back to the time of Abraham.

Reciprocity is an ingrained tract of Chinese culture, and the Chinese people are unlikely to forget all the good Christian schools brought to their country. Christian education was not totally a foreign operation but involved many Chinese Christians. It received support from the Chinese government, through the Ministry of Education, and from the Chinese gentry class.[67] At Christian schools, the best of the West and East met. And, despite the religious bias of their founders and home societies, mission schools represented the charitable side of Western culture. In the formative years of modern China, Christian education provided the much needed information on Western science, and many ideas that became constructs of a new culture. As strongholds of Western science and liberalism, mission schools left an enduring legacy and, in fact, became a "vitalizing and formative part of China's permanent heritage."[68]

## NOTES

1. *Zhongguo da baike quanshu* (Encyclopedia sinica) (Education) (Beijing: Encyclopedia Sinica Press, 1985), pp. 377-378; Albert Feuerwerker, "The Foreign Presence in China," in John K. Fairbank ed., *Cambridge History of China*, vol. 12, pp. 174-175; Jiang Shuge, *Zhongguo jindai jiaoyu zhidu* (Education system in modern China) (Shanghai: Commercial Press, 1934), p. 157. Another source indicates that in the 1920s Christian elementary schools were placed by the Chinese government into two categories: lower primary (four years) and higher primary (three years). Of the former, there were 5,607 schools with 150,779 students, and of the latter, 956 schools and 32,829 students. Students in Christian elementary schools accounted for 4.3 percent of the elementary school enrollment in China in that period. According to *Christian Education in China*, a study made by an Educational Commission representing the Mission Boards and Societies conducting work in China. (New York: Committee of Reference and Council of the Foreign Missions Conference of North America, 1922), pp. 67-68, 89.

2. Jessie G. Lutz, *China and the Christian Colleges, 1850-1950* (Ithaca: Cornell University Press, 1971), pp. 531-533; also see *Zhongguo dabaike quanshu* (Education), pp. 377-378; Ministry of Education, *Di yi ci zhongguo jiaoyu nianjian* (First yearbook on Chinese education) (Shanghai: Kaiming Shudian, 1934), vol. 4, pp. 44-47.

3. Lutz, *China and Christian the Colleges*, pp. 109-110.

4. Ibid, pp. 202-203; also John K. Fairbank, "Introduction: The Many Faces of Protestant Missions in China and the United States," in John K. Fairbank ed., *The Missionary Enterprises in China and America*. (Cambridge, Mass.: Harvard University Press, 1974), pp. 13-14; Elsewhere, statistics differed somewhat from this. See Zheng Dengyun, *Zhongguo jindai jiaoyu shi* (History of education in modern China) (Shanghai: East China Normal University Press, 1994), pp. 270-271.

5. See Albert Feuerwerker, "The Foreign Presence in China," in John K. Fairbank, *Cambridge History of China*, vol. 12, pp. 176-177.

6. In 1835, Mrs. Gutzlaff, wife of Dr. Karl Friedrich August Gutzlaff founded the first Christian school that took female students in Macao. In 1844, another Christian school for girls was opened in Ningbo by Miss Aldersey, followed by the first boarding school for girls in Fuzhou. See Mary R. Anderson, *A Cycle in the Celestial Kingdom or Protestant Mission Schools for Girls in South China: 1827 to the Japanese Invasion* (Mobile, Alabama: Heiter-Starke Printing Co., 1943), pp. 60-62.

7. Paul Cohen, "Christian Missions and Their Impact to 1900," John K. Fairbank ed., *Cambridge History of China*, vol. 10, p. 583.

8. Beijing University which pioneered in coeducation, for example, enrolled the first batch of female students only in 1920; Chen Qingzhi, *Zhongguo jiaoyu shi* (History of Chinese education) (Taibei: Commercial Press, 1968), pp. 686-687; Song Shu: "Biantong pian: Kaihuazhang" (Reform: enlightenment), no. 4, see Zheng Dengyun, *Zhongguo jindai jiaoyu shi*, pp. 117-118; Zheng Guanying, "Nu Jiao" (Women's education), *Shengshi weiyan* (Warning in a prosperous time), vol. 3; Yan Fu, "Lun fu shang chuangxing nuxuetang shi" (On the setting up of a school for girls in Shanghai), *Guowenbao* (National affairs), January 10, 11, 1898; in Chen Xuexun ed., *Zhongguo jindai jiaoyu wen xuan* (Essays on education in modern China) (Beijing: People's Education Press, 1993), pp. 58-59, 212-215.

9. Shi Jinghuan, "Jindai xifang chuanjiaoshi zaihua jiaoyu huodong de zhuanyehua," *Lishi yanjiu* (Historical studies), 6 (June 1989): 36.

10. See Earl H. Cressy, *Christian Higher Education in China: A Study for the Year 1925-1926.* (CCEA Bulletin. No. 20, Shanghai, 1928), p. 181.

11. Lutz, *China and the Christian Colleges*, pp. 511-512.

12. Milton T. Stauffer ed., *The Christian Occupation of China* (Shanghai, 1922), pp. 33-34; quoted in Lutz, *China and the Christian Colleges*, p. 224.

13. Mary Lamberton, *St. John's University, Shanghai, 1879-1951* (New York: United Board for Christian Colleges in China, 1955), pp. 77-81; Charles H. Corbett, *Shantung Christian College (Cheeloo)* (New York: United Board for Christian Colleges in China, 1955), pp. 139-143; Mrs. Lawrence Thurston & Miss Ruth M. Chester, *Ginling College* (New York: United Board for Christian Colleges in China, 1955), pp. 30-32; Lutz, *China and the Christian Colleges*, pp. 212-213.

14. Cobertt, *Shantung Christian College*, pp. 139-143; Thurston, *Ginling College*, pp. 30-32.

15. Jiang Shuge, *Zhongguo jindai jiaoyu zhidu* (Educational system in modern China) (Shanghai: Commercial Press, 1934), p. 160.

16. "Touxian tiaojian xia shi zhongguo jiaoyu quan" (China's educational sovereignty under conditions of surrender), *Guide Weekly*, vol. 63, May, 1924.

17. The Grand Anti-Christianity Alliance, *Fandui jidujiao yundong* (The Anti-Christian Movement), quoted in Lutz, *China and the Christian Colleges*, pp. 227-228;

Tatsuro and Sumiko Yamamoto, "The Anti-Christian Movement in China, 1922-1927," *Far Eastern Quarterly*, 12 (December 1953): 140-143.

18. Dwight W. Edwards, *Yenching University* (New York: United Board for Christian Higher Education in Asia, 1959), pp. 146-148.

19. John Coe, *Huachung University* (United Board for Christian Higher Education in Asia, 1962), pp. 43-44; Zheng Dengyun, *Zhongguo jindai jiaoyu shi*, p. 275.

20. Shu Xincheng, ed., *Jindai zhongguo jiaoyu shiliao* (Historical materials on Modern Chinese Education), 4 vols. (Shanghai, 1923), vol. 3, pp. 180-183.

21. Corbett, *Lingnan University* (New York: United Board for Christian Higher Education in Asia, 1963), pp. 89-94; also in Lutz, *China and the Christian Colleges*, p. 249.

22. *Zhonghua jiaoyu jie* (Chinese education) vol. 15, no. 5, 6, 9, and vol. 16, no. 3.

23. Central Institute for Educational Research, *Zhongguo xiandai jiaoyu dashihi* (Chronicle of Modern Chinese Education) (Beijing: Educational Science Press, 1988), pp. 83-84.

24. *Zhonghua jiaoyu jie*, vol. 14, no. 7.

25. *Jiaoyu zazhi*, vol. 18, no. 1; also see, Jiang Shuge, *Zhongguo jindai jiaoyu zhidu*, p. 161; Charles H. Corbett, *Shantung Christian College*, pp. 168-169.

26. *Zhonghua Jiaoyu* jie, vol. 14, no. 8; see, Central Institute for Education Research, *Zhongguo xiandai jiaoyu dashiji*, p. 97.

27. *Zhongguo qingnian yundong lishi ziliao*, 1926-1927.

28. *Daxueyuan gongbao* (Bulletin of the Ministry of Learning), vol. 1, no. 9.

29. Alice H. Gregg, *China and Educational Autonomy: The Changing Role of the Protestant Educational Missionary in China, 1807-1939* (Syracuse: Syracuse University Press, 1946): p. 127.

30. "Statements Distributed in Preparation for the Conference," *Chinese Christian Education: A Report of a Conference Held in New York City, April 6th*, 1925, under the joint auspices of the International Missionary Council and the Foreign Missions Conference of North America (New York, 1925), p. 5; "Tentative Findings of the Conference of Chinese Administrators in Christian Colleges and Universities," see ibid., pp. 18-20.

31. Mrs. Lawrence Thurston & Miss Ruth M. Chester, *Ginling College*, pp. 5, 64-5.

32. Tatsuro and Sumiko Yamamoto, "The Anti-Christian Movement in China, 1922-1927, *Far Eastern Quarterly*, 12 (December 1953): 136.

33. Corbett, *Shantung Christian University*, pp. 169-170; *Dongfang zazhi*, vol. 24, no. 6; see, Central Institute for Educational Research, *Zhongguo xiandai jiaoyu dashiji*, pp. 127-128.

34. *Jiaoyu zazhi* (Education journal), vol. 19, no. 7, July, 1927.

35. *Jiaoyu zazhi*, vol. 19, no. 2, February, 1927.

36. Lutz, *China and the Christian Colleges*, pp. 254, 259-261; Zheng Dengyun, *Zhongguo jindai jiaoyu shi*, pp. 272-276.

37. James H. Pott, "Christian Primary School Education in China," *Educational Review*, (July 1933): 247; Earl H. Cressy, "The Present Status of Christian Schools," *Chinese Recorder*, September 1936, p. 539.

38. *Dongfang Magazine*, vol. 24, no. 6, *Jiaoyu zazhi*, vol. 21, no. 3.

39. *Jiaoyu zazhi*, vol. 21, no. 12.

40. Corbett, *Shantung Christian College*, p. 174.

41. Lutz, *China and the Christian Colleges*, p. 269.

42. *Minguo ribao*, January 30, 1931.

43. *Jiaoyubu gongbao* (Bulletin of the ministry of education) vol. 2, no. 7.

44. *Jiaoyubu gongbao*, vol. 1, no. 5, vol. 6, no. 35, 36 (1929).

45. *Jiaoyubu gongbao*, vol. 1, no. 10; vol. 2, no. 27, 47 (1930).

46. *Jiaoyubu gongbao*, vol. 2, no. 26; *Minguo ribao* (The republic daily), May 4, 10, 17, 1930.

47. *Yijiusansan nian zhi Shanghai jiaoyu* (Education in Shanghai in 1933), see Central Research Institute for Educational Sciences, *Zhongguo xiandai jiaoyu dashiji*, p. 257.

48. Ministry of Education, "Revision of Private School Regulations," *Jiaoyubu gongbao*, vol. 5, no. 41, 42.

49. Mary Raleigh Anderson, *A Cycle in the Celestial Kingdom, or Protestant Mission Schools in South China: 1827 to the Japanese Invasion* (Mobile, Alabama: Heiter-Starke Printing Co., 1943), pp. 342-343.

50. E. W. Wallace, *The Place of Private Schools in a National System of Education.* (Shanghai: China Christian Educational Association Bulletin, no. 5, 1925).

51. M. Searle Bates, *Missions in Far Eastern Cultural Relations* (New York: Foreign Missions Conference of North America, 1943), pp. 11-12.

52. "Educational News," *The Chinese Recorder*, 71 (1940): 579.

53. Dwight W. Edwards & Y. P. Mei, *Yenching University* (New York: United Board for Christian Higher Education in Asia), pp. 365-368. A few of them such as Michael Lindsay, a British teacher who married a Chinese woman, and the William Bands's, who were also British, managed to flee Beiping and took refuge in Communist areas. They came out of Red China with glowing accounts of the Chinese Communists.

54. *Jiaoyu zazhi*, vol. 29, no. 6.

55. See Central Research Institute, *Jiaoyu dashiji*, p. 518.

56. Dwight W. Edwards & Y. P. Mei, *Yenching University* (New York: United Board for Christian Higher Education in Asia, 1959), pp. 376-377.

57. Lewis C. Walmsley, *West China Union University* (New York: United Board for Christian Higher Education in Asia 1974), pp. 92-94; 115-119.

58. Lutz, *China and the Christian Colleges*, p. 379.

59. Ibid., 376.

60. Thurston and Chester, *Ginling College*, p. 120.

61. The United Board for Christian Colleges in China sent 3.24 million to its member schools between 1945 and 1948. But due to the unfair exchange rate, the U.S. dollar in the fall of 1946 was at only 20 percent of its prewar value and by the fall of 1947, at only 15 percent. See Lutz, *China and the Christian Colleges*, p. 404.

62. Ibid., p. 408.

63. *Wen hui bao*, June 20, 1946.

64. *Yi shi bao*, December 30, 1946, *Ching-shih jih-pao*, December 31, 1946, and *Ta-kung pao*, January 10, 1947; see Lutz, *China and the Christian Colleges*, pp. 415-420.

65. John K. Fairbank, "Introduction: The Many Faces of Protestant Missions in China and the United States," in Fairbank ed., *The Missionary Enterprises in China and America*, pp. 13-14.

66. Oliver J. Caldwell, "Chinese Universities and the War," *School and Society* (February, 1942): 232-233; Lutz, *China and the Christian Colleges*, p. 494.

67. Walmsley, *West China Union University*, pp. 92, 126-127.

68. Corbett, *Shantung Christian College*, p. 266.

Xingtan where Confucius (551–479 B.C.) taught.

Bailudong (White Deer Cave) Shuyuan in Jiangxi for which Zhu Xi (1130–1200) wrote the famous rules comparable to the Benedictine Rules.

Examination Halls for the *keju* candidates, Nanjing, 1900s.

Sanwei Shuwu in Shaoxing, Zhejiang was a typical *sishu* in traditional China.

E. A. K. Hackett Medical College for Women, Canton, 1911.

Candidates for Christian Ministry, Shandong Christian College, 1910s.

St. John's University, Shanghai, 1910s.

Tianjin Nankai Middle School, founded in 1904 by Yan Xiu and Zhang Boling.

Jimei Middle School in Xiamen, Fujian province was set up by Chen Jiageng, an overseas Chinese businessman in 1918.

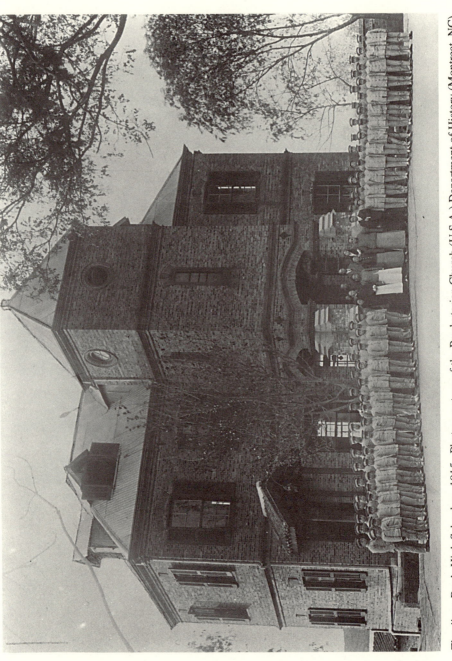

Zhenjiang Boy's High School ca. 1915. Photo courtesy of the Presbyterian Church (U.S.A.) Department of History (Montreat, NC).

七七民國會大會夏次一第合聯行實教督基
月年國會會夏次一第合聯行實教督基

Suzhou (Soochow) University, 1918. Photo courtesy of the Presbyterian Church (U.S.A.) Department of History (Montreat, NC).

Jukui Middle School in Sichuan province. The school began as Jukui Academy in 1870. It became private Jukui School in Republican era. In the 1950s, it was taken over by the new government.

Shenyang Experimental High School, set up in 1988, is, in fact, a private school.

Yanjing Huaqiao (Overseas Chinese) University in Beijing, 1984.

China University of Science and Technology Management, Beijing, 1985.

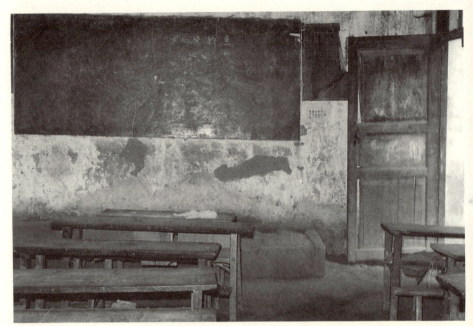

This classroom at Xindian Elementary School in Wanyuan county, Sichuan province speaks of the paucity of education in rural China today.

Private Guangya School, founded in 1992, is believed to be the first openly labeled private school since the 1950s.

Maple Leaf International School at Jinshitan (Golden Rock Beach) near Dalian, Liaoning province. As suggested by its name, the school has Canadian connections.

# 5

# Demise of the *Sili* and Rise of the *Minban*[1]

In the early 1950s the Chinese government abolished private schools, thereby creating one of the most abnormal periods in the history of Chinese education. Surprisingly, very few people raised serious questions about this move then and thereafter—while the Chinese people were unable to resist the awesome power of a revolution, observers outside China found it hard to visualize the whole picture of what was happening behind the bamboo screen due to a lack of information. In retrospect, this historical anomaly was by no means an accident, nor was it a vagary of Mao Zedong, chairman of the ruling party and president of the new state. Rather, it was the symbolic culmination of a social and political revolution and a by-product of an international situation fraught with tension.

## PRIVATE SCHOOLS IN THE 1950s

To understand the takeover of private schools in the early 1950s, one should not forget that, although the Chinese government in modern times encouraged the growth of public and private schools, no modern Chinese regime has wanted an independent school system. It has always been the goal of the state to incorporate private schools into a national educational program. In this regard, the Beijing government under Yuan Shikai and Nanjing government under Jiang Jieshi shared striking similarities. In times of disunity and economic growth, the government tended to lose its grip on private schools. But it never adopted a laissez faire policy vis-à-vis education. The Nationalist government's decision to turn some well-run private elementary schools into citizen schools (*guomin xuexiao*) during World War II was only a variation of the policy of bringing private schools into the national system. During the war, the Nationalist government took over several private universities and placed them under the Ministry of Education.[2] Shanghai Jiaotong (Communication) University and Guangzhou Jinan University managed to maintain their names but depended on government funds for survival. After championing private education for over twenty-five years, Fudan University was nationalized in January 1941, for financial reasons.

Even Nankai University failed to survive the trauma of the war. The war not only severely damaged its old campus in Tianjin but made it almost totally dependent on government support as part of the Southwest Associated University or Lianda. Sadly enough, when the war ended, Nankai found it impossible to resume operation as an independent private college. Zhang Boling begged Nanjing for continued governmental assistance. The government, on its part, was ready to confer public (*guoli*) status on all leading universities, including Nankai, in an effort to rebuild the nation's educational system. Jiang Jieshi personally suggested that Nankai be turned into a governmental university as a condition of receiving public funding, saying that the change would only demonstrate the government's commitment to Nankai. At Jiang's insistence, Nankai swallowed its pride and became National Nankai University in April 1946. Zhang Boling, then seventy years old, doggedly asked and secured Jiang's promise to allow Nankai to resume its independence ten years later. Jiang agreed. But his regime was driven to Taiwan in 1949 and Nankai has not been redeemed yet.[3]

During the interim between World War II and the civil war, China's private education at all levels showed some measurable growth. In less than one year, nearly 2,000 new private elementary schools were created along with 100 new private middle schools and 15 private post-secondary institutions. Even after the outbreak of the civil war in 1946, private education held on.[4] Yet when government troops began to collapse at the front in 1948, education in Nationalist China fell into disarray. The skyrocketing inflation of 1948 and 1949 hit private schools especially hard. In cities like Beijing and Shanghai, many private schools were brought to the verge of total shutdown. Only mission schools fared reasonably well because they raised money from outside sources. Famous universities like Nankai had to operate on loans from local banks.[5]

The Communists had drawn up a blueprint for education well before entering the cities. They foresaw a nationwide drive for industrialization under their leadership to fulfill the dream of generations of Chinese patriots since the nineteenth century. The program was ambitious for a nation hardly coming out of medieval backwardness and traumatized by prolonged war. To achieve the goals they set before themselves, the Communists had to overcome many obstacles, including a lack of well-trained personnel in modern science and technology. The Communist party membership included 700,000 relatively educated people, barely enough to even fill the administrative positions in the new bureaucracy. While many of well-educated people fled to Taiwan with the

Nationalist regime, over two million of them remained. Still, this was far short of the projected goal of the new government.

In December 1949 the First National Education Conference under the new government was held in Beijing. At the conference, the new leadership laid down the general philosophy of education in Communist China. "The education in the People's Republic of China is the education of new democracy. It is to raise the people's educational level, to train talents for the country's reconstruction, and to promote the attitude of serving the people while combating feudal, bureaucratic bourgeois, and fascist ideology. Such education is at once nationalist, scientific, and populist. It combines theory with practice, to serve the people, especially the workers, peasants, and soldiers, to assist the current revolutionary struggle and reconstruction." The new education, however, did not start with a clean slate. Rather, it had to be based on existing schools. The new leadership realized that remolding the old educational system was a very difficult task and would take a long time. It decided that an overall reform could be carried out "only after the accumulation of knowledge through individual reforms at different levels."[6] As to private education, the state vowed to "protect and support" private schools run by Chinese citizens. At the same time, it promised to provide leadership and to reform these schools gradually.[7]

Given the structure of the nation's education at the time, the new regime's policy toward private schools was necessarily prudent. In 1949, China had 205 colleges, of which 81 were private. In some regions, such as the southwest and the Shanghai area, private colleges outnumbered public colleges. In Wuhan and Nanjing, there were about as many private colleges as there were public colleges. At the time of the First National Conference on Education, China still had 1,467 private middle schools with 366,000 students, representing 48 percent of the nation's middle schools and 42 percent of its middle school student population. In Beijing, Tianjin, Shanghai, Nanjing, and Wuhan, private elementary and middle schools were in the majority, accounting for 56 percent of all schools and 84 percent of the student population. Some private schools, such as Jiangnan University in Shanghai and Huanan (South China) United University in Guangzhou, maintained institutional health despite the damage of the civil war. Some, like Dongnan (Southeast) Medical College in Shanghai, even tried to please the new regime by voluntarily relocating to rural areas.

Until mid-1950 the new regime had not completely decided how to deal with private schools. It pursued a policy of "salutary neglect" toward these schools in the very spirit of the "New Democracy." The policy made much sense when the nation's educational system had been weakened by a brain drain following the fall of the Nationalist government. To make up for this loss, the new government, through some of its sympathizers among the intelligentsia such as Hua Luogen, a world-renowned mathematician, appealed to Chinese scholars abroad to return to the new China. Only about two hundred answered the call. Before the new regime was firmly established, it seemed unwise, if not impossible, to take over all private schools immediately.

At the same time, by the end of the civil war, there had been both a quantitative and a qualitative decline in private education. Hubei province reported 98 private middle schools and 308 private elementary schools in 1948. In late 1949 before the Communist victory, the number of private middle schools fell to 52 and in 1950, only 35 remained. Most of these schools were in abysmal financial situations.[8] In southwestern China, the student body at private colleges dropped by two-thirds in the first two years of the People's Republic. Many private schools had trouble attracting students because the economy was in limbo and their traditional clientele, the urban middle class, was facing extinction.

Critics of private schools pointed out that many of them lacked the necessary conditions for quality education. The School of Science and Technology of Datong University in Shanghai, for example, had no faculty of its own; all courses were taught by adjunct professors. Zhonghua Industry and Business School in Shanghai was just a four-story building where eight hundred students enrolled in such fields as mechanical engineering, civil engineering, business administration, and accounting. The library of the Southwest China School of Fine Arts in Chongqing had only sixteen books. To the new regime which gave priority to industry and science, course offerings at private colleges were terribly lopsided. In a survey of forty-five private colleges, the new government found that only 23 percent had science and technology majors. Most focused on humanities, law, and business, which were deemed unessential for the economy.[9]

Most problems of private schools, however, were circumstantial and would have been solved along with economic recovery. The Common Program, laid out at the Chinese People's Political Consultative Conference in September 1949 and other documents of the Chinese Communist Party, called for a gradualist approach to socialist transformation and the preservation of China's still young capitalism under the "New Democracy." Had the leadership of the CCP adhered to such moderation, private schools would have had a good chance of recovery and even expansion. Unfortunately, the CCP decided to push forward a revolution against common sense, thereby bringing irretrievable damage to the nation's educational system.

**THE TAKEOVER**

In June 1950 the First National Conference on Higher Education met in Beijing. Participants in this conference drew up the Temporary Regulations on the Administration of Private Colleges which was approved by the forty-third regular session of the State Council later in the same year. Among other things, the document called for Chinese control of the administrative and financial affairs of all private colleges. Since the boards of many private schools were in disarray, the government urged the reorganization of the boards of private colleges and required all private colleges to reregister to establish their legal status. The nomination of presidents and vice presidents of these colleges by their school boards had to be approved by the education authorities of the regional governments. No private colleges were allowed to make any religious course mandatory or to force their students to participate in religious activities.[10] The last point was apparently directed against Christian colleges and was reminiscent of the policy of the Nationalist government in the 1920s and 1930s.

As many private schools faced grave financial and administrative difficulties, the State Council issued the Directive Concerning Aid to Unemployed Teachers and the Problem of School Closing. It asked local governments to assist existing private schools and help them carry out reforms to decrease operating costs and attract more students. According to the directive, local governments should extend financial aid to private schools to maintain their operation when necessary. In the meantime, the government should also persuade poorly managed private schools to merge with other schools.[11] The new regime's caution was also reflected in its efforts to keep schools out of revolutionary storms such as land reform. To its local administrators, Beijing counseled caution and patience. Teachers and students, regardless of family background, were to be exempt from struggle meetings, forced confessions, and political purges. Rather, the new regime wanted to win them over, to reform them through moral suasion and education.[12] These measures seemed quite reasonable and reminiscent of the policy of the Nationalist regime at its best.

However, the initial caution was soon replaced by heady political campaigns aimed at total control. In fact, the takeover of schools followed the footsteps of the triumphant red army. Before the Communists finished their conquest, local governments were appointing principals to schools. Political workers were setting up CCP cells, the Communist Youth League branches, and the National Student Federation chapters in schools with a view to consolidating the new regime.

With the end of the civil war, a social revolution started that aimed at creating an egalitarian economy. Drastic economic changes both in the cities and countryside led to the elimination of the middle class. In the countryside, the old social structure was turned upside down through land reform, which in many places proved to be a bloody liquidation of landlords and rich farmers. In the cities, the business community lingered on. But in the political campaigns such as the Five-Antis in 1951 and 1952, capitalists and small businessmen who had patronized private schools were targeted.[13] Although the new regime aimed primarily at controlling industry, private schools were nevertheless affected because the political campaigns destroyed much of their traditional clientele.

The international situation had much to do with the fate of Chinese education. Foreign aid was badly needed when the Communists assumed power. Yet in the early 1950s, any assistance from the West was impossible. Faced with menace from hostile forces at home and abroad, Mao Zedong and his colleagues adopted a "lean-to-one-side" foreign policy by forging an alliance with the

Soviet Union. Thus in the 1950s, a trickle of Soviet aid came to China, including thousands of Russian "experts." In the overall Sino-Soviet honeymoon atmosphere, China's school system leaned to one side as well. The school system of the Soviet Union, though far behind that of the West, was reverently regarded as a model by the Chinese Communists. While emulating the Soviet Union helped the new regime stand on its feet, this success entailed a price. One of the negative consequences was the abolition of private education.

Christian universities were the first casualties of the Communist takeover. During the civil war, Communist propaganda convinced the administrations and faculties of mission schools that they could remain independent if they agreed to cooperate with the new regime. In the general climate of toleration and good will, however, administrations of Christian colleges were reorganized, and foreigners lost their control over school affairs. Thus even though the new regime permitted Christian colleges to receive funds from the West, some policies of the new regime, such as the taxation of school property, made normal operation of Christian schools difficult and discouraged sponsoring organizations abroad.[14] In July 1949 a resolute municipal government of Beiping surpassed its Nationalist predecessor by prohibiting all religious courses at mission schools, on the ground that this time-honored practice violated the students' religious freedom. It also forbade foreigners to be headmasters or presidents of mission schools in the name of national sovereignty.[15]

Yet on the whole, mission schools seemed to accept the advent of the Communist era with amazing calm. On the campus of Yanjing University, for example, there was almost a consensus that the school should stay where it was in the hope that Christian educators could reach a modus vivendi with the new regime, whereby they could continue to work without sacrificing the essentials of the school's Christian purpose or its academic freedom. Such optimism was not totally unfounded. For example, even though the new authorities were unfavorable to Christian education, they nevertheless showed some restraint when students at Christian schools voluntarily participated in religious activities. At Qilu university, the student choir rendered Handel's Messiah on Christmas 1949 and sang Stainer's Crucifixion the following week.[16] When the students of Qilu University sent a petition to the Communist governor of Shandong against the occupation of some buildings by another institute, the later responded immediately and resolved the matter in favor of Qilu.[17]

Although the CCP recognized religious freedom in broad terms, mission schools, especially those sponsored by Americans, found themselves in a very awkward position because of the pro-Nationalist China policy of Washington during the Chinese civil war. By mid-1950 it had become apparent to Western observers that Christian colleges in China had to be totally sinified in exchange for their institutional survival. In the Resolutions Concerning the Leadership of Institutions of Higher Learning, adopted by the First National Conference on Higher Education, the Chinese government defined the task of all Chinese colleges as serving national reconstruction under the leadership of the CCP. The promise of instilling Marxian ideology among college students and shifting from liberal arts to scientific and technological education sent chills over mission school campuses.[18] Leaders of mission schools had little choice but to comply with the new regime in the hope that, while playing a role in the nation's new life, they could somehow maintain their distinctive identity. Yet such compliance proved extremely painful. To satisfy the new government, Christian schools had to secure emergency funds from abroad to pay taxes levied on school property and provide more scholarships to students from working class families. Their curricula were overhauled, and many teachers were unable to carry out the new programs. Christian colleges and high schools lost a significant portion of their students when they were recruited into the People's Liberation Army and the new government. The loss of students and frequent political meetings disrupted the academic routine. Worse still, on some campuses, past disputes and bad feelings against school administrations quickly heated up into power struggles.[19]

The Chinese participation in the Korean War in October 1950, against almost the entire West spelled the doom of Christian education in Red China. On mission school campuses all over the country, rallies and study sessions were held by party workers and student activists under the slogan of Resist America, Aid Korea. When the United States was demonized in official organs, students at mission schools moved quickly to draw a line between themselves and American imperialism. Meanwhile, the Truman administration intensified anti-American sentiments by freezing all Communist assets in the United States.

The first test of the will of the new Chinese government came on the eve of China's military operation in Korea. On October 12 the Ministry of Education ordered the takeover of Furen (Catholic) University in Beijing. Ma Xulun, the Minister of Education, held a press conference at which he announced the government's decision. Founded in 1925 by Catholic missionaries, Furen had been one of the oldest and finest Christian colleges in China. After 1949 Furen's financial resources shrank as a result of the church's disenchantment with the anti-Western stance of the new regime. When the school's new administration requested more funds, Roman Catholic church insisted on retaining its administrative authority over the school. To the Chinese government, this meant continuous Western encroachment on China's educational sovereignty. When the Chinese government refused to concede, the home mission cut off funding altogether in August 1950. The Chinese government promptly appropriated money at the request of the university administration. In September the Ministry of Education invited the representative of the Catholic mission for a meeting. At the meeting the Chinese government warned the Catholic mission of a takeover if it did not stop interfering in the administrative affairs of the school. The takeover took place in October as the Catholic mission stood firm on its position of maintaining control.[20]

During the bitter haggling, the Chinese government seemed to draw a fine line between the issue of educational sovereignty and religion. In his statement,

Minister Ma made it clear that the takeover was a political issue and had nothing to do with religion. Furen University was taken over as a private institution rather than as a mission school. The change was not intended to affect the lives of teachers or students. Under the general principle of religious freedom, government workers were instructed to be sensitive to people's religion.[21] On mission school campuses, participation in political study sessions was voluntary.

In late 1950, however, the reform of private education picked up its tempo. In December, the military authority in Chongqing dissolved the Chinese Popular Education Promotion Association founded by James Yan who was openly pro-Nationalist and anti-Communist. This decision was apparently a by-product of the Chinese decision to jump into the Korean fray and President Harry Truman's decision to deploy the Seventh Fleet of the U.S. navy in the Taiwan Strait. In the winter of 1950 and 1951, the anti-American campaign heated up. At its sixty-fifth regular meeting, the State Council passed the Resolution on American Funded Educational and Philanthropic Institutions and Religious Organizations; removing American influence on China's education now became part of the campaign to regain educational sovereignty. All ties between Chinese schools and the United States were to be severed. Missionary colleges and hospitals were either to be transformed into state-owned institutions or private institutions run by Chinese. In the latter case, the state would provide the necessary financial assistance.

As Americans became increasingly a liability to mission schools, a summary withdrawal of American missionaries seemed to be necessary to save these institutions. In 1951 the Religious Affairs Bureau implemented the Three-Selves Movement (*sanzi yundong*) for "self-government, self-support, and self-propagation" among Chinese Christians with a view to controlling the Christian church in China. In this campaign, the missionary enterprise was again condemned as part of Western cultural imperialism. This allegation brought the tide against Christian education to the point of no return. By May 1951 eight Christian colleges had lost all their American staff.[22]

Until this time, there were 20 foreign-funded colleges in China, excluding Furen University. These schools enrolled 14,536 students and hired 3,491 professors and other staff members. The 17 colleges that received money from the United States had 12,984 students (see Table 7). There were 514 foreign-financed middle schools with 160,250 students and 10,433 employees. The 255 middle schools that received aid from American missions had a total student body of 87,347 and a staff of 6,214. Foreign-financed elementary schools numbered 1,113, with student bodies of 188,376 and teaching staffs of 2,759.[23]

Following the resolution of the State Council, the Ministry of Education ordered all foreign-funded schools to register as public schools. All American administrators and board members were stripped of their power. American teachers were dismissed for "reactionary thoughts and words." Schools funded by foreigners other than Americans were allowed to continue to operate except the "especially reactionary ones." At the same time, in the patriotic education

**Table 7: Private Colleges, 1912-1949**

| Year | Private Total | Private Universities | Private Colleges | Private Post-Secondary Schools | Total of Private & Public | Percentage of Private Colleges |
|------|-------|--------------|----------|-------------------|------------------|-------------------|
| 1912 | 36 | 2 | — | 34 | 115 | 31.3 |
| 1913 | 35 | 2 | — | 33 | 114 | 30.7 |
| 1914 | 28 | 4 | — | 24 | 102 | 27.5 |
| 1915 | 34 | 7 | — | 27 | 104 | 32.7 |
| 1916 | 28 | 7 | — | 21 | 86 | 32.6 |
| 1917 | — | 7 | — | — | — | — |
| 1918 | 27 | 6 | — | 21 | 86 | 31.4 |
| 1919 | — | 7 | — | — | — | — |
| 1920 | 24 | 7 | — | 17 | 84 | 28.6 |
| 1921 | — | 8 | — | — | — | — |
| 1922 | — | 9 | — | — | — | — |
| 1923 | — | 10 | — | — | — | — |
| 1924 | — | 11 | — | — | — | — |
| 1925 | 29 | 13 | — | 16 | 105 | 27.6 |
| 1926 | — | 14 | — | — | — | — |
| 1927 | — | 18 | — | — | — | — |
| 1928 | — | 21 | — | — | — | — |
| 1929 | — | 21 | — | — | — | — |
| 1930 | — | 27 | — | — | — | — |
| 1931 | 47 | 19 | 18 | 10 | — | — |
| 1932 | 46 | 19 | 19 | 8 | 103 | 44.7 |
| 1933 | 51 | 20 | 22 | 9 | 108 | 47.2 |
| 1934 | 51 | 20 | 22 | 9 | 110 | 46.4 |
| 1935 | 53 | 20 | 24 | 9 | 108 | 49.1 |
| 1936 | 53 | 20 | 22 | 11 | 108 | 49.1 |
| 1937 | 47 | 18 | 20 | 9 | 91 | 51.6 |
| 1938 | 47 | 18 | 20 | 9 | 97 | 48.5 |
| 1939 | 45 | 18 | 19 | 8 | 101 | 44.6 |
| 1940 | 51 | 18 | 21 | 12 | 113 | 45.1 |
| 1941 | 52 | 18 | 20 | 14 | 129 | 40.3 |
| 1942 | 51 | 18 | 19 | 14 | 132 | 38.6 |
| 1943 | 50 | 18 | 19 | 13 | 133 | 37.6 |
| 1944 | 54 | 18 | 20 | 16 | 145 | 37.2 |
| 1945 | 54 | 16 | 22 | 16 | 141 | 38.3 |
| 1946 | 64 | 22 | 24 | 18 | 185 | 34.6 |
| 1947 | 66 | 23 | 24 | 19 | — | — |
| 1948 | 70 | 24 | 24 | 22 | — | — |
| 1949 | 75 | 25 | 27 | 23 | — | — |

Note: Unregistered private colleges are not counted.
Source: *Di er ci zhongguo jiaoyu nianjian*, vol. 2, pp. 119-120.

carried out in former Christian schools, the entire missionary enterprise in China was vehemently denounced. The government warned the students at former Christian schools that Western imperialists and their lackeys in China were still conducting all kinds of criminal activities to sabotage the people's government.[24]

The so-called "reorganization of higher education" (*yuanxi tiaozhen*) in 1952 and 1953 then dealt a fatal blow to Christian colleges. The reorganization was a revolutionary measure aimed at a highly centralized control of China's colleges after the Soviet model. The government wanted to create a higher educational system which would be more efficient and more geared to its industrialization program. There was also a clear political purpose: through the reorganization, the government put its own members and close allies into key positions and removed people of questionable loyalty from power. The reorganization paved the way for the party's policy of enlisting students from the working class and peasants.

Through the reorganization, Yanjing University, Jingu University (financed by Catholic missions), Beijing Union (Xiehe) Hospital, Mingxian College, the University of Nanjing, Jinling College, Beijing Union (Xiehe) University, Huanan (South China) College, Huazhong (Central China) University, the Wenhua College of Library Science and West China Union University were turned into governmental institutions. The University of Shanghai (Fujiang), Suzhou (Dongwu) University and seven other universities were taken over but remained private institutions.[25] By the end of 1952, three-fourths of all colleges had been reorganized. In 1953 the Ministry of Education added the final touches to the reorganization. By the end of this year, the number of colleges had dropped from 201 in 1952 to 181. The last private colleges were brought under state control.

The school takeover proceeded with surprising orderliness and calm; there was no significant resistance, at least on the surface. This is probably because of the great momentum of the Chinese revolution on the one hand and the weakness of China's liberal education on the other. Among China's intelligentsia, even the Western-educated professionals, socialism had considerable appeal. Besides, authoritarian government was not new to them. Nor was it the first time a newly established Chinese government had tried to shape the school system according to its will. To most Chinese teachers, nationalization of education was not necessarily a bad thing. They could live with a state-controlled school system under benevolent authoritarianism. The domestic and international situation, and the impressive record of the Communists up to the 1950s, were behind such seeming passivity.

## THOUGHT REFORM AND PRIVATE SCHOOLS

The new regime's sweep in the educational field can be explained against the broader background of the political campaigns of the early 1950s. On the whole, the CCP wanted to gain the willing cooperation of professionals, including teachers, and demonstrated much patience and even generosity. Openly acknowledging and emphasizing the importance of the country's small educated population, the central committee of the CCP required its local functionaries to listen to criticism and suggestion from professionals. The party apparently hoped to make as many converts as possible. It was not easy, however, to hammer a revolutionary ideology into the heads of largely Western-educated people.

In retrospect, it appears that Mao and other party ideologues attempted to brainwash intellectuals through a series of case studies. In other words, the party organs not only promulgated the official line, but also explained what constituted deviation from it by identifying and examining some negative examples. At the same time, party ideologues such as Liu Shaoqi developed techniques for converting intellectuals to the official ideology through the Thought Reform (Sixiang gaizao).

Ideological indoctrination was not a new subject for Mao and his allies. In Yanan during World War II, Mao brought the party into unprecedented unity through the Rectification Campaign (*zhengfeng*). Not only his rivals in the party were purged, but also dissidents among the motley band of intellectuals gathered in Yanan. Wang Shiwei, an independent-minded writer and outspoken critic of the official line in literature and art, was ruthlessly condemned in 1942 and executed five years later. In 1948 Communist authorities in Manchuria launched another anti-intellectual inquisition revolving around Xiao Jun, a well-respected novelist and loyal ally of the Communist Party. Driven by the dream of a Chinese utopia, Xiao reprimanded the party on a variety of issues including its pro-Soviet foreign policy and violence during the land reform. Idealism got him into trouble in the ceaseless factional struggle in the CCP.

In 1951 and 1952 the repudiation of Wu Xun, a beggar-philanthropist of the nineteenth century sent another disturbing signal. The May 20, 1951 issue of the *People's Daily* carried an editorial by Mao Zedong himself. Mao was disgusted by what he saw as Wu Xun's subservient attitude toward the feudal rulers and worship of the old tradition. In the production of the movie *Story of Wu Xun* (Wu Xun zhuan) and the warm critical acclaim it received, Mao detected a great ideological confusion among the country's cultural elite. Even after the onset of the campaign to discredit Wu Xun, there was significant resistance among educators.[26] As far as private education was concerned, this was not a good sign. For one thing, the campaign to discredit Wu Xun and the so-called Wu Xun Spirit further politicized education. Mao and his supporters firmly held that nothing, not even education, was beyond politics. In "What Have We Learned from the Discussion on Wu Xun?", the vice minister of education Qian Junrui related the Wu Xun spirit to what he called petty-bourgeois reformism.[27] Such radicalism must have shaken many Chinese educators.

In the increasingly heated warfare, even Tao Xingzhi, the Communists' erstwhile ally, was subject to defamation because Tao was a "bourgeois reformist," not a revolutionary, and because, among other things, Tao was a great admirer of Wu Xun. Another former ally of the Communists, Chen Heqin, who was known for his "active education" (*huo jiaoyu*), was criticized as a disciple of John Dewey. Chen's philosophy was considered wrong because it was devoid of "social content" and "political purpose." It was essentially identical to Tao Xingzhi's concept of "life as education." To ideologues in the CCP, both Tao's and Chen's careers reflected the "decadent educational philosophy" of the capitalist world.[28] Such diatribes were apparently necessary for the new regime to establish a new order. Unfortunately, political extremism also proved corrosive to the new political power.

In the general fury toward America, John Dewey and his educational theory came under fire. An article by Cao Fu in *The Peoples' Education* fired the first shot. Cao labeled Dewey's philosophy idealistic and called for the total liquidation of his influence in China as a legacy of cultural imperialism. Dewey's number-one disciple in China, Dr. Hu Shi, did not escape a similar indictment. The champion of China's liberal education and gradualist reform was easily labeled reactionary. But Hu was totally immune to the assault in his exile in Taiwan. In comparison, Yu Pingbo, an erudite expert on *A Dream of Red Mansions*[29] was picked out as a substitute. In 1954 two virtually unknown young scholars voiced their criticism of Yu in an academic journal. Party ideologues soon realized the value of the article and carried it in the influential *Guangming Daily*, followed by an avalanche of condemnation of Yu. On the whole, however, the party exercised restraints and used the campaign as a seminar on Marxism for China's intelligentsia. The most important message of the Communist government was its determination to bring China's educated population in line with the political orthodoxy. It would be unfair to say that political campaigns in the 1950s were designed to intimidate the populace, especially the intelligentsia. Yet all these campaigns undoubtedly resulted in a political atmosphere in which compliance was vital to the survival of any individual and institution. Opposition did not stand any chance and was extremely risky.

In August 1951 Beijing publicized the Resolution on Reforming China's Educational System. The document bore two prominent features. First, a Soviet-type five-year elementary school education replaced the old six-year program that had been divided into a four-year lower elementary school and two-year higher elementary school. Second, a variety of adult schools, at both the elementary and secondary levels were to be established to achieve mass literacy. The change represented an attempt to make education available to the workers and peasants who had been hitherto kept out of school, and was designed to broaden the government's base of support.[30] The implementation of the new system demonstrated the resolve of the Communist government to turn the school into a political tool. A takeover of private schools was imminent.[31] At the same time, Chinese educators were ready to embrace the change as they emerged from the soul-cleansing process of the Thought Reform.

## FINAL SWEEP

In 1952 Mao Zedong decided to takeover all private schools in China. A report from the party committee of the Beijing municipality in June 1952 found that most middle and elementary school students had difficulty in paying tuition, and that the existing scholarship and tuition waiver programs were inadequate. Mao wrote the following comment on the report, "If possible, we should take over all private middle and elementary schools."[32] The largess of a great leader thus sentenced one of the oldest institutions in China to death.

The Ministry of Education reacted promptly. In August, it decided to take over all private middle schools by the end of 1953 and all private elementary schools by the end of the following year.[33] In September, the ministry instructed its apparatus at all levels to proceed to turn all private schools under government control. Private schools run by foreigners were targeted first, followed by Chinese ones. Private middle schools were turned over before private elementary schools. Of the remaining 514 mission middle schools, 268 underwent reorganization in 1952. Fifty-one of these schools were seized by the government and 217 retained their private status under Chinese administration. Of the 1,133 mission elementary schools, 465 were reorganized. Fifteen percent of these schools were immediately taken over by the government while 85 percent retained their private status under Chinese administration. By the end of 1952, only 1,412 private middle schools and 8,925 private elementary schools remained. The last few were turned public by the end of 1956 when a "high tide of socialism" was gathering momentum in China.[34]

In the vast countryside, the *sishu* still dominated elementary education. In southern Anhui, for example, *sishu* numbered 3,768 in 1950, twice the total of the new-style elementary schools. Meanwhile, students and teachers at *sishu* accounted for one-third and three-fifths respectively of the region's totals. In some remote areas, the *sishu* was the only type of school for children. Evidently millions of Chinese farmers still trusted and supported the old form of elementary education whose program reflected the needs of rural China.

It was obvious that the continued existence of private schools was not only necessary but beneficial to both the new regime and the Chinese people. Mao Zedong seemed to have given the matter some second thoughts when he suggested in May 1953 that the *sishu*-type, experimental, and irregular schools be allowed to exist. The State Council likewise urged government agencies to provide assistance to private schools while encouraging private individuals and entrepreneurs to establish schools. As late as 1955, the People's Congress was still reasserting the country's need for schools set up by "private citizens."[35]

Oddly enough, the takeover of private schools proceeded any way. In the cities, the social revolution aimed at public ownership of the means of production was eliminating the economic conditions for the continuous existence of private schools, and the highly charged political atmosphere of the early 1950s paved the way for a centralized educational system. In Shanghai, which had the largest concentration of private schools, the administrations of eleven private middle schools and thirteen private elementary schools were thoroughly reorganized because of their alleged connections with the Nationalist government. Private schools in general were required to be run in a "democratic way." This meant that their finances would be subject to public scrutiny and government auditing. Profiting from education was not only immoral but politically dangerous. In the meantime, many private schools actually sought government takeover for economic and political reasons. Since private education was linked to an obsolete mode of production and ownership, administrators of private schools felt enormous pressure to get into line with the "new democracy."

In a petition to the government, the board, staff, and student body of two private schools in Liaoning province listed the following reasons for governmental control: (1.) while financial difficulties would keep some students out of school, governmental sponsorship would free the students from financial concerns; (2.) all students were willing to accept the authority of the government; (3.) changing to public status would enable the schools to fully utilize their facilities; (4.) the students would be able to break away from the yoke of feudal ideology and think freely; (5.) without proper political guidance, the students would not be able to elevate their political consciousness and would remain isolated from the working people; (6.) without the government's direct oversight, the schools would be slow in getting things done and were liable to mistakes that violated the government's educational policy; (7.) without enough income, the schools would not only cease to grow but gradually vanish; (8.) without the public status, the schools would not be able to take political and legal responsibility for the students; and (9.) their graduates would face tremendous difficulty in locating a job if they failed to enter college.[36]

The fear revealed in items 5 through 9 refracted the attitude of government officials who equated private schools with the old regime and even considered private education "reactionary." These officials had even less patience with the *sishu*. To them, the *sishu* was a remnant of the education of "feudal China." Its continued existence constituted an obstacle to socialist education and an insult to the new regime. *Sishu* teachers, by the same token, were "antiquated transmitters" of a moribund culture. Thus all *sishu* were shut down and many *sishu* teachers were forced to give up teaching for farming.[37] The fury of land reform made the takeover of the *sishu* an easy job.

The takeover of private schools signified the beginning of a period of aberration in Chinese education. Because of its lack of experience, the Communist government overestimated its abilities and assumed an impossible task. Even though the government admittedly put considerable resources into education, and China's school system experienced tremendous quantitative growth, the net result of abolishing private education was negative. The centralized educational bureaucracy proved incapable of planning for a field in which individual creativity was vital. For decades after the government takeover, individual initiative in higher education was stifled. The incessant political campaigns for ideological control were detrimental to the country's education for they ran counter to the spirit of modern science and the very heart of Confucian scholarship.

Only in recent years, have historians in mainland China begun to look at the events in the early 1950s objectively. Some historians argued that the government abolished private schools too soon and too fast on the ground that in the early 1950s, capitalism was still part of the Chinese economy.[38] This is essentially a moot point because first, the political climate in the early 1950s was not only against private education but against private business as well; and second, the abolition of private education, sooner or later, was administratively counterproductive and morally untenable. The radicalism of the 1950s not only created a hiatus in China's private education but also severely spoiled the intellectual climate for over two decades. Until now, most of the transformation of China's private education remains untold and scarcely studied. But the damage of this disastrous period can hardly be overestimated.

## *MINBAN* SCHOOLS: NEW WINE IN AN OLD BOTTLE

The efforts of the new government produced some impressive results in the first four years of the People's Republic. By the end of 1953, the number of elementary school students was 135 percent higher and of middle school students, 185 percent higher than the pre-revolutionary level. Yet on the whole, such progress barely matched the ambition of the new leadership, which was trying to accomplish too much too fast. Even given the youthful optimism of the CCP, the odds were piled up against it. China was still the home to some 250 million illiterate people. In 1954 the government candidly acknowledged that the economic backwardness of the country made it unrealistic to immediately implement compulsory elementary education, let alone secondary education. Moreover, despite increasing educational spending, many existing schools were in dire need of basic facilities and qualified teaching staff.[39]

From this discrepancy stemmed the concept of the *minban* (people-run) school. Although the concept of *minban* had different manifestations due to circumstances, a typical *minban* school was normally set up as a grassroots initiative with local funding to meet the needs of the local people. Its operation primarily depended on tuition in money or in kind. Most *minban* schools were expected to implement the government's plan for compulsory elementary education. Some, especially those in urban areas, were remedial and enrolled adults.

The idea of the *minban* school was not really new. The *shexue* (community school) of the Yuan and Ming periods and the *yixue* (charity school) of the Ming and Qing periods were prototypes of the *minban* school. The *shexue* began in the early years of the Yuan dynasty. Following a decree from the first Yuan emperor, a school was set up in every fifty households (a *she*), primarily for the children of farmers. In the early Ming, the *shexue* was promoted vigorously by the imperial government as a means of spreading learning and good morals (*jiaohua*). Undoubtedly, this type of school was designed as a tool of compulsory education to maintain social stability and achieve mass literacy. While the government took the initiative in launching the *shexue*, this endeavor came increasingly under the control of local gentry. The *yixue* in the Qing period was likewise intended to raise popular literacy and received strong governmental support. Many *yixue* were run on local donations. Tuition of the *yixue* was low and often waived for children of poor families. The purpose was to turn children into law-abiding subjects (*anshen liangmin*) by teaching them Confucian orthodoxy.[40]

Due to their populist ideology, the Communists were among the most enthusiastic promoters of mass education. As early as the 1920s, Mao Zedong sympathized with the *sishu* and hailed the enthusiasm of the farmers in Hunan province in setting up schools. In 1938 Mao Zedong developed his theory about mass education in Yanan, saying that government alone could not fulfill the task of elevating the people's educational level and arousing their nationalist consciousness. In 1944 the government of the Shaanxi, Gansu and Ningxia Border Region laid down the principle of "people-run school with government assistance" (*minban gongzhu*), which placed financial responsibility for elementary education into the hands of villagers and the local elite. At the same time, the government asserted its authority in guiding *minban* schools and opposed a laissez faire policy (*ren qi zi liu*) in education.[41]

In the early 1950s, while abolishing private schools in the cities, the new government began to call for the establishment of *minban* schools, especially in rural areas. In a November, 1952 directive, the Ministry of Education recognized that there was a widespread public interest in setting up *minban* schools and urged local governments to support such enthusiasm. Mao Zedong himself endorsed the idea in May 1953. The *minban* school had an especially vigorous start in the countryside because the rural cooperatives seemed to have sufficient resources to invest in them. In 1957 a directive from the Ministry of Education called for the opening of more channels of schooling to meet the demands of an ever-increasing number of school-age children. Public participation in education was described as a valuable addition to the government's endeavors. The ministry wanted    industrial enterprises, government agencies, social organizations, colleges, urban communities, and rural cooperatives to open and operate schools.

The document set off the first wave of *minban* schools in the People's Republic.[42] By the end of 1957, an incomplete survey indicated that there were at least 426,000 students enrolled at *minban* middle schools (compared to a total of seven million middle school students). The number of *minban* elementary school students was four times as great (total enrollment was 64 million).[43] Remedial schools and night schools popped up as well since governmental middle schools and high schools were unable to absorb the entire student population. The Education Ministry instructed its local functionaries to turn on the green light even to schools set up and run by private citizens.[44] In this general spirit, the government began to woo overseas Chinese to help in education. In the Measures Concerning Overseas Chinese Investment in Education, the State Council applauded overseas Chinese for their interest in promoting education in coastal provinces such as Fujian and Guangdong.

Without government funding, *minban* schools in the 1950s, at least those in the cities, charged higher tuition than public schools. For the same reason, these schools had poorer facilities and generally inferior teaching staff. Many *minban* schools had to rent classrooms or borrow desks and chairs from students' parents.[45] The *minban* concept may have been favored by Chairman Mao and some party ideologues, but in practice it was never well-received by the intelligentsia or educational bureaucrats, who preferred the regular governmental schools. It served at most as an expedient supplement to China's stratified school system. While the education bureaus at all levels paid little attention to the *minban* schools' financial difficulties, parents in urban areas were reluctant to send their children to these schools.

Despite their self-sufficiency, *minban* schools had limited administrative autonomy, as their principals usually had to be approved by the local education authority. Academically, *minban* schools before the Cultural Revolution (1966-1976) had virtually no freedom. Just as the *shexue* or *yixue* were required to teach Confucian values, *minban* schools had to follow the curriculum designed by the Education Ministry and the political line of the government. Besides, while private schools in imperial China were steered by the civil service examination, urban *minban* schools in the 1950s and 1960s had to tailor their program to prepare students for government-administered exams.

In early 1958 the *minban* approach was further confirmed when Liu Shaoqi, then vice-chairman of the ruling party and president of the state, advocated a "two-track" school system in China. In addition to regular schools, Liu suggested, there should be a part-time school system in both urban and rural areas to answer the needs of workers and peasants. The part-time system, equally important as the regular system, should be institutionalized.

In the same year, the Central Committee of the CCP and the State Council issued the Directive for Educational Affairs. The goal of mass education, the document suggested, could only be achieved by the concerted effort of the central government, local government, industrial enterprises, rural cooperatives, schools, and in fact the entire populace. Only by running the two systems at the same time, could China's education bridge the gap between learning and practice, and between manual and mental labor.[46] In the cities, large industrial enterprises and public institutions began to run spare-time schools for their employees under their own educational administration. Although their students were adults, the curricula of these schools were similar to those of regular middle schools and technical high schools. In the countryside, a similar system developed with fewer resources but with equal enthusiasm.

The *minban* school, as an embodiment of the Communists' "mass line" of the Yanan period, thus made up for the government's financial deficiencies. Prominent Communist officials could not hide their pride about this accomplishment: "Our education has truly become the business of the people, truly serving the interest of the working class and truly in the hands of the people. The expansion of education among the laboring class bears great significance to the development of socialism and the future of national construction."[47] Such vision of utopia initiated a great leap forward in China's education. In 1958 a multitude of schools of all types mushroomed. There were 68,000 *minban* middle schools nationwide by mid-1958, and elementary education was popularized in 1,240 counties, largely through *minban* schools.[48] In 1959 the number of colleges increased to 1,289 and their enrollment grew to 962,000. Altogether, the country had 96 million people in school by the end of this year, 30 million of them in spare-time schools.

The number of *minban* schools increased in the cities in the early 1960s due to the country's economic difficulties and decreases in educational spending. Between 1961 and 1964, the government implemented a policy of readjustment, which led to a reduction in governmental schools all over the country. The development of education, the Ministry of Education explained in a 1962 document, had outpaced economic growth and become too much for the economy to sustain. The document reiterated Liu Shaoqi's idea of the two-track school system, encouraging a variety of educational institutions run by the people under the government's control. Most elementary and secondary education, the documented specified, should be run by the state, supplemented by *minban* schools, including those run by private citizens. Even higher education in such special fields as religion, fine arts, and traditional Chinese medicine could be set up by social organizations (*renmin tuanti*) or even private citizens.[49]

Such relaxed policies, combined with the government's retreat in formal education, brought about an increase in *minban* schools in urban areas. In Guangzhou, for example, the city government enacted regulations that encouraged neighborhood groups to run schools in private homes and abandoned factory buildings. The proliferation of *minban* schools created a potential problem for the government. Since these schools did not receive financial support from the government, they were apt to depart from the official line. Some operated without a permit from the educational authorities, and some cheated their students for a profit. Especially difficult to supervise were the correspondence schools. The Ministry of Education thus ordered the shutdown of all unregistered *minban* schools and called for greater restraints on the remaining ones.[50]

Still, *minban* schools remained a significant supplement to the public school system. In Shanghai, the number of *minban* elementary schools never dropped below 20 percent of the city's total number of schools between 1958 and 1962. *Minban* middle schools enrolled 14.2 percent of the city's middle school students. Some *minban* schools became model schools for their academic accomplishments and, as a whole, these schools alleviated the pressure on the government. In urban areas, the number of *minban* schools declined when the cities pulled themselves out of the depression. Yet it is hard to tell whether *minban* schools in urban areas would have totally disappeared if it had not been for the Cultural Revolution.[51]

One amazing yet little-known phenomenon was the short revival of the *sishu* in the rural areas. Between 1962 and 1963, the *sishu* quietly resurfaced in several provinces, especially Hubei and Hunan, due to the reduction of public and *minban* schools run by the people's communes. In remote mountains, farmers began to hire educated persons to teach their children and the term *sishu* was used probably for convenience. Apparently at some *sishu*, materials contrary to the political orthodoxy were adopted and teachers were of problematic backgrounds. Local governments, in a quandary, reported to Beijing. In its response to the reports from the educational bureau of the provincial governments of Hubei and Hunan, the Ministry of Education favored neither abolition nor a laissez faire approach. Instead, it asked local functionaries to guide and administer these *sishu* in accordance with the educational policy and regulations of the central government. Teachers at the *sishu* had to be citizens of the People's Republic and academically qualified.[52] *Sishu* teachers could choose their own teaching materials as long as they did not contain reactionary or superstitious materials.[53]

## SIGNIFICANCE OF THE *MINBAN*

A typical *minban* school theoretically was not a private school. But on the continuum of China's educational system, it was much closer to a private school than to a public school. It was a stopgap measure designed first to achieve mass literacy as a means to speed up socialist industrialization and, second, to assure central control over education without a financial burden for the Chinese government. Thus the *minban* school was ideologically desirable and administratively manageable. For parents who could not send their children to a governmental school, a good *minban* school was their last hope. In urban areas where the admission policies of high schools and colleges became blatantly discriminatory against children from politically "inferior" families, *minban* schools served as a safety valve to diffuse the discontent of the victims of political injustice. Even though *minban* schools were known for their shabby campuses and poor facilities, their diplomas were recognized by the government. Because of this, they promised students job opportunities.

However, given the sociopolitical conditions of the 1950s and 1960s, *minban* schools, especially those in urban areas, in reality offered little hope of upward mobility to their students. In general, these schools tended to have two types of students: the academically poor and the politically unreliable. With the exception of 1962, Chinese education in the 1960s was heavily charged by politics. In the cities, mediocre students could go to good schools if they were from a politically dependable family. Thus children from "good" families ended up in a *minban* school only when they had extremely poor academic records. At the same time, a top student would be rejected by a public school simply because he or she had a questionable family background. This policy was based on the Maoist theory of class struggle and was supposedly intended to level off the gap between the privileged under the old regime and the "laboring people." In 1964 and 1965 academic criteria were completely dropped and replaced by political criteria. Many good students from "bad" families ended up in a *minban* middle or high school to keep alive their dream for college education, however forlorn it may have been.

While many half-study, half-work schools perished in the difficult years following the Great Leap Forward, *minban* primary and middle schools refused to go away, largely because they fulfilled the need of the Chinese government for mass education. By the end of 1964, the government found that, of the 220 million Chinese youth between seven and twenty-five years old, only 27 percent were in school. The insufficiency of the public school system justified the *minban* approach in the country's educational system. The central committee of the CCP again emphasized the need for more *minban* schools, both full-time and half-study, half-work. By tapping the energy of the masses, the committee believed, a variety of schools could be established at little cost to the state.[54]

The Cultural Revolution between 1966 and 1976, by paralyzing China's school system, only increased the need for *minban* schools. One of the primary targets of the Cultural Revolution was China's school system. A person with unusual intelligence but limited formal education, Mao distrusted the educational system and his distrust of the system increased throughout the early 1960s, when he lost grip on the vast bureaucracy. As far as Mao was concerned, regular schools had been ruining China's youth by detaching them from the productive activities of the real world. The onslaught on the Chinese school system during the Cultural Revolution appears ridiculous and insane in retrospect. But education was indeed a battleground between Mao and his radical followers on the one hand, and relatively moderate party bureaucrats on the other.

It did not take the Red Guards long to cripple the country's educational system. In three months, all semblance of order and normalcy was gone. Beijing's radicals cheered the victory; however, it proved much more difficult to build a new, truly revolutionary school system upon the rubble of the old. In fact, the radical Cultural Revolution group, headed by Mme. Mao Zedong, never formulated a comprehensive program for the nation's education, even though their ideas seemed to have prevailed with Mao's endorsement. In the overall chaos, educational officials from the top ranks of government to local functionaries resorted to improvisation.

*Minban* education received a shot in the arm from Mao's populism and the ideal of an educational system genuinely serving the needs of the people. Although the Cultural Revolution smacked of totalitarianism, it nevertheless created a pseudoanarchy in administration. Schools were reopened in 1970, only after millions of the Red Guards and older students were sent to the countryside to be re-educated by the "poor and lower-middle" peasants. Between 1970 and 1976, however, schools were unstable as the political atmosphere was volatile. The bureaucracy never recovered from the initial blows of the Cultural Revolution and incessant power struggle in the ruling party kept educational administrators in fear. Urged by the radicals close to Mao, the educational administration underwent a process of decentralization. Provincial and municipal education bureaus assumed much authority. Even the people's communes and production brigades were asked to assume responsibility for maintaining schools. In general, a rural people's commune had a public elementary school with a teaching staff paid by the local government. Schools at the production brigade level could be either public or *minban*, or a combination of both. At the height of the Cultural Revolution, there was even a trend to turn all public schools in rural areas into *minban*.[55] *Minban* teachers' workloads were converted into "work points" on the basis of which they shared in the village's produce. In some localities, *minban* teachers received limited governmental subsidies.

The government's financial destitution forced enterprises in urban areas to establish schools for the children of their employees as well. Thus overall the educational revolution in the 1970s led to a growth in the proportion of *minban* schools in China's educational system. In 1977, *minban* teachers accounted for 40 percent of the country's middle school teachers. In elementary schools, nearly 70 percent of the teachers were in *minban*.

The end of the Cultural Revolution set off a trend back to normalcy in China's education. *Minban* schools and the educational populism they embodied became quickly obsolete. When the nationwide entrance examination for higher education was reinstituted in the winter of 1977 and 1978, most *minban* schools found themselves unable to compete with governmental schools. Starting in 1979, the reform in rural China also had an impact on *minban* education. When the people's communes were still functioning, rural *minban* schools could often draw financial support from the production brigades. When the people's communes ceased to work, as they did in the early 1980s, the state had to either assume the salaries of *minban* teachers, or let the schools be privatized.

During the Cultural Revolution, the ruling party reinforced its control of education through its local administrations. At the same time, the school system became seriously disoriented. The key to this paradox was the fundamental contradiction between Mao's view of education as a tool of proletarian politics and the dynamics of modern education that evolved around science and technology. Throughout the 1950s and 1960s, the problem was also reflected in the conflict between the less-educated political elite and the intelligentsia. Mao won a decisive victory in the Hundred Flower Campaign of 1957 after he had stigmatized 400,000 educated Chinese as "rightists." Yet the intrinsic law of modern education repeatedly asserted itself even at a time when Mao stood at the pinnacle of his power. *Minban* schools were, after all, schools. As such, they had an intrinsic tendency to stress academic excellence rather than political dogma. Thus at the end of the Cultural Revolution, some *minban* schools, especially those in urban areas, were operating at a level comparable to the better public schools.

Few would deny that China's system of formal education was devastated by the Cultural Revolution. At the end of what was called the "ten years of turmoil," Chinese schools were in ruins. Aimed at an overhaul of China's school system, the Cultural Revolution only revealed the gulf between Mao's perception of what Chinese schooling should be and the laws inherent in modern education. Cultural-Revolution populism offered little help to a country already mired in poverty and backwardness. The cost of the revolution proved expectedly unacceptable to the intelligentsia, who not only lamented their own loss of prestige but were seriously concerned with the widening gap between China and the outside world in science and technology. When Premier Zhou Enlai introduced the goals of the Four Modernizations in 1974, he voiced the feelings of four million Chinese intellectuals.

In post-Mao educational reform, *minban* schooling came under heavy pressure. In the realm of regular education, it would decline as a result of the general trend back to standardization, normalcy, and centralization. The newly restored elitism among Chinese educators would prove highly unfriendly to *minban* schools. To them, *minban* schooling was not only irregular but inferior as well. Thus the proud swan of the Cultural Revolution era became once again the ugly duckling. In rural areas, the goal of a *minban* school in every village was allowed to lapse. No one was inclined to promote so 'irregular' a form of schooling."[56] Yet the concept of the "people-run school" refused to go away. Instead, it demonstrated both vitality and adaptability in an era of relative openness and ideological relaxation.

# NOTES

1. The term *sili* means private while *minban* literally means people-run.

2. Xiamen University had been taken over by the government in 1936. See, Wang Yanan, "Guoli xiamen daxue gaijin qingkuang baogao" (Report on the progress at Xiamen national university), *Xin Jiaoyu* (New education), 2 (November 15, 1950): 18.

3. Wang Wenjun, Liang Jisheng, Yang Xuan, Zhang Shujian, Xia Jiashan, *Nankai daxue xiaoshi ziliao xuan, 1919-1949* (Documents on the history of Nankai University). (Tianjin: Nankai University Press, 1989), pp. 88-97; Zheng Zhiguang and Yang Guangwei, *Zhang Boling zhuan* (Biography of Zhang Boling) (Tianjin: Tianjin People's Press, 1989), pp. 112, 119; *Nankai daxue xiaoshi* (History of Nankai University) (Tianjin: Nankai University Press, 1990), pp. 325-326.

4. *Di er ci zhongguo jiaoyu nianjian* (Second yearbook on Chinese education) (Shanghai: Commercial Press, 1948), vol. 2, Chapter 6, p. 118.

5. Hu Yan, "Zhongguo jinxiandai sili xuexiao" (Private schools in modern China), in Zhang Zhiyi ed., *Sili minban xuexiao de lilun yu shijian* (Theory and pracitice of private and *minban* schools) (Beijing: Chinese Workers Press, 1994), p. 27.

6. Central Institute for Educational Research, *Zhonghua renmin gongheguo jiaoyu dashiji, 1948-1982* (Chronicle of education in the People's Republic of China, 1949-1982) (Beijing: Educational Science Press, 1983), pp. 7-8.

7. Ibid., pp. 7-8.

8. Hu Yan, "Zhongguo jinxiandai sili xuexiao," in Zhang Zhiyi ed., *Sili minban xuexiao de lilun yu shijian*, p. 27.

9. Mao Lirui & Shen Guanqun, *Zhongguo jiaoyu tongshi* (General history of Chinese education) (Jinan: Shandong Education Press, 1988), vol. 6, pp. 24-26.

10. Central Institute for Educational Reaserch, *Dashiji*, p. 26.

11. Ibid., p. 22.

12. Ibid., p. 23.

13. The Five-Antis was a concerted attack on bribery, tax evasion, theft of state assets, cheating in labor or materials, and stealing of state economic intellligence.

14. Jessie G. Lutz, *China and the Christian Colleges, 1850-1950* (Ithaca: Cornell University Press, 1971), pp. 444-446.

15. Beiping Municipal Government, "Beiping shi sili xuexiao lingshi guanli banfa" (Provisional regulations on private schools) (July, 1949), see Zhang Zhiyi, ed., *Sili minban xuexiao de lilun yu shijian*, p. 72.

16. Charles H. Corbett, *Shantung Christian College (Cheeloo)* (New York: United Board for Christian Colleges in China, 1955), p. 263.

17. Dwight W. Edwards, *Yenching University* (New York: United Board for Christian Higher Education in Asia, 1959), p. 420; Corbett, *Shantung Christian University*, p. 264.

18. Stewart Fraser comp. & ed., *Chinese Communist Education, Records of the First Decade* (Nashville, 1965), pp. 92-97.

19. Clarence B. Day, *Hangchow University: A Brief History* (New York: United Board for Christian Colleges in China, 1955), pp. 136-137; Edwards, *Yenching*, pp. 429, 431-432; S. B. Thomas, "Recent Educational Policy in China," *Pacific Affairs*, 23 (March 1955): 30; Chao Wei-ming, "Lin Xian Yang: Mei di guo zhuyizhe di zhongshi zougou" (Lin Xianyang: Faithful running dog of the American imperialists), *Jiefang ribao* (Liberation daily), March 29, 1951.

20. Central Institute for Educational Research, *Dashiji*, pp. 27-28.

21. Ibid., pp. 22, 27-28.

22. Lutz, *China and Christian Colleges*, p. 463.

23. Central Institute for Educational Research, *Dashiji*, pp. 31-32.

24. Xu Li, "Qian tianzhujiao xuexiao dangqian de aiguo zhuyi jiaoyu" (Patriotic education at former Catholic schools), *Xin Jiaoyu*, 4 (October 15, 1951): 7; Lutz, *China and the Christian Colleges*, pp. 461-484; Lu Xingwei ed., *Shanghai putong jiaoyu shi* (History of basic education in Shanghai) (Shanghai: Shanghai Education Press, 1994), pp. 34-37.

25. Central Institute for Educational Research, *Dashiji*, pp. 35-36.

26. Bureau of Education, Shandong Provincial Government, "Taolun pipan dianying wu xun zhuan he wu xun jingshen de zongjie baogao" (Report on the campaign to denounce Wu Xun), *Xin Jiaoyu*, 4 (October 15, 1951): 31-32.

27. *People's Daily*, August 27, 1951.

28. Cao Fu, "Huo jiaoyu pipan" (Critique of the active education), *Xin Jiaoyu*, 4 (November 15, 1951): 3-7.

29. *A Dream of Red Mansions* (Honglou meng) by Cao Xueqin is a novel of the 18th century.

30. "Zhongyang renmin zhengfu zhengwuyuan guanyu gaige xuezhi de jueding" (Decision of the State Council concerning the reform of the educational system) *Xin Jiaoyu*, 4 (October 15, 1951): 1-3.

31. "Wei shenme bixu gaige xuezhi" (Why must the educational system be changed)? *People's Daily*, August 10, 1951; Sheng Tilan, "Xuezhi gaige de jingshen he yiyi" (Essence of the new educational system), *Xin Jiaoyu*, 4 (October 15, 1951): 8-9.

32. Liu Yingjie ed., *Zhongguo jiaoyu dashidian*, vol. 1, p. 80.

33. Central Institute for Educational Research, *Dashiji*, pp. 59, 63.

34. Zhang Hongzhi, "Jieshou jieguan yuanyou xuexiao" (Takeover of old schools), in Liu Yingjie et al., *Zhongguo jiaoyu dashidian: 1949-1990* (Book of major educational events in China) (Hangzhou: Zhejiang Education Press, 1993), vol. 1, pp. 79-83.

35. Sa Zhaoxiang, "Yunxu siren banxue" (Private individuals allowed to set up schools), Liu Yingjie et al., *Zhongguo jiaoyu dashidian*, pp. 92-93; State Council, "Guanyu zhengdun he gaijin xiaoxue jiaoyu de zhishi" (Directive for Reforming and improving elementary education) (November 26, 1953); Qu Baokui, Lei Xiaozhu, Yu Guang & Huang Rongchang ed., *Zhongguo jiaoyu gaige* (Educational reform in China) (Beijing: People's Education Press, 1991), p. 132.

36. Board, staff, and students of Wenhui and Wenhua Schools, "Petition to the Government for Turning Private Wenhui and Wenhua Schools into Governmental Schools," April 23, 1949, Shenyang Municipal Government Permanent Files, Education, 1949; Lu Xingwei ed. *Shanghai putong jiaoyushi*, pp. 32-34.

37. Ministry of Education Permanent Files, 1950, vol. 76.

38. Mao Lirui & Shen Guanqun ed., *Zhonguo jiaoyu tongshi*, vol. 6, p. 29.

39. Public Relations Department, Central Committee of the CCP, "Guanyu gaoxiao he chuzhong biyesheng congshi laodong shengchan de xuanchuan tigang" (Communication outlines concerning the issue of elementary and middle school graduates participating in productive activities), *Renmin ribao* (People's daily), May 29, 1954.

40. Mao Lirui & Shen Guanqun ed., *Zhongguo jiaoyu tongshi*, vol. 3, pp. 444-446.

41. Mao Zedong, *Mao Zedong lun jiaoyu gongzuo* (Mao Zedong on education), (Beijing: People's Education Press, 1958), p. 33; Zheng Dengyun, *Zhongguo jindai*

*jiaoyu shi* (History of education in modern China) (Shanghai: East China Normal University Press, 1994), pp. 438-439.

42. Jean C. Robinson, "Decentralization, Money, and Power: The Case of People-Run Schools in China," *Comparative Education Review*, 30 (January, 1986): 78.

43. Central Institute for Educational Research, *Dashiji*, p. 198; State Statistical Bureau ed., *Ten Great Years* (Beijing: Peking Foreign Language Press, 1960), p. 192.

44. Ibid., p. 110.

45. Robinson , "Decentralization, Money, and Power," 82.

46. Central Institute for Educational Research, *Dashiji*, p. 223.

47. Yang Xiufeng "Educational Revolution and Progress: 1949-1959," *Jian guo shi nien* (Ten years since the founding of the People's Republic of China) (Hong Kong: Chi Wen Publishing Co., 1959). vol. 2, pp. 101-102.

48. Lu Dingyi, "Jiaoyu bixu yu shengchan laodong xiang jiehe" (Education must be combined with productive activities), *Hongqi* (Red Flag), July 1958, p. 6.

49. Central Institute for Educational Research, *Dashiji*, pp. 306-307.

50. Ibid., 342.

51. Lu Xinwei ed., *Shanghai putong jiaoyushi*, pp. 333-338; Jonathan Unger, *Education under Mao: Class and Competition in Canton Schools, 1960-1980* (New York: Columbia University Press, 1982), p. 17.

52. Ex-landlords and rich farmers were classified as enemies of the people, not citizens.

53. Central Insitute for Educational Research, *Dashiji*, pp. 319; 324-325; 328.

54. Ibid., pp. 370-371, 377; "Nuli banhao bannong bandu xuexiao" (We need to administer half-study, half-farm schools better), *Renmin ribao*, May 30, 1964.

55. *Remin ribao*, November 14, 15, 1968; January 6, 1969.

56. Robinson, "Decentralization, Money, and Power," 52.

# 6

# Resurgence of Private Schools in Post-Mao China

The post-Mao reforms in China between 1979 and 1995 resulted in many fundamental changes affecting almost every aspect of Chinese society. Chinese education likewise underwent significant metamorphosis. However, while the educational reform in this period came under close scrutiny by China experts in the West, the steady revival of private education, one of the most dramatic phenomena in Chinese society, remained relatively unexplored. As education was such a crucial component of Chinese culture, the reemergence of private schools not only shed much light on the state of China's school system but had far-reaching implications for the changing role of the Chinese government, the shifting Chinese culture, and even Chinese society as a whole. Moreover, while certainly a product of the post-Mao liberalization, private education added a tremendous impetus to China's social, political, economic, and cultural transformations.

## INITIAL REVIVAL

Chinese society in the 1980s and 1990s saw a gradual retreat of the ruling Communist party from the radical ideology of the Maoist era. As the Cultural Revolution had led the country and the government into a dead end and created tremendous popular apathy, if not outright antagonism, toward the ideological orthodoxy, a policy of political decompression was necessary for the survival of the CCP. In an effort to heal the wounds inflicted by the Cultural Revolution and reestablish its credit among the Chinese people, the Communist party under Deng Xiaoping yielded greater freedom to the Chinese people while repudiating the Ten Years of Turmoil. Through the *boluan fanzheng* (rectification of past errors) campaign, the party tried to change its image from a party of revolutionaries to one of builders and from a party of cadres to one of managers.[1]

Political relaxation brought about an unprecedented outpouring of enthusiasm in fields such as education. The Chinese intelligentsia, while agonizing over the devastation of the Cultural Revolution and the widening gap between China and the rest of the world in science and technology, had great expectations for the country's schooling in the new era. The ruling party, smarting from the blows of the Cultural Revolution era, was more ready than ever before to respect the expertise and opinions of China's educated elite and allow them to play a greater role in the Chinese people's cultural and social life. Thus the Dengist regime and Chinese intelligentsia found a common ground in liquidating the anti-intellectualism of the Cultural Revolution. At the same time, ideological liberalization in an era of economic reform also made the educated elite bolder than ever in reshaping Chinese society.

In formal education, the backlash to the Cultural Revolution was an immediate return to normalcy, highlighted by the reinstitution of the nationwide entrance examination for higher education in 1977 and 1978. While the entrance examination was not perfect, it nevertheless helped boost the morale of the teachers and raise the hopes of the youth. Under the general goal of modernization, the Chinese government attempted to improve the country's school system by implementing reforms such as the responsibility system for college presidents and school principals and the system of academic degrees. These measures stemmed from the ruling party's recognition of the limits of ideology and allowed further changes in the educational system to adapt to the rapidly developing economy. Needless to say, such liberalization helped create an intellectual and social climate conducive to the revival of private education.

The economic reform in the post-Mao era further spurred China's educational reform. In the countryside, the household responsibility system (*baochan daohu*) unleashed an enthusiasm among Chinese farmers that had not been seen since the land reform of the early 1950s. While leading to the demise of the people's commune, the policy revitalized the agricultural sector and gave the Deng Xiaoping administration great leverage for further reform. In the cities, reformers of the post-Mao era tried to diversify the economy by allowing the private sector to grow and by attracting foreign investment. Reform measures such as the contract responsibility system (*chengbao jingying zhi*), leasing-management system (*zulin jingying zhi*), and joint-stock system (*gufen zhi*) were experimented with throughout the 1980s and 1990s with a view to rejuvenating state-owned enterprises. At the same time, the new leadership cautiously recognized market mechanisms and attempted to free China's industry from an obsolete model of central planning.[2]

These changes had a multifaceted impact on China's educational system. On the whole, they opened up a vast market for skilled labor which, in turn, rekindled public interest in learning. At the same time, the new orientation of the Chinese economy relentlessly exposed the chronic illness of the school system and compelled it to make necessary readjustments. While governmental schools admittedly made great strides in meeting the needs of the economic reform, private education proved a more powerful answer to the challenge of China's burgeoning market economy.

In the early 1980s various forms of nongovernmental schools popped up all over the country, especially in the cities. These schools targeted a vast market of people in their twenties and thirties who wanted to pass the entrance examination for higher education or to complete their high school education through remedial work for a diploma, which would help them find a better job or gain greater opportunities at their work place. Even in the countryside, educators opened up nongovernmental schools, often with the endorsement of the local authorities. There seemed to be at least a tacit understanding between organizers of such schools and government officials that these private schools helped check the rising illiteracy in the country. Many retired teachers taught at such schools for a second source of income as well as personal fulfillment. The minor democratic parties (*minzhu dangpai*), which had large memberships among educators and other professionals, were especially active, since education was a field where they could exercise the greatest influence and encounter the fewest problems with the ruling party.[3] Even though nongovernmental schools charged a tuition, they attracted an increasing number of students due to the flexibility of their schedules and practicality of their programs. These schools found a convenient model in the tradition of *minban* education which was not only ideologically correct but also administratively elastic.

A salient feature of private education in this period was its vocational orientation. Many of the early private schools offered a great variety of courses in fields such as foreign languages, accounting, bookkeeping, home economics, architecture, tailoring, and industrial management. These course answered the needs of the rapidly expanding market for skilled labor. Without their own campuses, most nongovernmental schools leased their classrooms and offices from existing public schools and colleges. Efficient management made possible considerable financial returns out of relatively small investments. Although organizers of such schools were often educators, people from other backgrounds also participate. In 1985, for example, a farmer-turned-entrepreneur in Anhui province set up a vocational school with a curriculum geared to the needs of an emerging demand for practical skills.[4] Some of these programs were cooperatively run by vocational and technical schools, both private and public, and by business enterprises. In such cases, the schools designed the curriculum according to the needs of their clients while the businesses financed the programs.[5] This model broke open the straitjacket of central planning and revitalized many state-owned schools, while contributing to the country's economic transformation.

In the general awakening of private education, the first private colleges since 1952 came into being as well. In 1982, Zhonghua Societal University (*Zhonghua shehui daxue*) was born in Shanghai, a city with a rich heritage of private schools. Thereafter, private higher education woke up rapidly. By the end of 1982, over one hundred private post-secondary institutions had been set up in major cities. The majority of these schools were for adult education and they scored impressive results. In 1985 there were over 30,000 adult technical training schools in China enrolling a total of 4,420,000 students. In 1990, the number of such schools rose to over 46,000 and their total enrollment was nearly 13,000,000. Some private citizens even attempted to establish universities that combined regular correspondence courses with periodic tutoring. In 1985 the first two independent correspondence colleges were founded, enrolling almost 10,000 students; and in 1990, four such colleges were offering dozens of majors to well over 15,000 students from all walks of life, including prisoners.

Governmental colleges, with their strong faculties and prestigious positions, showed special interest and unusual energy in this drive, especially after 1982 when the Ministry of Higher Education implemented the nonformal college education examination (*Gaodeng jiaoyu zixue kaoshi*). Reminiscent of the *keju* in imperial China, this system was designed to expand the benefits of higher education with the minimal possible investment. It appealed to many adults who did not want to sacrifice their jobs and family life to obtain a college diploma. With no limitation on age and formal education, it opened up higher education to an enormous number of Chinese citizens who would not have had a chance in regular colleges and inspired great enthusiasm in higher learning. In 1979, 72 public colleges offered correspondence and evening programs largely geared to this public interest. In 1987, 367 state-run colleges participated, with a total enrollment of 459,474. By the end of 1990, 15 million candidates had participated in the nonformal college education examination in 102 majors. Over half a million had obtained their three-year college degree and 3,785 their four-year college diploma.

Resulting from spontaneous efforts and often initiated by individual departments, such programs were seldom incorporated into the government's plan. Most of their students were self-supporting even though some students were sent by their employers, or *danwei*, under a contract and obligated to return to their work units upon graduation. These self-paying and contract students opened up new sources of revenue for colleges and bettered the lives of college professors. Nonformal higher education revealed the great potential of colleges, leading China's higher education toward a vast market while increasing its social function.[6] Many of these programs proved to be the embryos of private colleges and postsecondary schools.

Overall, responses of the reformist Chinese government to such changes were positive, for some obvious reasons. First, it is a constitutional right of citizens of the People's Republic of China to found and operate schools as long as the schools accept the general policy of the ruling party. Article Four,

Chapter Nineteen, of the Constitution recognized the right and value of educational enterprises run by "social forces" and individual citizens. This principle set the keynote for subsequent legislation in the 1980s and 1990s. Second, nongovernmental schools were a great addition to governmental schools which were handicapped by a lack of funding and space to absorb the flood of candidates created during the wasteful years of the Cultural Revolution. The schools set up by nongovernmental agencies met the nation's needs by bridging the enormous gap between the goal of modernization and the existing mass ignorance. In the Resolution on the  Reform of the Educational System (May 27, 1985), the ruling party recognized the key role of education in modernizing China and established the principle of Training First, Employment Later in building a work force. While promoting vocational education, the party called for the participation of "collectives, individuals as well as all other social forces."[7] In the 1986 Compulsory Education Law, the state reiterated its vow to encourage "enterprises, institutions, and other quarters of the society to set up various schools."[8] These documents not only reaffirmed the *minban* tradition in schooling, but turned on a green light for all sorts of private educational enterprises.

It is also important to remember that private education revived in the general euphoria and enlightened atmosphere of the post-Mao era which affirmed the value of  knowledge and the role of China's intelligentsia. In a culture that prizes education, the outpouring of enthusiasm was a direct reaction to the anti-intellectualism of the Maoist era. And, although the backlash to the Cultural Revolution proved disturbing from time to time, such schools seemed quite innocuous to the ruling party. Thus in 1987 and 1988, the State Education Commission issued a series of documents, including the Provisional Regulations Concerning Educational Institutions Run by Social Forces and Provisional Regulations on the Finance of Educational Institutions Run by Social Forces. With these documents, the government allowed state-owned enterprises and institutions, the democratic parties, popular organizations, economic collectives, and learned societies to set up educational institutions. Private citizens were allowed to do so with special permission from the educational office at various levels of the government. Foreigners, overseas Chinese, educators, and businessmen from Hong Kong and Taiwan were invited as well, which indicated the government's confidence and forward-looking attitude.[9]

Problems admittedly developed in nongovernmental schools from the very beginning and consequently they came under public criticism and government censure. For instance, some of the nongovernmental schools were established primarily for profit and tended to suffer from mismanagement. Others, for a lack of revenue controls, violated some well-established bookkeeping and accounting rules. Some private colleges and postsecondary schools lowered academic standards for financial reasons thereby cheapening the college diploma. Since all college students expected to be assigned a job upon graduation, and some *minban* colleges or programs apparently promised their self-paying students job assignments, personnel departments of local governments came under pressure to place an unexpected number of college graduates. Moreover, many state-funded colleges diverted considerable resources to continuing education classes, thereby lowering the quality of their regular programs. To make matters worse, numerous institutions publicized their evening degree programs and correspondence courses with deceptive advertising even though they did not meet state requirements.

The State Education Commission was forced to apply a brake to educational reform while warning private schools of their legal responsibilities. These warnings had only a limited effect on the frenzy for higher education, however. Thus in 1990 and 1991, the State Education Commission further tightened its controls. While charging some *minban* colleges with creating "social instability" and "defaming" China's higher education, it required these schools to be approved twice: after obtaining permission to operate from a provincial or municipal education commission, they then had to apply to the State Education Commission for approval of any program that lasted more than a year.[10]

Overall, the gains far outweighed the losses. When official organs were criticizing the Cultural Revolution for devastating China's education, there was no reason to crack down on nongovernmental schools. Still thinking in the framework of a planned economy, the government even tried to accept into its personnel planning tuition students in some fields such as medicine.[11] Yet until the early 1990s, private education developed under various guises and, in many cases, remained a parasite on the public school system. It took time for private education to shape its identity, and an auspicious moment to assert its independence.

## EXPLOSION OF PRIVATE SCHOOLS

The first openly labeled "private" school since the mid-1950s was probably Private Guangya School in Dujiangyan, Sichuan province.[12] Opened in June 1992, by Qing Guangya, a successful and farsighted entrepreneur, Guangya School caused an instant sensation. A visionary and innovative administrator, Qing gave his school a unique identity by building a picturesque campus and implementing a revolutionary teaching philosophy in the classroom. He shocked many conventional minds by openly admitting the allegedly "aristocratic" nature of his school. Although located in the remote southwest, Guangya School nevertheless hit the headlines in  both the Western and Chinese media and attracted a constant flow of teachers from all over China and from foreign countries. The founding of this private school was coincided with China's recovery from the ideological retrogression in the wake of the Tiananmen Square Incident of June 4, 1989. Following elder statesman Deng Xiaoping's South China tour earlier that year, it signified  the beginning of a new phase in

China's educational reform and ushered in an unprecedented wave of private schools.

According to incomplete official statistics, by the end of 1995, there were 20,780 private kindergartens, 3,159 private primary and secondary schools, and 672 private vocational and technical schools. In addition, there were 1,230 private colleges with an average enrollment of 2,400 students. The China University of Science and Technology Management, for example, enrolled over 7,000 students in 88 programs, surpassing that of most public institutions of higher education. Moreover, 25 private colleges were authorized in 1996 by the State Education Commission to issue diplomas to their graduates, which not only indicated the qualitative growth of private colleges but also suggested a great leap in the government's attitude toward private education as a whole.[13]

One of the conditions favoring the expansion of private schools was the country's growing affluence. Since the onset of the post-Mao reforms, China's economy grew at an average rate of 9 to 10 percent per year. In the meantime, it also underwent a structural transformation marked by a growing private sector. In mid-1994 China had nearly 32 million self-employed persons (*getihu*) who possessed a total capital of around 100 billion yuan. In addition, there were 328,000 private companies with a total employment of over half a million people and with combined assets of over 100 billion yuan. The savings of the Chinese people grew steadily as well. Even though inflation threatened the value of the legal tender, Chinese citizens still kept well over 2 trillion yuan in state banks in 1994.[14] Out of the drive for wealth there emerged a small middle class in Chinese society. A country that exalted egalitarianism and glorified a puritanical life style, China in the early 1990s boasted its own millionaires and billionaires.[15]

The middle class furnished China's private education with the necessary socioeconomic conditions in at least two respects. First, members of the class, who understood the importance of education, demanded that private schools better the lots of their children; and second, they had the necessary capital to found private schools. For those parents who had bitter a childhood during the Cultural Revolution, sending their children to luxurious private schools was an indirect compensation for their own loss. The government's one-child-per-family policy in urban areas further intensified the desire to provide one's only child with the best education possible. The reemergence of private schools also bore witness to the unique Chinese obsession with education, which made it possible for some reputable school founders to borrow millions of yuan from parents who were eager to insure their children's future by investing in education.[16] Besides, private investors procured valuable land at favorable prices by setting up schools and, as the government granted tax-exempt status to school-run enterprises, some entrepreneurs could maximize their profits by attaching their business to a private school. Private boarding schools, moreover, met the needs of many parents who had very irregular work schedules. By placing their children at a private boarding school, they could make frequent business trips and conduct their business in such places as night clubs and restaurants. Sending children to the best private schools was also a status symbol that may well translate into practical advantages.

Thus between 1992 and 1995, businessmen with foresight and dreams found education a field of investment with the promise of at least moderate financial return and psychological gratification. Especially after 1992, individuals and businesses vied with one another to put money into the haphazard construction of private schools, the best of which cost hundreds of millions of yuan. The first phase of investment in the Asia Pacific International School in Shenzhen alone, for example, required 160 million yuan, or $20 million. In urban centers and some coastal provinces, private schools even attracted foreign capital, especially form overseas Chinese businessmen. Even though the Chinese government never objected to funding from overseas Chinese, the practice stopped during the Cultural Revolution and did not revive until the late 1970s. In Fujian and Guangdong, private schools bearing the names of their benefactors were common. Many of these schools were independent and bona fide private schools.[17]

As a part of China's educational reform, the emergence of private schools was contingent on the state of the country's public education. Between 1977 and 1995, China's public education made great strides. Acutely aware of the gap between China and the West, the post-Mao Chinese government vowed to make education one of its top priorities and allocated a considerable amount of human and material resources to improve the nation's education. School teachers' salaries, for example, were raised significantly to offset the rising cost of living. Propaganda machines promoted teachers as part of the "working class," a sharp contrast to their nickname, the "stinking ninth" (*Chou laojiu*), during the Cultural Revolution. The core curriculum was upgraded to meet the challenge of the twenty-first century and criteria were standardized to promote teaching excellence in the classroom.

For all its achievements, however, public education in China left much to be desired. For one thing, the government found it increasingly hard to meet the needs of all schools despite, and perhaps because of, its ambition. As a result, China's public schools, especially those in rural areas suffered from a severe financial anemia. Studies in the early 1990s deplored the woeful inadequacy of the government's investment in public education; while the international average of educational spending in a country with China's economic level was 3.3 percent of its GNP,[18] China's educational budget between 1950 and 1985 rarely exceeded 3 percent and was overall 0.7 percent less than the international average.[19] Shortages of funding proved to be devastating to China's public school system. At middle schools and primary schools, there was little money left for anything other than the absolute necessities, such as teachers' salaries and chalk. Because of this, many urban and rural public schools were plagued by poor maintenance and shortage of instructional supplies. Nationwide, 8 percent of school buildings were rated hazardous. In Hunan province alone, there were 2.615 million square meters of unsafe building space in the secondary and primary schools, of which over one million square meters were classified as "most dangerous."[20]

The poor conditions of public schools and economic polarization, especially in rural China, resulted in a rising student dropout rate and loss of teachers. In 1988 the middle school dropout rate reached 8 percent in Fujian province, and more than 139,000 students dropped out of school in Zhejiang. According to government sources, the overall dropout rate in middle schools and primary schools in China in the late 1980s was 2.8 percent, and between 1986 and 1988, three million elementary school students left school, primarily for financial reasons.[21]

While reformers in Beijing were well aware of the importance of improving teachers' standards of living, in many localities, teachers' real incomes declined due to a variety of factors, including official negligence. In the early 1990s, the salaries of Chinese teachers were merely one-quarter of what teachers made in other countries at a similar level of economic development and less than half of what teachers earned in India. Professors at the most prestigious universities made less money than the uneducated street vendors of popsicles and baked sweet potatoes.[22] The lack of material reward devastated teachers' morale and discouraged competent high school graduates from applying to normal universities and teachers colleges. In some regions, there were more openings for students at these colleges than there were applicants. The net result was the aging of the teaching staff and a shortage of qualified teachers, especially in rural schools. Worse still, due to a maladjusted economy and official neglect, late pay for school teachers became a common occurrence. In 1993 the problem of delayed pay affected school teachers in twenty-eight provinces and, in Hunan province, 65 percent of teachers had their pay withheld for several months.[23] All this contributed to an unprecedented outflow of teachers from public schools at a time when good teachers were vital to system. By the end of 1992, over 430,000 school teachers nationwide had fled the classroom for other jobs.[24]

Despite a lack of good schools and a lack of space in universities, basic education in urban China was probably more competitive and more elitist than in most countries. For decades, the entire system traveled on the narrow rails of a promotion-oriented educational program. Students had to take entrance exams before entering high school and college. When the latter-day *keju* became excessive, it tended to stifle creativity in the classroom and hamper the development of healthy personalities.[25]

The so-called key-point middle school (*zhongdian zhongxue*), for example, at once demonstrated the strength of China's school system and the limits of its educational elitism. Key-point schools make up about 2 to 4 percent of all middle and high schools. Favored by the state, these schools were known for their superior teaching staffs and facilities. Most elementary graduates and middle school graduates had to take exams to be admitted to these schools. As there were often over ten times as many candidates as there were openings, competition was fierce. In recent years a vicious circle of incessant tests and excessive workloads wreaked havoc on the students' mental and physical health and caused widespread concerns. Each year, hundreds of thousands of high school graduates had to go through the "examination hell" in "Black July" to find a niche in a governmental university. Due to the pressure of exams, the integrity of the curricula at schools become hard to maintain, since schools would cut the non-core subjects so that students would have more time to prepare for matriculation.

Like the *keju* in imperial China, the arbitrary mode of "education for the sake of promotion to the next level of schooling" detached millions of Chinese students from the reality of life. Students who spent years preparing for exams hardly developed the practical skills necessary for the challenges of the work place. Those who failed in the college entrance examination at the end of basic education thus were double losers: while being rejected by colleges, these youth possessed few of the skills required by the fast-changing job market.[26] Although parents complained, many teachers worried, and the State Education Commission repeatedly admonished, few schools mustered enough courage to break this circle.

Concomitant with the shrinking educational expenditure was the unequal access to education. By the 1990s, egalitarianism in education had become an ideal of the past and public education in China was no longer free. Urban and rural public schools charged various fees to ameliorate the school system's budgetary difficulties and to narrow the gap in standards of living between teachers and other professionals.[27] Better schools, especially the key-point schools, took an increasing number of students at "negotiated prices" which, in many cases, amounted to well over ten thousand yuan per year. For the average salaried families such fees were exorbitant. Of course, people with position and power could always squeeze their children in through the "back door." The big losers were the children whose parents had neither influence nor money.[28]

In areas with a stagnant economy, these fees directly contributed to the declining number of students. In a county in Sichuan province, youth who were not in school because they could not afford the fees made up 74 percent of school-age children. If not for the government's repeated warnings, this educational exaction would have long spiraled out of control. These problems in the public school system, on the one hand, and the country's renewed drive for further openness following Deng Xiaoping's South China tour of 1992, on the other, explained the explosion of private schools.

Although it is difficult to make any generalization about the types of private schools in the 1990s, we can nevertheless put them into three categories in terms of their funding and operation. The first type of private schools were founded and controlled by private investors. Some of these investors were former educators; however, most of them were successful businessmen. For these investors, private schools were both a philanthropic and potentially lucrative endeavor. The second type of private schools were set up by Chinese individuals or business firms in collaboration with foreign investors. Many schools set up by joint ventures between Chinese and foreign partners fell into this category. The third type were founded and operated by Chinese enterprises and institutions in the very tradition of the *minban* school. In a culture where connections with the government were crucial, many private schools involved government officials or agencies in their administration or boards.[29] The advantage of such schools was obvious. With inside connections, they could not only circumvent government regulations but also enjoy favorable treatment in land procurement and tax exemptions.

As in the early years of private education in China, the quality of private schools depended on the personality of their founders. Most founders were extremely pragmatic and equipped with an insight into both the market place and education, although some may have had little formal education themselves. As education was their conscious choice, most of these people had an intense desire, if not a sense of mission, to succeed. Such leadership was largely responsible for the rise of private schools in the 1990s.[30]

The temptation and challenge of private education drew many talented and ambitious administrators as well. The top choices of investors when hiring staff were usually retired principals of key-point schools who had both experience and prestige. An ideal administration had a two-tier structure; the senior headmasters were assisted by younger officials, some of whom had advanced degrees in education or school administration. Compared with administrators of public schools, headmasters and top administrators of private schools were often more aggressive and more willing to cross conventional lines to get things done. Typically, they had to spend much of their time and energy traveling between government offices, sometimes resorting to extralegal activities to expedite their work. The need for survival, combined with the desire to succeed, translated into the miraculous expansion of private schools.

In most cases, the financial independence of private schools led to administrative flexibility and creativity in the classroom. In comparison, public schools were often held back by inept administrations and handicapped by excessive government intervention that had little to do with the quality of education. In addition, an outdated personnel system and a system of promotion based on seniority inhibited the introduction of innovative approaches and novel ideas into the classroom. Private schools, in comparison, enjoyed greater autonomy in curriculum design and administrative affairs which led to better teaching and greater competitiveness. At private schools, teachers' salaries were more likely to be based on performance or the ability to attract and retain new students than on seniority. Whereas in a public school, punishment was rarely meted out for poor performance, in a private school, a mediocre teacher was unlikely to stay for long. When enrolling students, private schools usually ignored the artificial boundaries of school districts so as to recruit students who had no access to a key-point school, either because of their homes' locations or because of their less-than-superb academic records.

Teaching was never a highly remunerative profession in China even though the government raised teachers' salaries several times since the late 1970s. As private schools offered a salary that was generally 50 percent higher than public schools, many private schools were able to hire good teachers. The hiring of teachers was facilitated by the government's new policy on retirement, under which female teachers could retire with full pensions at fifty and male teachers at fifty-five. Many retired elementary and middle schools teachers, still in the prime of their lives, came to private schools for a second income and self-fulfillment. For private schools, employing retired and part time teachers who were still holding a job at public schools exempted them from paying benefits such as medical insurance. In addition to competitive salaries, a growing number of private schools also offered excellent housing and benefits including medical insurance and retirement pension programs.

With few exceptions, all private schools had to fulfill the core curriculum laid down by the State Education Commission if they wanted their students to be competitive in various exams. The results of these exams meant life and death to them. Private schools were also subject to the authority of the local education commission. In the early 1990s, the superintendent's office (*Duxue shi*) of the municipal and county education commission extended its authority into the private sector to ensure conformity to governmental regulations. The office's priorities were, first, to ensure that the core curriculum for the nine-year compulsory education was properly followed; second, to eliminate obvious political heresies; and third, to monitor schools' revenues and expenditures.

However, due to their financial independence, private schools maintained considerable administrative autonomy. Because of this, some private schools were able to depart from the well-established promotion-oriented and teacher-centered learning in public schools. At these private schools, teachers were encouraged to employ Western-style teaching, and students were given much more opportunity to voice their opinions. Although its pedagogical merit was obvious, this approach was nonetheless risky in a system that was geared to exams; unless it translated into good test scores. Open-minded theoreticians cheered for such private schools because, by making students the center of the learning process and by offering an assortment of extracurricular activities, they were molding truly "well-rounded" individuals.

## PRIVATE HIGHER EDUCATION IN THE 1990s

Private higher education entered a period of expansion as well after 1992. The growth of private higher education largely reflected the acceleration in China's economic reforms after Deng Xiaoping's South China Tour. It also resulted from the determination of the ruling party to push educational reform forward. In the Resolution on the Reform of the Educational System (1985) the central committee of the CCP pointed out that the inadequacy of education had not changed "compared to the need for socialist modernization." In the 1990s the same problem remained and became even more acute (see Table 8). The only sensible solution was to further reduce state control over higher education and extend the autonomy of institutions of higher education under the government's guidelines and plans.

**Table 8: Competition for Places in Public Universities, 1988-1992**

| Year | High School Graduates | Freshmen Admitted | Rejected Applicants |
|------|----------------------|-------------------|---------------------|
| 1988 | 3,316,000 | 670,000 | 2,646,000 |
| 1989 | 3,295,000 | 597,100 | 2,698,000 |
| 1990 | 3,251,000 | 608,900 | 2,642,000 |
| 1991 | 3,038,000 | 619,900 | 2,418,000 |
| 1992 | 3,087,500 | 754,200 | 2,333,000 |
| Total | 15,987,600 | 3,250,100 | 12,737,500 |

Source: Study Team, China National Institute of Educational Research, *A Study on NGO-Sponsored and Private Higher Education in China*, (Beijing, 1995), p. 43.

Like private elementary and secondary schools, private colleges were also assisted by some chronic problems in public schools. Although much progress had been made in reforming the system of higher education since the late 1970s, changes in governmental colleges proved far from adequate because of their academic inertia and administrative inflexibility. In fact, economic reform in the 1980s and 1990s exposed a "macro-disarray" in China's higher education in its structure of levels, disciplines, and programs. For years, rigid governmental administrations had created a curious phenomenon: while China suffered from a critical shortage of specialized personnel, there was at the same time a surplus of graduates in some dying fields. As many public universities concentrated on very narrow fields of study, their graduates often lacked the ability to effectively handle practical work.[31]

Obviously, the shortage of talented personnel impeded economic development. To scholars and reform-minded officials, the solution lay in the structural reform of the educational system, and private colleges with vocational orientation offered a powerful remedy for the malaise of the public sector. Since the mid-1980s, vocational colleges serving local economic needs were set up by existing educational institutions, business enterprises, and private citizens. Even though some private colleges were sponsored by public institutions, they received virtually no funding from the state and were de facto private. These colleges enrolled nonresidential, self-paying students for whom the schools were not responsible for job placement. In Jiangsu province alone, eighteen such colleges were established between 1982 and 1987, with 143 distinctive programs and 11,400 students. They had a total teaching and administrative staff of 3,200, of which 1,300 were full-time teachers.[32] By the early 1990s, postsecondary vocational schools had become well-entrenched as the norm and the cutting edge of private higher education. Most private college administrations demonstrated foresight in shaping their programs and agility in responding to market signals. They especially targeted fields in short supply, such as mechanical engineering, electronics, automation, finance, accounting, advertising, business administration, foreign trade, and foreign languages. For their own survival and their students' adaptability, many private colleges also favored interdisciplinary studies.

The flexibility of private colleges stemmed primarily from the diversity and practicality of their course offerings and a multi-level structure that included four-year colleges and other programs of various durations. In addition to high school graduates, private colleges also recruited their students from the work force and the unemployed. To meet the needs of the market and their clientele, private colleges developed highly applicable programs and, while public institutions were hamstrung by cumbersome administrations and too many auxiliary personnel, private colleges were characterized by administrative and managerial efficiency. As such, they were able to utilize the latent resources of public institutions and direct them toward societal needs. By doing so, private colleges at once supplemented and challenged public institutions. They helped expose the inertia in public higher education and introduced competition into this formerly stagnant field.

Beneficial to the growth of private colleges was the Chinese government's will to further decentralize higher education. While determined to control higher education through macroscopic management, the state was ready to share the business with a growing civil society. At the root of this concession was the government's financial and managerial inability to maintain an educational system that was big enough to meet the needs of the nation and diversified enough to serve the goal of modernization. Between 1988 and 1992, for example, nearly 20 million students graduated from high school. Only a meager 3.2 million, or 16 percent, were admitted to public colleges, not to mention the much greater number of students who had been knocked out of the relentless competition at the elementary and secondary levels. According to the fourth national census in 1990, only 1,442 out of 100,000 Chinese adults had either taken some college courses or completed college. Thus there was a vast market for private colleges. Because of this, the Chinese government sought to redesign the educational system to make it more responsive to the nation's economic needs; this could be achieved only through a combination of government and private initiatives.

The revival of private higher education also benefited from some specific reforms in public institutions such as changes in admission and job assignment policies. Starting in the mid-1980s, the government allowed colleges and universities to enroll employer-contracted students and self-financed students after they fulfilled the governmental quota, in accordance with societal demands and the capacity of the schools. Beijing Institute of Architectural Engineering, for example, pioneered in accepting contracted students on a trial basis and accomplished remarkable results. Between 1986 and 1993, its enrollment of tuition students rose from 10 percent to 34 percent of the student population with an annual income of 1.5 million yuan from private sources. About 70 to 80 percent of these funds were used to cover current costs and the rest was used for faculty subsidies.[33]

In 1993 after much delay and hesitation, the Chinese government decided to overhaul the existing job assignment system for college graduates to meet the needs of the "socialist market economy." Instead of guaranteeing job placement for every graduate, the government decided to let the freshmen of the class of 1997 pay for their own college education and find jobs for themselves upon graduation through a "two-way selection," or *gongxu jian mian* (the meeting of supply and demand). Under the general principle of "paying to go to college, no placement guarantee, equal competition, and two-way selection,"[34] three types of admission were introduced: the planned admission (*jihua zhaosheng*), admission from designated areas (*dingxiang zhaosheng*), and employer-sponsored education (*weituo peiyang*). This shift in policy signified the government's recognition of the inadvisability of monopolizing China's higher education and its willingness to allow market mechanisms to regulate the field.[35] In 1994, 154,000 tuition students enrolled in public colleges. This number represented 15.6 percent of the total enrollment and 26.9 percent state-planned enrollment. Tuition requirements and gradual abolition of job assignment responsibilities at governmental institutions opened a new horizon for private higher education.

## IMPACT OF PRIVATE SCHOOLS

Private schools came under public scrutiny and even encountered animosity almost from their very inception not merely because of the public prejudice against wealth nurtured by the Maoist revolution but also because of the socioeconomic polarization that resulted from the Dengist reform. While the fortunes of millionaires and billionaires made a mockery of the old economic system, Chinese consumers were hit hard by double-digit annual inflation beginning in the late 1980s. Numerous state-owned enterprises slipped into the doldrums and laid off large proportion of their employees. According to government sources, in late 1994 up to 44.5 percent of state firms were losing money, despite an annual growth rate of about 10 percent in the overall national economy.[36] Eager to push the country toward a "socialist market economy," the State Council finally decided in 1994 to enforce the bankruptcy law which had passed in 1988 but remained unsure where to reassign the employees of shut-down factories. Chinese workers, who received heavy doses of state-sponsored welfare and enjoyed a prestigious position during the Maoist era, were not psychologically prepared for this downturn in fortunes. Sporadic strikes and demonstrations that challenged the legitimacy of the government took place in some cities.

In 1992 through 1995, the controversy over private schools heated up with the emergence of the so-called "elite schools." Usually with a strong financial backup, these private schools were equipped with such enviable facilities as computer labs, language labs, indoor gyms, swimming pools, and piano studios. While having obvious commercial values, ultra-modern facilities such as computer labs enabled these schools to implement programs that prepared their students for the challenge of the twenty-first century. Compared with the shabby and crowded classrooms at public schools, classrooms at the elite schools were well-lit and spacious. While a classroom at a typical urban public school held well over sixty students, the average size of a class at an elite school was less than thirty.

Like some elite private schools of the Nationalist era, the elite schools of the 1990s emphasized foreign languages, especially English, as the medium of instruction. Because of this, foreign teachers were coveted by these schools both for their real and advertising value. Although the employment of foreign teachers at elementary and secondary schools was a sensitive issue and was generally discouraged by the government, the elite private schools could always secure special permission or simply circumvent government requirements with their connections (*guanxi*). Some even established exchange programs with schools in foreign countries with a view to attracting students from rich families. And, like their predecessors in the Nationalist era, most elite private schools in the 1990s were boarding schools, and some had air-conditioned student dorms. This enabled them to organize a variety of extracurricular student activities that were impossible at most public schools.

In the midst of popular anxiety and frustration, the salaried class quickly turned against the luxurious private schools because of their inaccessibility. Jinghua Primary School in Beijing, for example, charged each new student a 14,000-yuan tuition plus a one-time capitalization fee of 30,000 yuan. Xiaozhuang Experimental International School in Jiangsu, established jointly by Xiaozhuang Normal School and the Liheng Company of Hong Kong, charged a one-time building fee of 24,000 yuan and a yearly tuition of 6,000 yuan. Private Zhonghua Yinghao School in Guangzhou asked for an entrance fee of 300,000 yuan, which was refundable upon graduation.[37] To the average Chinese, such fees were astronomical. Yet to the parents of the students, the cost was just pocket change. The arrogance of China's nouveau riche flew directly into the face of China's salaried classes. To losers in the post-Mao economic reform, this was an affront. A veteran cadre complained: "We have worked for the country and for the state for more than half a century, and poured out every ounce of our energy and life's blood for the good of the public, but our children cannot afford to attend a school like that. These schools are catering to the newly rich, the upstarts."[38]

Hostility toward these private schools was intensified by the poverty of the public school system. In numerous poverty-stricken areas children were kept out of school because their parents were unable to pay a meager sixty-yuan annual tuition. In 1992 the rate of student dropouts in Yilong county, Sichuan province, climbed as high as 48 percent. In 1991, in Sichuan province alone, nearly a million students dropped out of school. In the same year, the nationwide dropout rate among elementary school students was 2.2 percent and among secondary school students, it was 5.8 percent. That meant 2.4 million middle school and 2.7 million elementary school students quit school each year. After all, China in the 1990s was still home to 80 million poor people who were suffering from a decline in the delivery of basic public social services such as health care and education.

In reality, genuinely elite schools were few, making up probably less than 10 percent of private schools established between 1990 and 1995. Most private schools charged an annual tuition less than eight thousand yuan or one thousand dollars. They certainly did not target the average workers in state-owned enterprises but rather the millions of *getihu* and employees in private and foreign business. In terms of facilities, most elite schools in China were still inferior to the average public school in the United States or other advanced Western countries, and it would take decades for them to meet international standards.

Sober-minded scholars pointed out that, under the economic conditions in China, it was a "worthy experiment to bring market economics into the realm of the educational system" because private schools broke the monopoly of the state and helped "redistribute the resources of education." [39] The question was not whether China needed these elite schools but whether China had a market for them. Without denying the profiteering of some private schools, we have to say that, on the whole, private education provided a meaningful channel for capital which might otherwise have been invested in such unworthy enterprises as gambling and pornographic publications. It was, overall, a positive development.

On the whole, the Chinese government demonstrated both foresight and courage. Shortly after the emergence of private schools, the government began to hail them as an "integral part of the socialist education..., a strategic measure to strengthen the basic education and an unshakable responsibility of the government at all levels." [40] In a culture that puts a premium on education, it was hard to find fault with setting up schools even though by non-governmental agents. Although party ideologues were not totally silent, younger officials in Beijing and local education commissions were certainly much less concerned about Marxist orthodoxy. A new generation of college-educated bureaucrats was trying to carve out a new path for schooling in China. At the same time, the mushrooming of private schools forced the government to readjust its policy toward basic education.

In 1993 the State Education Commission dispatched two fact-finding missions, one to the United States and the other to Japan, to investigate private education. Reports by these delegations urged the government to recognize the need for private schools in China and recommended the establishment of regulations and a system of accreditation. By doing so, the government could not only channel private capital into education but also limit profit making in private schools. To ensure the healthy growth of private education in China, the reports also called for government supervision in finances and the quality of instruction.[41] The delegation to Japan, in particular, recommended transforming some financially troubled public schools into private institutions. More significantly, the report pointed to the urgent need for a private education law which, after more than ten years since the reemergence of private education in the People's Republic, was conspicuously absent. The delegation found that China's current socioeconomic situation was similar to that of Japan in the 1950s and 1960s and that it could learn much from its neighbor.

In general, education commissions were willing to recognize the limited autonomy of private schools. Yet at the same time officials required private schools to follow state educational guidelines, policies, and legislation. Private schools were instructed to emphasize moral education through organizations such as the Young Pioneers, the Communist Youth League, and the Students Union. To ensure instructional quality in the classroom, local education commissions asked private schools to participate with public schools in officially monitored exams and tried to implement programs of accreditation for private schools.

At the same time, the government was rightfully critical of private schools for making a profit. Profiteering in education was considered immoral because teaching in general had been a self-denying profession throughout China's history, and schools at all levels were thought to have social responsibilities. Both reformers and conservatives in the CCP agreed that schools in China should remain "socialist in nature." Strictly speaking, however, this argument meant little since few Chinese in the public or private sector were certain about what a socialist market economy actually meant. Nor were they sure how to maintain the egalitarian ideal in a time of rapid polarization in wealth. If the ruling party to allowed part of the population to become rich ahead of others, if it acquiesced in the conspicuous consumption of a minority, then why did it censure private schools?

For ideological and administrative expediency, in 1995 the State Education Commission suggested that private schools change the adjective "private" (*sili*) to *minban*, probably because the former suggested a non-socialist quality while the latter smacked of the populism of the ruling party, even though populism had in effect been jettisoned by the majority of its membership. There was also the fear that investors in private schools were running private schools as private estates, regardless of the schools' social responsibilities. In China's burgeoning education market, however, it was not easy to eliminate profit making.

Moreover, to the urban population, the term *minban* had long been discredited as something inferior, while "private" was ostentatiously attached to the names of non-government schools and proudly advertised. Chinese officials noticed that in Japan, profit and nonprofit private schools were treated differently. While non-profit schools were recognized by both the education administration and the commerce department and enjoyed tax exemptions, profit-making schools were subject to taxation as business endeavors. However, in China, it was difficult to make such a distinction because the government had yet to develop the mechanisms to regulate the market.[42]

In many respects, the rapid proliferation of private schools caught the government unprepared. Provincial and municipal education commissions were already short-handed in managing public education. For all their enthusiasm, the commissions approved more private schools than they could effectively supervise. The semi-laissez-faire state of private education showed at once the confidence of the Chinese government and its inadequacy. For good private schools, this was a blessing, for it allowed them to expand without burdensome government interventions. But the growth of private schools was uneven. Many private schools were set up promptly without meeting pertinent requirements and some were largely speculative schemes. Thus starting in 1994, education commissions at all levels were urged to reexamine their approval procedures and to redefine criteria for certifications. Their effort to bring private schools under control, however, proved difficult because of the latter's relative autonomy and their own personnel shortage.

At the same time, the vitality demonstrated by private schools magnified the administrative and instructional weaknesses of public schools. The magnetism of private schools attracted an increasing number of good teachers from public schools, adding a further destabilizing factor to the already shaken system. Although private schools helped to keep the best teachers from "jumping ship,"[43] administrators of public schools were in general displeased. The limited "brain drain" to the private sector may have affected the quality of instruction at public schools as some education officials claimed. In reality, however, public school administrators were most upset by their own inability to maintain personnel control. Therefore they increasingly pressed the government to side with them on matters of personnel transfer. Their hysteria was not in vain. When disputes occurred between a private and public school over a good teacher, government officials and education commissions usually leaned toward their old domain. Although the free flow of labor was quite common in industry and commerce, in education most government officials were not committed to this ideal because they feared chaos. In the mid-1990s the liberalization of education still remained a very touchy issue.

Furthermore, government attempts to control education were motivated by ideological as well as pragmatic concerns. More than the government in any other culture, the Chinese government saw schools as institutions to imbue the minds of the younger generation with politically correct ideas. Education was expected to contribute to social stability rather than to challenge the status quo, to create and maintain consensus rather than to foment dissension. Private schools, by virtue of their autonomy, often made education officials uneasy. In all public schools, for instance, patriotism was emphasized through classroom instruction and such activities as Monday morning flag-raising ceremonies. Young Pioneers in all elementary schools and middle schools were essential in promoting the official line. In private schools, however, these ceremonies could be overlooked or quietly sacrificed for academic excellence. It was certainly mind-boggling to government officials when some private schools openly and unabashedly called themselves "aristocratic."

Opposition to the elite schools was often associated with public displeasure with the wanton corruption in China. In a developing economy, unequal access to power meant unequal access to opportunities. Loopholes in political institutions and laws and moral laxity among officials, enabled a small number of people to reap huge profits through very questionable activities. Even though Beijing launched ostensible campaigns against official corruption, the temptation of wealth still continued to corrode the ruling party's morale. Children in private schools were invariably from well-to-do families, and those in very expensive private schools were usually from the nouveau riche, whose wealth was often amassed by bending the principles. Moreover, even though education was considered the noblest and most corruption-free field, private school administrators frequently found themselves in a moral twilight zone, especially in dealing with government agencies whose attitude sometimes meant life and death for private schools. In this sense, private schools that prospered on the growing gulf between the rich and poor only magnified the problems that were besetting Chinese society in the 1990s. At the heart of the issue was whether China could enjoy the benefits of the market without being polluted by its intrinsic evils.

Like other sectors of the market economy, private education was subject to irrational desires and speculative errors. Thus there was an oversupply of private schools in some areas, especially on the coast, where investment in private schools continued unabatedly between 1992 and 1995. In Guangdong province, for example, there were over six hundred private schools in 1994, thirty-one of which were labeled as "elite." While the elite schools were designed to enroll a total of seventy thousand students, less than seven thousand had signed up.[44] Because of this oversupply, competition among private schools became ugly and wasteful. The provincial education commission therefore either decided, or was instructed, to withhold approval of the cataract of applications for private school licenses, even though this decision made people wonder whether the government was willing to respect market mechanisms in education.

The government, unhappy with the semi-anarchical situation in private education, could not ignore public resentment of the elite private schools. Top officials of the State Education Commission called for certain controls over private schools and urged the government to help such schools change their orientation or, if the schools refused to listen, to shut them down.[45] In 1994 a circular from the State Education Commission called profiteering in education "intolerable." It forbade schools from pursuing a profit or raising capital for endeavors rather than education. It required private schools to spend all their legal income on their own development and operation. Moreover, it called for the organization of supervisory committees for the financial affairs of these schools which would be composed of parents and donors. The State Education Commission also instructed its local agencies to rigorously audit all private schools' financial management.[46]

## PROSPECTS FOR PRIVATE EDUCATION

After a visit to Jingshan Middle School in Beijing in 1983, Deng Xiaoping with left these words: "Education should be geared to the needs of modernization, the world and the future." Since the Cultural Revolution, it has been the goal of the Chinese government to make nine-year compulsory education universal and to eliminate illiteracy among the young and middle-aged. In big cities and coastal provinces, the government would like to implement a twelve-year compulsory schooling for all citizens by the end of the twentieth century. Yet a 1994 survey indicates that China still has over 180 million illiterate people and 2.6 million teenage dropouts and, while there are only 11.7 engineers out of 10,000 Chinese, 40 percent of China's industrial work force has had no more than nine years' education. Such numbers are quite sobering and even more daunting when one realizes that, in some economically backward provinces, the annual income of a peasant family is about two hundred yuan, which makes the school fee of thirty yuan a big allocation of family income.[47] In the cities, education also faces severe challenges, especially since the majority of state-owned enterprises are running in the red and the government has not come up with any magic formula for rejuvenating them. Thus for the foreseeable future, Beijing has to face the problem of operating a huge educational system in a poor country.

Obviously, it will be extremely difficult for public schools alone to achieve the government's goals especially if China's economy is further commercial-ised. The government has already made it clear that it is not going to carry the financial burden for education all by itself and that it would like to share it with individuals and institutions that have the interest, money, and expertise to set up and run schools and universities. Therefore, there will be ample room in the future for private education in China. Between the 1910s and the end of World War II, more than one-third of all China's students studied in private schools. In contemporary Japan, private schools enroll 11.2 percent of the total student population. In China today, the students at private schools probably make up less than 1 percent of the total student population, not to say that before the year 2,000, the total enrollment in China's elementary and secondary schools will increase by 34 million.[48] Private higher education, in particular, faces unprecedented opportunities because, beginning in fall, 1997, all public universities and colleges in China require their students to pay tuition. This change puts private colleges in a better position to compete governmental schools. The golden age of private education in China is indeed yet to come.

It is anticipated that there will be a continuous, though sometimes uneven, growth of private schools in China in the next decade. Along with this growth, Chinese society will become more open and Chinese culture more diverse. But, given the treacherous nature of Chinese politics, increasing economic disparities and the government's need to maintain ideological control, the development of private education may experience some temporary setbacks. So far the relationship between private schools and the government has been by and large constructive and this should continue in the future. In all likelihood, the government will try to maintain macro-control over private education, which is not necessarily a negative thing even though some private schools would like retain as much autonomy as possible. It would take a fundamental change in the government's attitude to treat private schools as an integral part of the nation's educational system. For the time being, private schools are still treated somewhat like illegitimate children. For example, while the Japanese government finances private schools, local education commissions in China are taking administrative fees from private schools to support the local government's understaffed bureaus and underpaid employees. Such a policy, if not stopped soon, is bound to inflict damages to private education.

The growth of private schools will also be affected by changes in public schools. A few public schools have had one foot in the educational market for years by taking tuition students. The challenge of private schools has forced the government to further recognize the power of market mechanisms. Starting in 1995, the government launched a pilot program among some urban key-point high schools by giving them greater autonomy in decision making and requiring them to become financially self-sufficient in two to three years. These state-owned and people-run (*guoyou minban*) schools are run by individual administrators under contract with the government and thereby enjoy much greater administrative autonomy.

This is another giant step forward from the principal responsibility system implemented in the mid-1980s, which gave the principals of selected schools all administrative powers except for such matters as firing teachers and making large-scale investments.[49] The measure satisfies both the strategic and tactical needs of the government. On the one hand, it lifts some burden from the government, thereby enabling it to focus its financial resources on the remaining public schools. It also frees the education commission from part of its routine so that it can exercise macro-control over the school system as a whole.[50] On the other hand, the *guoyou minban* schools also serve as a counterweight to private schools. Since these schools are still state property, their autonomy could be easily withdrawn by the government.

At present, it is still too early to foretell the future of the pseudo-privatization of public schools. But it is predictable that, with a veteran teaching staff and established reputations, these schools will prove fierce rivals to private schools and give the government important leverage in administering the school system. It is as if the "household responsibility system" has been extended into China's education. The policy is likely to help release the heretofore dormant energy among public school administrators and teachers. But large-scale privatization of public schools is highly unlikely, for public education has been a well-guarded turf of nation-states everywhere, and the Chinese government has a big stake in maintaining it.

Above all, private schools, though a popular trend in today's China, have to pass the test of the market. The growth of the Chinese economy since 1979 has been rapid but uneven, and the market for private schools is yet to be expanded. Unlike public schools, which still comfortably eat from the "big iron bowl" of the state, private schools are subject to the whim of the market place. Commercialization of schools often leads to inflated advertising and impossible goals, thereby smearing the image of private education. A lack of planning in many cases has also resulted in various problems in fund-raising and operation. Given today's intensifying competition and the relative inexperience of their investors and leaders, not all private schools are going to survive. In some areas, relentless competition is already driving some less efficient nongovernmental schools out of the market. For their collective survival, it is imperative that private schools increase their mutual contacts and form national as well as regional associations. Through such associations, they can not only to promote their common cause more effectively, but also develop rules to avoid cutthroat competition.

Ultimately the healthy and steady growth of private education in China will require the protection of law. Although the Education Law passed in early 1995 sets the legal framework for schools, details regarding the status and rights of private schools have yet to be worked out.[51] In a culture that imposes many obligations on the people but grants them few rights, the government tends to bend its own rules. For examples, Article 25, Chapter 3, of the Education Law prohibits any school or educational institution from making a profit. The term "profit" needs to be defined precisely or it can be wielded as a weapon by the state. Given the magnitude of China's judicial reform, and the Chinese people's lack of experience with a market economy, it will take years for the state and private citizens to figure out how to play by the rules of the game.

In this regard, the Nationalist government in Taiwan has much to offer to Beijing. Based on pre-1949 legislation, the refugee government passed the Private Education Law in 1974 and details for its implementation in 1975. While guaranteeing the right of citizens to establish and run private schools in a civil society, this legislation also established the role of private schools as institutions of "public service" (*gongyi shiye*). In 1950, there was practically no private education in Taiwan. By the 1990s, private schools accounted for over

33 percent of all schools on the island. In tertiary education, private institutions made up the majority.[52] Such impressive progress resulted from the general improvement in Taiwan's economic and social conditions and the dynamic and creative leadership of the Nationalist government.

Private education had been a norm of schooling in China for over two millennia. It underwent a very abnormal period in modern times and became one of the major casualties of a profound political and social revolution set off in the nineteenth century. Its resurgence from a temporary demise not only bears testimony to the great resiliency of Chinese civilization but signifies the beginning of an era in which the Chinese state will have to recognize the autonomy of schools as a necessary part of a growing civil society and a modern educational system. Viewed historically, private education, by being part of China's economic reform and cultural openness, is spearheading the country's educational reform and, by asserting the crucial role of educators in the nation's social and political life, it is leading China back toward its glorious tradition.

## NOTES

1. Jie Chen and Peng Deng, *China since the Cultural Revolution* (Westport: Praeger, 1995), p. 34.

2. Ibid., pp. 39-63.

3. Jiang Fang, "Shinian Changsang, Yipai xinlu: Chongqing shi shehui liliang banxue de huigu yu zhanwang" (Ten years of reform has yielded fruits: Past and future of  schools run by social forces in Chongqing), Chongqing Municipal Education Commission ed., *Chunfeng huayu* (Spring wind brought rains) (Chongqing, 1992), pp. 181-188; Luan Wencheng, "Guanyu nongchun siren banxue de shijian yu tansuo (Experiments in private education in rural areas), in ibid., pp. 191-197.

4. "Farmer-Sponsored Schools," *Beijing Review* (10-16 October , 1994), pp. 33; also see John Cleverley, *The Schooling of China: Tradition and Modernity in Chinese Education* (North Sydney: Allen & Unwin Pty. Ltd., 1991), p. 336; Suzanne Pepper, *China's Education Reform in the 1980s: Policies, Issues, and Historical Perspectives* (Berkeley: Institute of East Asian Studies, University of California at Berkeley Center for Chinese Studies, 1990), pp. 102-111.

5. See Cheng Jieming, *Zhongguo dalu jiaoyu shikuang* (State of education in mainland China) (Taibei: Taiwan Commercial Press, 1993), pp. 184-197.

6. Ibid., pp. 211-216.

7. Division of Vocational and Technical Education, State Education Commission, *Quanguo zhiye jiaoyu gongzuo huiyi wenjian huibian* (Collection of documents of the national conference for vocational and technical education) (Beijing: Beijing Normal University Press, 1986), pp. 410-412; see *Chinese Education*, 24 (Fall, 1990): 8-15.

8. See Shi Ming Hu and Eli Seifman eds., *A Documentary History of Education in the PRC, 1977-1986* (New York: AMS Press, 1987), p. 228.

9. State Education Commission, "Temporary Regulations Concerning Schools Sponsored by Social Forces," July 8, 1987.

10. State Education Commission, "Notice Concerning Advertising by Some Minban Colleges," July 26, 1990.

11. State Education Commission, "Notice Regarding Some Problems in Schools by Non-Governmental Agents," October 17, 1988.

12. According to some, Shenyang Experiment High School, founded in July 1988, is the first of this kind. The school is not as prominent as others since it did not have its own campus but had to rent classrooms from others, "Private Schools: A New Trend in Education," *Liaoshen Wanbao* (Liaoning-Shenyang Evening News), January 5, 1994.

13. Project Team, *A Study on NGO-Sponsored and Private Higher Education in China* (Beijing: China National Institute of Educational Research, 1995), p. 61; Li Yuehong & Xu Jiangshan, "Jiang Shuyun he ta de daxue" (Jiang Shuyun and her university), *Renmin Ribao*, April 13, 1995; Wang Mingda, "Report at the First Conference on the Management of Private Schools," *Minban Jiaoyu tongxun* (Newsletter of private and NGO-sponsored education), vol. 9, no. 6, 1996, p. 1.

14. Study Team, China National Institute of Educational Research, *A Study on NGO-sponsored and Private Higher Education in China* (Beijing, 1995), pp. 8-12.

15. Bi Cheng, "Woguo sili xuexiao shijian yu lilun de tansuo" (Theory and practice of private schools in our country), in Zhang Zhiyi ed., *Sili minban xuexiao de lilun yu shijian* (Theory and practice of private and *minban* schools) (Beijing: Chinese Workers Press, 1994), pp. 227-228, 230-231.

16. Wen Jing, "Fengbei wadi qi" (Huge monument in marshy lands), *Yingkou ribao* (Yingkou daily), December 6, 1995; Zhao Xianzhi, "Xinhua xuetuan: Sixue de qiji" (Xinhua school group: miracle in private education), *Liaoning ribao* (Liaoning daily), May 2, 1996.

17. Liu Yingjie ed., *Zhongguo jiaoyu dashidian, 1949-1990* (Book of major educational events in China) (Hangzhou: Zhejiang Education Press, 1993), pp. 2135-2140, 2144-2147.

18. On average, educational expenditures accounted for 4.2 percent of the GNP in countries with a per capita GNP of $300-$500, 4.4 percent in countries with a per capita GNP of $500-$1,000, 4.5 percent in countries with a per capita GNP of $1,000-$2,000, and 5.8 percent in countries with a per capita GNP of over $5,000.

19. Ho Zuoxiu & Mao Junqiang, "Is Our Education Funding above Average among Countries of a Comparable Level of Development?" *Chinese Education*, 25 (Fall, 1992): 76, 89, 93.

20. Yuan Liansheng, "On the Deficiency of Our Educational Funding: An Analysis of the Amount and Percentage of Our Educational Investment, 1977-1987. *Chinese Education and Society*, 25 (Winter, 1992-93): 28-29; Huang Yao, "In Search of New Mechanisms in Solving Problems of Educational Finance," in ibid., 36-53.

21. Yang Shaojiang, "Gaibian jiaoyu jingfei buzu, xianzai shi zhenzheng luoshi dao xingdong de shihou le" (Reversing the insufficiency of funds for education: Now is the time for action), *Shijie jingji daobao* (World economic herald), 424 (January, 1989): 6-7.

22. Wu Wen & Luo Daming, "Heavy Laden Wings: A Sad Contemplation on China's Education," *Chinese Education and Society*, 28 (January-February, 1995): 27.

23. Zhu Junjie and Xia Zhilun, "Tuoqian zhongxiaoxue jiaoshi gongzi xianxiang touxi" (Reasons for the delay in school teachers pay: an analysis), *Jiaoyu yanjiu* (Studies in Education), 4 (April 1994): 36-40; also see State Education Commission Special Topic Study Group, "Shehui zhuyi shichang jingji yu jiaoyu tizhi gaige" (Socialist market economy and the reform of the educational system), *Jiaoyu yanjiu*, 1 (January 1994): 5-6.

24. Wu Wen & Luo Daming, " Heavy Laden Wings," 93; Research Group, State Education Commission, "Shehui zhuyi shichang jingji yu jiaoyu tizhi gaige," *Jiaoyu yanjiu*, 1 (January, 1994): 5.

25. Yang Dongping, "Zhongguo jiaoyu de weiji suozai: Touzi duanque, xiaoyi dixia, gaige geng man" (China's Crisis in education: Inadequate investment, low returns, and slow reform), *Shijie jingji daobao*, no. 392, May 23, 1988, pp. 1, 3; see *Chinese Education*, 23 (Summer, 1990): 16-17.

26. Wu Wen & Luo Daming, "Heavy Laden Wings," 18, 22.

27. Ibid., 20.

28. Ibid., 26.

29. Zeng Tianshan, "Woguo gong si li xuexiao bingchun fazhan de qianjing" (Prospects for the coexistence and development of public and private schools in our country), in Zhang Zhiyi ed., *Sili minban xuexiao de lilun yu shijian*, pp. 210-211; Zhu Weiguo & Ding Yong, "Zhengque bawo shichang jizhi zai minban xuexiao banxue zhong de zuoyong" (Correctly handle market mechanisms in the management of *minban* schools), *Jiaoyu yanjiu*, 182 (March, 1995): 30-31.

30. Ibid., 31-32.

31. Liu Yifan, "Gaodeng jiaoyu gaige de jige wenti" (Some issues concerning the reform of higher education), *Jiaoyu yanjiu* (Educational research), 186 (July, 1995): 3-6; Zeng Qiang, Chen Yuejin, Tang Zhihui & Liu Xiguang, "Impoverished Education," *Chinese Education*, 23 (Summer, 1990): 17; Yang Dongping, "Zhongguo jiaoyude weiji suozai," pp. 1, 3.

32. Dai Shujun, "Zhiye daxue keyi fazhan wei gaodeng zhiye jishu jiaoyu de lianheti" (Vocational universities can develop into post-secondary vocational education consortia) *Gaodeng zhiye jiaoyu* (Studies on higher education) (March 1, 1987). pp. 5, 6.

33. Wu Xiu, "Dui putong gaoxiao zhaosheng fenpei zhidu gaige de sikao," *Chinese Education and Society*, 27 (May-June, 1994): 54; also see Yu Changan, "Chengdu: College and University Students Enter the Job Market," in ibid., 75-78; Deng Haiyun, "The Metratrend Toward the Labor Market: An Analysis of the Job Market for 1993 College and University Graduates," in ibid., 79-91.

34. Rao Digang, Chen Haizhun, & Wang Shenghao, "Policy Analysis of the Early State (1985-1991) of Reform of the Job Assignment System for Colleges Graduates," *Chinese Education and Society*, 27 (May-June, 1994): 38-40.

35. Xu Xiu, "Dui putong gaoxiao zhaosheng fenpei zhidu gaige de sikao " (Reflections on the reform of admission to colleges and universities and the job assignment system for their graduates) *Zhongguo gaojiao yanjiu* (Studies in Chinese higher education), April, 1992, pp. 46-48; see *Chinese Education and Society*, 27 (May-June, 1994): 53.

36. Wu Yunhe, "Economy Steady with 11 percent Rise in GDP," *China Daily*, October 19, 1994.

37. Wu Tingfeng, "Woguo shehui liliang banxue ruogan wenti tantao" (Reflections on the *minban* education in our country), *Jiaoyu yanjiu yu shiyan* (Educational studies and practice), 1 (1995): 1-6; Wu Wen and Luo Daming, "Heavy Laden Wings," 71-74.

38. Wu Wen & Luo Daming, "Heavy Laden Wings," 82.

39. Ibid., 79, 96; Gu Meiling, "Sili xuexiao yu shichang jingji" (Private schools and the market economy), *Journal of Sichuan University* (Social Science), 1 (1994): 12-14; Zhang Xiaoming, "Wei shehui liliang banxue diwei zhengming" (Give private school its right place), *Chengren jiaoyu* (Adult education), 6 (June, 1994): 23-24.

40. Municipal Education Commission of Shenyang, "Provisional Regulations Concerning People-Run Secondary, Elementary and Vocational Schools," February 24, 1993.

41. Shao Jinrong, Zhang Wen, & Zhang Xiaodong, "Meiguo sili xuexiao zhuanti diaoyan baogao" (Special report on private schools in the United States), *Educational References*, no. 1-2, January 31, 1994, pp. 1-22.

42. Dong Mingchuan et al., Riben sili jiaoyu kaocha baogao (Report of the History and State of Private Education in Japan), *Educational References*, no. 1-2, January 31, 1994, pp. 23-42.

43. Wu Wen & Luo Daming, "Heavy Laden Wings," 93.

44. *Chinese Youth Daily*, February 20, 1995.

45. *Chinese Education*, January 12, 1995; *China Daily*, February 21, 1995.

46. State Education Commission, "Guanyu minban xuexiao xiang shehui chouji zijin wenti de tongzhi" (Circular concerning the fundraising by private schools), November 1, 1994, Guo Qijia ed., *Zhonghua renmin gongheguo jiaoyufa quanshu* (Complete collection of educational statutes in the People's Republic of China) (Beijing: Beijing Institute of Radio and TV Broadcasting, 1995), pp. 385-386.

47. Lin Shiwei, "Girls Get a Hand to Stay in School," *China Daily*, September 15, 1994.

48. State Education Commission Special Topic Study Group, "Shehui zhuyi shichang jingji yu jiaoyu tizhi gaige," *Jiaoyu yanjiu*, 1 (January 1994): 6.

49. Jing Lin, *Education in Post-Mao China* (Westport: Praeger, 1993), pp. 79-85; also see Liu Guowei and Yi Xiaofeng, "Guanyu zhongxue li de dangzheng fenkai" (On the separation of administrative power and party power in middle schools), *Renmin jiaoyu* (People's Education), 6 (1988): 19-20.

50. See Wang Xiaoquan, "Chengbanzhi–Gongban xuexiao zouchu kunjing de xuanze" (The contract system: Way for public schools to get out of their current plight), *Zhongguo jiaoyu bao* (Chinese educational news), August 5, 1995.

51. See Li Lianning, "Woguo jiaoyu fazhi jianshe de lichengbei" (A milestone in educational legislation in China), *Jiaoyu Yanjiu*, 5 (May 1995): 3-8, 30.

52. Zheng Danhua & Suo Guangyi, "Taiwan sili jiaoyu" (Private education in Taiwan), in Zhang Zhiyi ed., *Sili minban xuexiao de lilun yu shijian*, pp. 98-124; Zhang Jiayi, "Taiwan diqu sili gaodeng xuexiao fazhan zhuangkuang" (State of private higher education in Taiwan), in ibid., pp. 25-43

# Glossary

Aiguo nuxue 爱国女学 Patriotic Women's School
anshen liangmin 安身良民 law-abiding people
bagu wen 八股文 eight-legged essay
Bailudong shuyuan 白鹿洞书院 White Deer Cave Academy
baochan daohu 包产到户 household responsibility system
boluan fanzhang 拨乱反正 rectification of past errors
Cai Xuan 蔡玄
Cai Yuanpei 蔡元培
Cen Chunxuan 岑春煊
Chen Duxiu 陈独秀
Chen Heqin 陈鹤琴
Chen Jiageng 陈嘉庚
Chen Jiongming 陈炯明
Chen Yi 陈颐
chengbao jingying zhi 承包经营制 contract responsibility system
chou laojiu 臭老九 stinking ninth
Chun-qiu 春秋 Spring-Autumn period
Chunyu Kun 淳于髡
cunshu 村塾 village school
Dai Zhen 戴震
dangzheng 党正 township head
danwei 单位 work unit
dasitu 大司徒 prime minister
Daxueyuan 大学院 Ministry of Education of the GMD regime in Canton
Ding Wenjiang 丁文江
dingxiang zhaosheng 定向招生 college admission from designated areas
Donglin shuyuan 东林书院
dongzhang 洞长 dean of a private academy in traditional China
Duxueshi 督学室 school superintendent's office

fazheng zhuanke xuexiao 法政专科学校 school of law and political science

Fei jidujiao xuesheng datongmeng 非基督教学生大同盟 Grand Alliance of Non-Christian Students

Fei zongjiao datongmeng 非宗教大同盟 Non-Religious Grand Alliance

fu shanzhang 副山长 vice dean of a private academy in traditional China

Fu Zuoyi 傅作义

fuxue 府学 provincial school

Gao Panlong 高攀龙

Gaodeng jiaoyu zixue kaoshi 高等教育自学考试 Nonformal College Education Examination

getihu 个体户 self-employed person

gongxu jianmian 供需见面 meeting of supply and demand

gongxue 公学 nongovernmental school

gongyi shiye 公益事业 public service

Gu Xiancheng 顾宪成

Gu Yanwu 顾炎武

guanli weiyuanhui 管理委员会 board of managers of a Christian college

guanxi 关系 connections

guanxue 官学 governmental school

gufen zhi 股份制 joint-stock system

Guimao xuezhi 癸卯学制 School System of 1904

guoli daxue 国立大学 national university

guoli 国立 public or national

guomin xuexiao 国民学校 citizen school

guoxue 国学 national school

guoyou minban 国有民办 state-owned and people-run

Guozijian 国子监 Capital University in imperial China

Hanlin 翰林 Imperial Academy in traditional China

He Lian 何廉

Hu Shi 胡适

Hu Wei 胡渭

Huang Yanpei 黄炎培

Huang Zongxi 黄宗羲

huijia xingxue 毁家兴学 set up schools with one's entire fortune

huo jiaoyu 活教育 live education

jiaguan 家馆 private school in one's residence

Jiang Guanyun 蒋观云

Jiang Mengling 蒋梦麟

Jiang Tingfu 蒋廷黻

jiangshu 讲书 lecturer at a private academy

jiansheng 监生 qualified candidate for the Capital university or Guozijian jiaoguan 教馆 private school in a student's house

jiaohua 教化 learning and good morals

Jiaoyu xingzheng weiyuanhui 教育行政委员会 Education Administration Committee

jiashu 家塾 private school in a teacher's house

jiaxue 家学 family school

jihua zhaosheng 计划招生 colleges' planned admission

jinglu 精庐 early private academy

jingshe 精舍 early private academy

jingxue 经学 textual study of Confucian classics

jinshi 进士 advanced scholar

Jixia xuegong 稷下学宫 Palace School at Jixia

junzi 君子 gentleman

juren 举人 elevated man

Kang Youwei 康有为

keju 科举 Civil Service Examination System

Kong Qiu or Confucius 孔子

kongtan 空谈 pure talk

Li Duanfen 李端芬

Li Tianlu 李天录

li 礼 propriety

Lianda 联大 Southwest Associated University

Liang Qichao 梁启超

liangzhi 良知 Man's innate capacity to know good

Ling Yutang 林语堂

Liu Kunyi 刘坤一

Lixue 礼学 Neo-Confucianism

Lu Xun 鲁迅

luxue 律学 law school in ancient China

Ma Xiangbo 马相伯

Ma Xulun 马叙伦

mengguan private elementary school

mengxue 蒙学 elementary school or basic literacy

minban gongzhu 民办公助 people-run with governmental assistance

minban 民办 people-run

minzhu dangpai 民主党派 democratic parties

Mo Zi 墨子

paifang 牌坊 archway

Qian Dehong 钱德洪

Qing Guangya 卿光亚

Qiu Jin 秋瑾

*Quanxue pian* 劝学篇 An exhortation on Learning

Quanxue suo 劝学所 Education-Promoting Office

ren qi zi liu 任其自流 laissez faire policy

ren 仁 benevolence

renmin tuanti 人民团体 civic organization

Rong Qing 荣庆

Ruan Yuan 阮元

Sanzi yundong 三自运动 Three-Selves Movement

shangshu 尚书 prime minister

shanzhang 山长 dean of a private academy

she 社 a unit of fifty households

Sheng Xuanhuai 盛宣怀

shengyuan 生员 students of provincial, prefectural, and county schools

shexue 社学 community school

shi 士 educated gentleman

shu 塾 a school

Shu Xincheng 舒新城

shushi 塾师 a *sishu* teacher

shushu 书塾 private elementary school

shuyuan 书院 private academy in traditional China

si yi 四夷 barbarian lands

sili xuexiao 私立学校 private school

Simenxue 四门学 governmental school in the capital of ancient China

Sishu gailiang hui 私塾改良会 Sishu-Reform Society

Sishu guanli weiyuanhui 私塾管理委员会 Sichu-Management Committee

sishu 私塾 private school in traditional China

situ 司徒 prime minister

Sixiang gaizhao 思想改造 Thought Reform

Taixue 太学 Capital University in imperial China

Tao Menghe 陶孟和

Tao Xingzhi 陶行知

Tian Pian 田骈

*Tongmeng xun* 童蒙训 Precepts for children

Tongmenghui 同盟会 Revolutionary Alliance organized by Dr. Sun Yat-sen in 1905

tongsheng 童生 candidate for the degree of budding scholar

tongwenguan 同文馆 foreign language school in the late Qing period

*Tongzi li* 童子礼 Children's decorum

Wang Ji 王畿

weituo peiyang 委托培养 employer-sponsored education

*Wu Xun zhuan* 武迅传 Story of Wu Xun

Wu Xun 武迅
Wu Yifang 伍廷芳
wujiao 五教  five fields of learning
xiang 庠 local school in ancient China
xiangxue 乡学  village school
xianxue 县学  county school
*Xiaoer yu* 小儿语  Children's language text
*Xiaoxue* 小学  Rudimentary readings of Confucian classics edited by Zhu Xi
    and Liu Zicheng
xiaoxuetang 小学堂  elementary school
*Xinxue* 新学  New learning
*Xinzheng* 新政  New Policy in late Qing
xiucai 秀才  budding scholar
xu 序 local school in ancient China
Xu Zunming 徐遵明
Xuebu 学部  Ministry of Learning in late Qing period
xuetang 学堂  new school
xuetian 学田  school land
*Xuewu gangyao* 学务纲要  Guidelines for Educational Affairs in 1904
Yan Ruoqu 阎若璩
Yan Xishan 阎锡山
Yan Xiu 严修
Yan Yangchu 晏阳初
Yan Yuan 颜元
Yang Sisheng 杨斯盛
yishu 义塾  charity school
yiwu 夷务  barbarian or foreign affairs
yixue 义学  charity school
Yongzheng 雍正  Emperor Yongzheng
Yuan Shikai 袁世凯
*Yuanxi tiaozheng* 院系调整  Reorganization of Higher Education
yungong yunneng 允公允能  faith in public service and talents
Zhang Baixi 张百熙
Zhang Boling 张伯苓
Zhang Taiyan 章太炎
Zhang Xueliang 张学良
Zhang Zhidong 张之洞
Zhang Zuolin 张作霖
*Zhengfeng* 整风  Rectification Campaign
*Zhengwu yuan* 政务院  State Council
zhiye jiaoyu 职业教育  vocational education

zhong xuetang 中学堂 middle school

zhongdian zhongxue 重点中学 key-point middle/high school

Zhonghua minguo daxueyuan 中华民国大学院 Ministry of Education of the Nanjing Government

Zhonghua shehui daxue 中华社会大学 Zhonghua Societal University

Zhou Enlai 周恩来

zhouxue 州学 prefectural school

zhouzhang 州长 prefectural magistrate

Zhu Xi 朱熹

zhuanke xuexiao 专科学校 professional school

zhujiao 助教 assistant professor

zhulu dizi 著录弟子 titular student

Zongli yamen 总理衙门 Foreign Affairs Office in the late Qing period

zongxue 宗学 clan school or school for children of aristocratic families

Zouding xuetang zhangcheng 奏定学堂章程 Memorial on Schools by Zhang Baixi, Zhang Zhidong, and Rong Qing in 1903

zulin jingying zhi 租赁经营制 leasing-management system

Zuo Zongtang 左宗棠

zuoguan 坐馆 private school in traditional China, normally in the residence of the students

# Selected Bibliography

**SOURCES IN CHINESE**

### Newspapers and Periodicals

*Beijing wanbao* (Beijing evening news)
*Bijiao jiaoyu yanjiu* (Studies in comparative education)
*Dagong bao* (Dagong daily)
*Dongfang zazhi* (Orient magazine)
*Guangming ribao* (Guangming daily)
*Jiaoyu kexue* (Educational science)
*Jiaoyu lilun yu shijian* (Theory and practice in education)
*Jiaoyu yanjiu* (Studies in education)
*Jiaoyu yanjiu yu shiyan* (Research and experiments in education)
*Jiaoyu zazhi* (Education magazine)
*Lishi yanjiu* (Historical studies)
*Minban jiaoyu tongxun* (Newsletters on *minban* education)
*Minguo ribao* (Republican daily)
*Pujiao yanjiu* (Studies in basic education)
*Renmin jiaoyu* (People's education)
*Shi bao* (Time)
*Waiguo zhong xiao xue jiaoyu* (Elementary and secondary education in foreign countries)
*Xin jiaoyu* (New education)
*Zhong xiao xue guanli* (Administration in elementary and secondary schools)
*Zhongguo jiaoyu bao* (Chinese education)
*Zhonghua jiaoyu jie* (Chinese education)

**Books and Articles**

Basic Education Section, State Educational Commission. *Jiunian yiwu jiaoyu jiaoxue wenjian huibian* (Documents on nine-year compulsory education). Beijing: Beijing Normal University Press, 1994.

Cai, Yuanpei. *Cai Yuanpei xuanji* (Selected works of Cai Yuanpei). Beijing: Zhonghua shuju, 1959.

Central Institute for Educational Research. *Shi yi jie san zhong quanhui yilai zhongyang jiaoyu wejian xuanbian* (Selected documents from the central government since the third plenum of the third congress of the CCP). Beijing: Educational Sciences Press, 1992.

——. *Zhonghua renmin gongheguo jiaoyu dashiji, 1949-1982* (Chronicle of education in the People's Republic of China, 1949-1982). Beijing: Educational Science Press, 1983.

——. *Zhongguo xiandai jiaoyu dashiji* (Major educational events in modern China). Beijing: Educational Science Press, 1988.

Chen, Heqin. *Wo de bansheng* (First half of my life). Shanghai: Shijie Shuju, 1941.

Chen, Jingpan. *Zhongguo jindai jiaoyushi* (History of education in modern China). Beijing: People's Education Press, 1983.

Chen, Qingzhi. *Zhongguo jiaoyushi* (History of Chinese education). Taibei: Commercial Press, 1968.

Chen, Xuexun ed. *Zhongguo jindai jiaoyu wenxuan* (Writings on education in modern China). Beijing: People's Education Press, 1983.

Chen, Xuexun. *Zhongguo jindai jiaoyu dashiji* (Major educational events in modern China). Shanghai: Shanghai Education Press, 1981.

——. *Zhongguo jindai jiaoyushi jiaoxue cankao ziliao* (Teacher's guide to the history of education in modern China). Beijing: People's Education Press, 1986.

——, & Zhou Decheng ed. *Zhongguo jiaoyushi yanjiu* (Studies in the history of Chinese education). Shanghai: East China Normal University Press, 1995.

Cheng, Jieming. *Zhongguo dalu jiaoyu shikuang* (State of education in mainland China). Taibei: Taiwan Commercial Press, 1993.

——. *Zhongguo jiaoyu gaige* (Educational reform in China). Hong Kong: Commercial Press, 1992.

Cheng, Shixing. *Zhongguo xiandai jiaoyushi* (History of education in modern China). Taipei: Sanmin Press, 1981.

Chongqing Educational Commission. *Chunfeng hua yu* (Documents on non governmental schools in Chongqing). Chongqing, 1992.

Chu, Hanmin. *Zhongguo di shuyuan* (China's academies). Beijing: Commercial Press, 1991.

Chu, Shipei. *Zhongguo daxue jiaoyu fazhanshi* (History of the evolution of Chinese universities). Taiyuan: Shanxi Education Press, 1993.

Deng, Peng. *Fei Zhengqing pingzhuan* (A biography of John K. Fairbank). Chengdu: Tiandi Press, 1997.

Deng, Xiaoping. *Deng Xiaoping lun xuexiao jiaoyu* (Deng Xiaoping on formal education). Beijing: China People's University Press, 1990.

*Di er ci zhongguo jiaoyu nianjian* (Second yearbook on China's education). Shanghai: Commercial Press, 1948.

*Di san ci zhongguo jiaoyu nianjian* (Third yearbook on China's education). Taibei: Zhongzheng Shuju, 1958.

Division of Vocational and Technical Education, State Education Commission. *Quanguo zhiye jiaoyu gongzuo huiyi wenjian huibian* (Collections of documents of the national conference for vocational and technical education). Beijing: Beijing Normal University Press, 1986.

*Di yi ci zhongguo jiaoyu nianjian* (First yearbook on China's education). Shanghai: Kaiming Shudian, 1934.

Fan, Wenlan ed. *Zhongguo tongshi* (General history of China). 10 vols. Beijing: People's Press, 1994.

Gu, Shusen. *Zhongguo lidai jiaoyu zhidu* (Educational systems in China's history). Nanjing: Jiangsu People's Press, 1981.

Guo, Moruo. *Wo de younian* (My childhood). Shanghai: Guanghua Shuju, 1930.

Guo, Qijia ed. *Zhonghua renmin gongheguo jiaoyufa quanshu* (Complete collection of educational statutes in the People's Republic of China). Beijing: Beijing Institute of Radio and TV Broadcasting, 1995.

Hong, Yonghong ed. *Xiamen daxue xiaoshi* (History of Xiamen University). Xiamen: Xiamen University Press, 1990.

Hu, Chang-tu. *Chinese Education under Communism.* New York: Bureau of Publication, Teachers College, Columbia University, 1962.

Hu, Shi. *Sishi zishu* (Memoir at forty). Shanghai: Yadong Tushuguan, 1941.

Huang, Zhong. *Woguo jindai jiaoyu ti fazhan* (Development of education in our nation's recent history). Taipei: Taiwan Commercial Press, 1980.

Jia, Fuming. *Quanmin jiaoyu yu zhonghua wenhua* (People's education and Chinese culture). Taipei: Wunan Press, 1992.

Jiang, Shuge. *Zhongguo jindai jiaoyu zhidu* (Educational system in modern China). Shanghai: Commercial Press, 1934.

Kao, Ji. *Zhongguo gaodeng jiaoyu sixiangshi* (History of thought on higher education in China). Beijing: People's Education Press, 1992.

Li, Changhua. *Qingji sichuan kai min qi yun tongji yanjiu: 1895-1911* (Enlightenment in Sichuan in the late Qing). Taibei: Institute of History, National University of Political Science, 1980.

Li, Guilin. *Zhongguo jiaoyushi* (History of Chinese education). Shanghai: Shanghai Education Press, 1989.

———. *Zhongguo xiandai jiaoyushi* (History of education in modern China). Changchun: Jilin Education Press, 1990.

Li, Shuhua. "Cong *sishu* dao xuetang" (From *sishu* to school). *Zhuanji wenxue* (Biographical literature), 17 (1970): 61-64.

Li, Zongtong. "Cong *jiashu* dao Nankai Zhongxue" (From *jiashu* to Nankai Middle School). Zhuanji Wenxue, 4 (1964): 43-45.

Liu, Yifan. *Zhongguo dangdai gaodeng jiaoyu shilue* (Brief history of higher education in modern China). Wuhan: Central China Polytechnic Press, 1991.

Liu, Yingjie ed. *Zhongguo jiaoyu dashidian* (Book of major educational events in China). 2 vols. Hangzhou: Zhejiang Education Press, 1993.

Lu, Xingwei ed. *Shanghai putong jiaoyushi* (History of education in Shanghai). Shanghai: Shanghai Education Press, 1995.

Lu, Yanchen. *Zhongguo jindai nuzi jiaoyushi* (History of women's education in modern China). Taibei: Wenshizhe Press, 1989.

Ma, Xulun. *Wo zai liushi sui yiqian* (My first sixty years of life). Shanghai: Shenghuo Shudian, 1947.

Mao, Lirui ed. *Zhongguo jiaoyushi jianbian* (Brief history of Chinese education). Beijing: Educational Science Press, 1984.

——, Lirui, Qu Junong & Shao Heting ed. *Zhongguo gudai jiaoyushi* (History of education in pre-modern China). Beijing: People's Education Press, 1981.

——, Shen Guanqun ed. *Zhongguo jiaoyu tongshi* (General history of Chinese education). 6 vols. Jinan: Shandong Education Press, 1988.

Mao, Zedong. *Mao Zedong xuanji* (Selected works of Mao Zedong). 5 vols. Beijing: People's Press, 1991.

*Nankai Daxue xiaoshi* (History of Nankai University). Tianjin: Nankai University Press, 1990.

*Nankai Daxue xiaoshi ziliao xuan* (Sources on the history of Nankai University). Tianjin: Nankai University Press, 1989.

Project Team. *A Study on NGO-Sponsored and Private Higher Education in China*. Beijing: China National Institute of Educational Research, 1995.

Qu, Baokui, Lei Xiaozhu, Yu Guang & Huang Rongchang ed. *Zhongguo jiaoyu gaige* (Educational reform in China). Beijing: People's Education Press, 1991.

Qu, Xingui & Tang Liangyan ed. *Zhongguo jindai jiaoyushi ziliao huibian* (Sources on the history of education in modern China). Shanghai: Shanghai Education Press, 1991.

Ren, Shixian. *Zhongguo jiaoyu sixiangshi* (History of educational philosophy in China). Taibei: Commercial Press, 1987.

Shen, Congwen. *Congwen zizhuan* (Biography of Shen Congwen). Shanghai: Kaiming Shudian, 1946.

Shu, Xincheng. *Wo he jiaoyu* (Education and I). Taibei: Longwen Press, 1980.

——. *Zhongguo jindai jiaoyushi ziliao* (Sources on the history of education in modern China). 3 vols. Beijing: People's Education Press, 1961.

——. *Zhongguo xiandai jiaoyushi* (History of education in modern China). Shanghai: Shanghai Shudian, 1934.

Song, Enrong ed. *Jindai zhongguo jiaoyu gaige* (Educational reform in modern China). Beijing: Educational Science Press, 1994.

——, & Zhang Xian ed. *Zhonghua minguo jiaoyu fagui xuanbian* (Educational statutes in Republican China). Nanjing: Jiangsu Education Press, 1990.

Sun, Peijun & Li Guoqing ed. *Zhongguo jiaoyu sixiangshi* (History of Chinese educational philosophy). Shanghai: East China Normal University Press, 1995.

Tong, Baoliang. *Zhongguo jiaoyu shigang* (Outline history of Chinese education). Beijing: People's Education Press, 1990.

Wang, Li & Qiao Muying ed. *Tianjin shi Nankai Zhongxue jianxiao jiushi zhounian jinian zhuankan* (Ninetieth anniversary of Tianjin Nankai Middle School). Tianjin: Nankai Middle School, 1995.

Wang, Wenjun, Liang Jiesheng, Yang Xuan, Zhang Shujian & Xia Jiashan. *Nankai daxue xiaoshi ziliao xuan, 1919-1949* (Documents on the history of Nankai University). Tianjin: Nankai University Press, 1989.

Wei, Yiqiao ed. *Zhongguo mingxiao* (Famous middle schools in China). Shenyang: Liaoning University Press, 1992.

Wu, Ni. *Zhongguo gudai sixue fazhan zhu wenti yanjiu* (Studies on private education in pre-modern China). Beijing: Social Science Press, 1996.

Xiong, Ming'an. *Zhonghua minguo jiaoyushi* (History of education in Republican China). Chongqing: Chongqing Press, 1990.

Xiong, Xianjun. *Zhongguo jiaoyu xingzhengshi* (History of educational administration in China). Wuhan: Central China Polytechnic Press, 1996.

Xu, Lianda ed. *Zhongguo lidai guanzhi cidian.* (Dictionary of government offices in imperial China). Hefei: Anhui Education Press, 1991.

Yang, Pusheng. *Zhongguo shuyuan yu wenhua chuantong* (Private academies And cultural heritage in China). Changsha: Hunan Education Press, 1992.

Yu, Penfa. *Zhongguo jiaoyu fazhanshi* (History of the growth of China's education). Wuchang: Central China Polytechnic Press, 1991.

Zhang, Boling. *Sishi nian Nankai xuexiao zhi huigu* (Recollections about Nankai in the past forty years). Taibei: Biographical Literature Series, no. 26, 1968

Zhang, Weixuan, Liu Wuyi & Xiao Xing ed. *Gongheguo fengyun sishi nian* (Forty years of the People's Republic of China). 2 vols. Beijing: China University of Political Science and Law, 1989.

Zhang, Zhengfan. *Zhongguo shuyuan zhidu kaolue* (A brief study of the *shuyuan* in China). Nanjing: Jiangsu Education Press, 1985.

Zhang, Zhiyi ed. *Sili minban xuexiao de lilun yu shijian* (Theory and practice of private and *minban* schools). Beijing: Chinese Workers Press, 1994.

Zheng, Dengyun. *Zhongguo jindai jiaoyushi* (History of education in modern China). Shanghai: East China Normal University Press, 1994.

Zheng, Shixing. *Zhongguo xiandai jiaoyushi* (History of education in modern China). Taibei: Sanmin Shuju, 1982.

Zheng, Zhiguang ed. *Zhang Boling zhuan* (A biography of Zhang Boling). Tianjin: Nankai University Press, 1989.

*Zhongguo da baike quanshu* (Encyclopedia sinica). Beijing: Encyclopedia Sinica Press, 1985.

*Zhongguo xiandai jiaoyu jia zhuan* (Biographies of great educators in modern China). Changsha: Hunan Education Press, 1986.

Zhou, Yudong. *Zhongguo xiandai jiaoyushi* (History of education in modern China). Shanghai: Shanghai Shudian, 1989.

Zhu, Youxian. *Zhongguo jindai xuezhi shiliao* (Historical documents on the educational system in modern China). Shanghai: East China Normal University Press, 1990.

## SOURCES IN ENGLISH

### Newspapers and Periodicals

*Beijing Review*
*China Daily*
*Chinese Education*
*Chinese Education and Society*
*Comparative Education*
*Comparative Education Review*

**Books and Articles**

Anderson, Mary Raleigh. *A Cycle in the Celestial Kingdom or Protestant Mission Schools for Girls in South China: 1827 to the Japanese Invasion.* Mobile, Alabama: Heiter-Starke Printing Co., 1943.

Ayers, William. *Chang Chih-tung and Educational Reform in China.* Cambridge, Mass.: Harvard University Press, 1971.

Bastid, Marianne. *Educational Reform in Early Twentieth-Century China.* Translated by Paul J. Bailey. Ann Arbor: University of Michigan Press, 1988.

Biggerstaff, Knight. *The Earliest Modern Government Schools in China.* Port Washington, NY: Kennikat Press, 1961.

Bodde, Derk. *Chinese Thought, Society, and Science.* Honolulu: University of Hawaii Press, 1991.

Borthwick, Sally. *Education and Social Change in China: The Beginnings of The Modern Era.* Stanford: Hoover Institution Press, 1983.

Burton, Charles. *Political and Social Change in China since 1978.* Westport: Greenwood Press, 1990.

Chang, Hao. *Liang Ch'i-ch'ao and Intellectual Transition in China, 1890-1907.* Cambridge, Mass.: Harvard University Press, 1971.

Chen, Jie & Peng Deng. *China since the Cultural Revolution: From Totalitarianism to Authoritarianism.* Westport: Praeger, 1995.

Chen, Theodore Hsi-en. *Education and Nation Building in China 1929-1937.* Los Angeles: University of Southern California Press, 1969.

China Christian Educational Association. *The Christian College in New China: The Report of the Second Biennial Conference of Christian Colleges and Universities in China, Shanghai College, February 12 to 16, 1926.* Bulletin no. 16. Shanghai, 1926.

——. *Statistical Report: Christian Colleges and Professional Schools of China, 1929-1930.* Bulletin no. 27. Shanghai, 1930.

——. *Statistical Report: Christian Colleges and Professional Schools of China, 1930-1931.* Bulletin no. 28. Shanghai, 1931.

——. *Statistical Report of Christian Colleges and Universities in China, 1924.* Bulletin no. 8. Shanghai, 1925.

*Chinese Christian Education: A Report of a Conference Held in New York city, April 6, 1925, under the Joint Auspices of the International Missionary Council and the Foreign Missions Conference of North America.* New York, 1925.

Chow, Tse-tsung. *The May Fourth Movement: Intellectual Revolution in Modern China.* Cambridge Mass.: Harvard University Press, 1960.

Cleverley, John F. *The Schooling of China: Tradition and Modernity in Chinese Education.* North Sydney: Allen & Unwin Pty. Ltd., 1991.

Coe, John L. *Huachung University.* New York: United Board for Christian Higher Education in Asia, 1962.

Cohen, Paul A. *China and Christianity: The Missionary Movement and the Growth of Chinese Antiforeignism, 1860-1870.* Cambridge, Mass.: Harvard University Press, 1963.

Conference of China Education International. *Perspectives on Contemporary Education in China.* Proceedings of the First Conference of China Education International Held at the State University of New York at Buffalo, July 13, 1988. Amherst, NY:

Publication Division, Comparative Education Center, Faculty of Educational Studies, State University of New York at Buffalo, 1988.

Corbett, Charles H. *Shantung Christian College (Cheeloo)*. New York: United Board for Christian Colleges in China, 1955.

Dai, Shujun. "The Development of Higher Vocational and Technical Education in China," *Chinese Education*, 24 (Spring 1991): 8-25.

Day, Clarence B. *Hangchow University: A Brief History*. New York: United Board for Christian Colleges in China, 1955.

Deng, Haiyun. "The Megatrend toward the Labor Market: An Analysis of the Job Market for 1993 College and University Graduates," *Chinese Education and Society*, 27 (May-June 1994): 79-92.

Deng, Peng. *China's Crisis and Revolution through American Lenses, 1944 1949*. Lanham: University Press of America, 1994.

Division of Vocational and Technical Education, State Education Commission. *Quanguo shiye jishu jiaoyu gongzuo huiyi wenjian huibian* (A collection of documents of the National Work Conference for Vocational and Technical Education). Beijing: Beijing Normal University Press, 1986.

Edwards, Dwight W. & Y.P. Mei. *Yenching University*. New York: United Board for Christian Higher Education in Asia, 1959.

Fairbank, John K. *The Missionary Enterprise in China and America*. Cambridge, Mass.: Harvard University Press, 1974.

——. *China: A New History*. Cambridge, Mass.: Harvard University Press, 1993.

——, & K. C. Liu. *Cambridge History of China*. Vol. 12, Late Qing. New York: Cambridge University Press, 1985.

Feuerwerker, "The Foreign Presence in China," in *Cambridge History of China* ed. By John K. Fairbank and K. C. Liu, vol. 12. New York: Cambridge University Press, 1985.

Foreign Missions Conference of North America. *Addresses on China at the 34th Annual Session*. New York, 1927.

Frank, Wolfgang. *The Reform and Abolition of the Traditional Chinese Examination System*. Cambridge, Mass.: Harvard University Press, 1963.

Gregg, Alice Henrietta. *China and Educational Autonomy: The Changing Role Of the Protestant Educational Missionary in China, 1807-1937*. Ann Arbor: University of Michigan Press, 1993.

Hamrin, Carol Lee. *China and the Challenge of the Future: Changing Political Patterns*. Boulder: Westview Press, 1990.

Hicks, George, ed. *Broken Mirror: China after Tiananmen*. New York: St. James Press, 1991.

Ho, Pingti, *The Ladder of Success in Imperial China*. New York: Columbia University Press, 1962.

Hsu, Imannuel Y. *Rise of Modern China*. 2nd ed. New York: Oxford University Press, 1975.

Hu, Shi Ming & Eli Seifman eds. *A Documentary History of Education in the PRC, 1977-1986*. New York: AMS Press, 1987.

Huang, Yao. "In Search of New Mechanisms in Solving Problems of Educational Finance," *Chinese Education*, 25 (Winter 1992-1993): 36-53.

Kuo, Ping-wen. *The Chinese System of Public Education*. New York: AMS Press, 1975.

Lamberton, Mary. *St. John's University, Shanghai, 1879-1951*. New York: United Board for Christian Colleges in China, 1955.

Latourette, Kenneth S. *A History of Christian Missions in China.* New York: The MacMillan Company, 1929.

Lee, Shiao-yun. *Chinese Education after Mao.* M.A. Thesis, San Diego State University, 1983.

Li, Shouxin. "The Level of Educational Expenditure in Our Country," *Chinese Education,* 25 (Winter 1992-1993): 7-20.

Lin, Jing. *Education in Post-Mao China.* Westport: Praeger, 1993.

Liu, Kuang-ching. *American Missionaries in China.* Cambridge, Mass.: Harvard University Press, 1966.

Lofstedt, Jan-Ingvar. *Chinese Educational Policy: Changes and Contradictions, 1949-1979.* Stockholm: Almgvist & Wiksell International Humanities Press, 1980.

Lutz, Jessie G. *China and the Christian Colleges, 1850-1950.* Ithaca: Cornell University Press, 1971.

Miyazaki, Ichisada. *China's Examination Hell.* Trans. Conrad Schirokauer. New York: Weatherhill, 1976.

Nelson, Wilbur K. *Education Goals in China: With Emphasis on the Relationship of Public and Private Schools on Taiwan during the Period 1949-1962.* Ph. D. Thesis. Claremont Graduate School, 1963.

Pepper, Suzanne. *China's Education Reform in the 1980s: Policies, Issue, and Historical Perspectives.* Berkeley: Institute of East Asian Studies, University of California at Berkeley Center for Chinese Studies, 1990.

Price, R. F. *Education in Communist China.* London: Routledge and Kegan Paul, 1975.

Rao, Digang, Chen Haizhun & Wang Shenghao. "Policy Analysis of the Early Stage (1985-1991) of China's Reform of the Job Assignment System for College Graduates," *Chinese Education and Society,* 27 (May-June 1994): 37-50.

Rawski, Evelyn Sakakida. *Education and Popular Literacy in Ch'ing China.* Ann Arbor: University of Michigan Press, 1979.

Reynolds, Douglas R. *China, 1898-1912: The Xinzheng Revolution and Japan.* Cambridge, Mass.: Council on East Asian Studies, Harvard University, 1993.

Sabados, Eugene Mathew. "Education in Communist China with Emphasis Upon the Top and Bottom of the Educational Ladder." M.S. Thesis, Danbury State College, 1962.

Schwartz, Benjamin. *In Search of Wealth and Power: Yan Fu and the West.* Cambridge, Mass.: Harvard University Press, 1964.

——. "The Intelligentsia in Communist China," *Daedalus,* Summer, 1960, pp. 604-621.

Scott, Roderick. *Fukien Christian University, A Historical Sketch.* New York: United Board for Christian Colleges in China, 1954.

Shirk, Susan L. *The Politics of Education in Post-Mao China.* Washington D.C.: China Council of the Asia Society, 1979.

State Education Commission. "Instructions on the Work of Job Assignment for College and University Graduates," *Chinese Education and Society,* 27 (May-June 1994): 7-10.

——. "Opinions on Reform in Admission and Job Assignment for College Students," *Chinese Education and Society,* 27 (May-June 1994): 11-18.

State Education Leaders Delegation. *China's Schools in Flux.* London: Macmillan, 1980.

Stauffer, Milton T. ed. *The Christian Occupation of China.* Shanghai, 1922.

Study Team, China National Institute of Education Research. *A Study on NGO Sponsored And Private Higher Education in China.* Beijing, 1995.

Taylor, Joseph. *History of West China Union University, 1910-1935*. Chengdu, China, 1936.

Topical Research Group, Institute of Chinese Vocational University Education. "The Development of Vocational Universities with Unique Chinese Features," *Chinese Education*, 24 (Spring 1991): 27-71.

Thurston, Matilda & Ruth M. Chester. *Ginling College*. New York: United Board for Christian Colleges in China, 1955.

Tsang, Chiu-sam. *Society, Schools and Progress in China*. New York: Pergamon Press, 1968.

Unger, Jonathan. *Education under Mao: Class and Competition in Canton Schools, 1960-1980*. New York: Columbia University Press, 1982.

Wales, Largo Ann. *Characteristics of Education in the People's Republic of China as Viewed by American Educators during 1974-1981*. Ph.D. Thesis, Seattle University, 1983.

Wallace, E. W. *The Place of Private Schools in a National System of Education*. Shanghai: China Christian Educational Association Bulletin, no. 5, 1925.

Walmsley, Lewis c. *West China Union University*. New York: United Board for Christian Higher Education in Asia, 1974.

Wang, Y. C. *Chinese Intellectuals and the West, 1872-1949*. Chapel Hill: University of North Carolina Press, 1966.

World Bank. *China: Issues and Prospects in Education*. Washington, D.C.: World Bank, 1985.

Wu, Fesheng. "Problems in China's Rural Educational Reform," *Chinese Education*, 22 (Winter 1989-1990): 49-58.

Wu, Wen & Luo Daming. "Heavy laden Wings: Sad Contemplation on China's Education," *Chinese Education and Society*, 28 (January-February 1995): 9-96.

Xu, Xiu. "Reflections on the Reform of Admission to Colleges and Universities and the Job Assignment System for Their Graduates," *Chinese Education and Society*, 27 (May-June 1994): 51-56.

Yamamoto, Tatsuro and Sumiko. "The Anti-Christian Movement in China, 1922-1927," *Far Eastern Quarterly*, 12 (1953): 133-147.

Yang, Dongping. "China Crisis in Education: Inadequate Investment, Low Returns, and Slow Reform," *Chinese Education*, 23 (Summer 1990): 15-17.

Yang, Shaojiang. "Reversing the Insufficiency of Funds for Education: Now Is the Time for Action," *Chinese Education*, 23 (Summer 1990): 31-32.

Yuan, Liansheng. "On the Deficiency of Our Educational Funding: An Analysis of the Amount and Percentage of Our Educational Investment, 1977-1987," *Chinese Education*, 25 (Winter 1992-1993): 21-35.

Zeng, Qiang, Chen Yuejin, Tang Zhihui, and Liu Xiguang. "The Impoverished Education," *Chinese Education*, 23 (Summer 1990): 18-21.

Zhang, Xiadao. "A Preliminary Exploration of the Issue of Job Assignment for College Graduate Science Majors," *Chinese Education and Society*, 27 (May-June 1994): 57-74.

Zhou, Taixuan. "Fei zongjiao jiaoyu yu jiaohui jiaoyu" (Non-religious education and Christian education), *Zhonghua jiaoyujie* (Chinese education). XIV, no. 8 (February, 1925).

Zhu, Kaixuan. "Some Issues Concerning Job Assignment for College Graduates," *Chinese Education and Society*, 27 (May-June 1994): 19-21.

# Index

**About the Author**

PENG DENG, a native of China, is Associate Professor of History at High Point University in North Carolina.

ISBN 0-275-95639-3

90000>

EAN

9 780275 956394

HARDCOVER BAR CODE